YORK MEDIEVAL TEXTS

General Editors

ELIZABETH SALTER & DEREK PEARSALL
University of York

For Tom—*joy mot he have*

Sir Gawain and the Green Knight

edited by.

R. A. WALDRON

University of London, King's College

 EDWARD ARNOLD

© R. A. WALDRON 1970

First published 1970 by
Edward Arnold (Publishers) Ltd
41 Maddox Street, London W1

Cloth edition SBN: 7131 5493 4
Paper edition SBN: 7131 5494 2

Printed in Great Britain by Billing & Sons Limited
Guildford and London

Preface

The present series of *York Medieval Texts* is designed for undergraduates and, where the text is appropriate, for upper forms of schools. Its aim is to provide editions of major pieces of Middle English writing in a form which will make them accessible without loss of historical authenticity. Texts are chosen because of their importance and artistic merit, and individual volumes may contain a single work, coherent extracts from a longer work, or representative examples of a genre. The principle governing the presentation of the text is to preserve the character of the English while eliminating unnecessary encumbrances such as obsolete letters and manuscript errors. Glossary and explanatory notes operate together to clarify the text; special attention is paid to the interpretation of passages which are syntactically rather than lexically difficult. The Introduction to each volume, like the rest of the apparatus, is designed to set the work in its proper literary context, and to provide the critical guidance most helpful to present-day readers. The intention of the series is exclusively literary: the Editors hope to attract a wider audience not only for works within the accepted literary canon, but also for those which have until now been regarded as 'specialist' in appeal, or which have been presented as if they were.

This volume adds to the series the complete text of a poem which, though an acknowledged masterpiece of medieval literature, makes abnormal demands upon the reader by reason of its subtle exploitation of a difficult dialect of Middle English and of the special idiom of alliterative verse. There is no short cut through the difficulties—they are the poem itself—but the present edition is designed to enable the modern reader to reach a sensitive first-hand understanding of the text as the only basis for valid literary judgement. The Introduction by-passes speculation on sources and analogues and deals directly with the poem's stylistic qualities and moral content. In conjunction with the Select Bibliography it provides a guide to the relevant *Gawain*-criticism of the past decade and also advances independent critical judgements, notably on the central issue of the degree and nature of Gawain's fault.

Acknowledgements

I am indebted to the Trustees of the British Museum, to the Council of the Early English Text Society and to the Oxford University Press for permission to print the text from the facsimile of B.M. MS Cotton Nero A.x. I also owe an incalculable debt to my colleagues and students at King's College, London, with whom I have discussed both specific and general problems in the interpretation of the poem over the past twelve years. Finally, it gives me great pleasure to record my gratitude to the General Editors, who have made many valuable suggestions.

R.A.W.

Contents

Abbreviations

CT	*Canterbury Tales*, edited by F. N. Robinson in *The Complete Works of Geoffrey Chaucer* (London, 2nd edn., 1957)
EDD	*English Dialect Dictionary*
EETS	Early English Text Society
EME	Early Middle English
ELH	*ELH: A Journal of English Literary History*
Fr	French
FMLS	*Forum for Modern Language Studies*
GGK	*Sir Gawain and the Green Knight*
JEGP	*Journal of English and Germanic Philology*
L	Latin
ME	Middle English
MED	*Middle English Dictionary*
MLN	*Modern Language Notes*
MLQ	*Modern Language Quarterly*
MLR	*Modern Language Review*
MP	*Modern Philology*
MS	Manuscript
NQ	*Notes and Queries*
Neophil.	*Neophilologus*
NT	*New Testament*
OE	Old English
OED	*Oxford English Dictionary*
OF	Old French
OIcel	Old Icelandic
OT	*Old Testament*
PMLA	*Publications of the Modern Language Association*
PQ	*Philological Quarterly*
RES N.S.	*Review of English Studies*, New Series
SOED	*Shorter Oxford English Dictionary*
Spec.	*Speculum*
TG, TG-Davis	see *Bibliography: Editions*

Select Bibliography

Facsimile

Pearl, Cleanness, Patience, and Sir Gawain, reproduced in facsimile from MS Cotton Nero A.x., with introduction by Sir Israel Gollancz (London, EETS, 1923)

Editions

Sir Gawain & The Green Knight, edited by J. R. R. Tolkien and E. V. Gordon (Oxford, Clarendon Press, 1925; corrected reprint, 1946) (*TG*). Second Edition, revised by Norman Davis, 1967 (*TG-Davis*)

Sir Gawain and The Green Knight, re-edited from MS Cotton Nero, A.x., in the British Museum, by Sir Israel Gollancz, with introductory essays by Mabel Day and Mary S. Serjeantson (London, EETS, 1940)

Pearl. Sir Gawain And The Green Knight, edited with an introduction by A. C. Cawley (Letchworth, Dent, 1962)

Translations

Prose, by Glyn Jones (London, Golden Cockerel Press, 1952)

Verse, by Brian Stone (Harmondsworth, Penguin Books, 1959) and by Marie Borroff (London, Longmans, 1968)

Textual Notes

In addition to the articles mentioned in the notes to the present edition, the following important textual commentaries have been used extensively:

C. T. Onions, *NQ* 146 (1924), 203–4, 244–5, 285–6

Elizabeth M. Wright, *JEGP* 34 (1935), 157–79, 339–50

C. A. Luttrell, *Neophil.* 39 (1955), 207–17; 40 (1956), 290–301; *NQ* 207 (1962), 447–50

Books and Critical Essays

R. W. Ackerman, 'Gawain's Shield: Penitential Doctrine in *GGK*', *Anglia* 76 (1958), 254–65

Larry D. Benson, *Art and Tradition in 'Sir Gawain and the Green Knight'* (New Brunswick, N.J., 1965). See Fox, 1968; Howard and Zacher, 1968

S. Bercovitch, 'Romance and Anti-Romance in *GGK*', *PQ* 44 (1965), 30–37. See Howard and Zacher, 1968

A*

Robert J. Blanch, editor, '*Sir Gawain*' *and* '*Pearl*': *Critical Essays* (Bloomington and London, 1966). Contains Burrow, 1959; Friedman, 1960; Markman, 1957; Green, 1962; Howard, 1964

M. W. Bloomfield, '*GGK*: An Appraisal', *PMLA* 76 (1961), 7–19. See Howard and Zacher, 1968

Marie Borroff, '*Sir Gawain and the Green Knight*': *A Stylistic and Metrical Study* (New Haven and London, 1962). See Fox, 1968; Howard and Zacher, 1968

R. H. Bowers, '*GGK* as Entertainment', *MLQ* 24 (1963), 333–41. See Howard and Zacher, 1968

D. S. Brewer, 'Courtesy and the *Gawain*-Poet', in *Patterns of Love and Courtesy: Essays in Memory of C. S. Lewis*, edited by John Lawlor (London, 1966), 54–85

John Burrow, 'The Two Confession Scenes in *GGK*', *MP* 57 (1959), 73–9. See Blanch, 1966

John Burrow, Reply to Hills, 1963, in *RES* N.S. 15 (1964), 56. See Howard and Zacher, 1968

John Burrow, *A Reading of* '*Sir Gawain and the Green Knight*' (London, 1965). See Fox, 1968

Cecily Clark, '*GGK*: Characterization by Syntax', *Essays in Criticism* 16 (1966), 361–74. See Fox, 1968

P. Delany, 'The Role of the Guide in *GGK*', *Neophil.* 49 (1965), 250–5. See Howard and Zacher, 1968

G. J. Engelhardt, 'The Predicament of Gawain', *MLQ* 16 (1955), 218–25. Reprinted in *Middle English Survey: Critical Essays*, edited by Edward Vasta (Notre Dame, 1965)

Dorothy Everett, *Essays on Middle English Literature* (Oxford, 1955), 68–85. See Fox, 1968

Denton Fox, editor, *Twentieth Century Interpretations of* '*Sir Gawain and the Green Knight*' (Englewood Cliffs, N.J., 1968). Contains an introductory essay and edited extracts from Everett, 1955; Benson, 1965; Burrow, 1965; Howard, 1964; Borroff, 1962; Speirs, 1949; Spearing, 1966; Clark, 1966; and others

A. B. Friedman, 'Morgan le Fay in *GGK*', *Spec.* 35 (1960), 260–74. See Blanch, 1966

R. H. Green, 'Gawain's Shield and the Quest for Perfection', *ELH* 29 (1962), 121–39. See Blanch, 1966; also reprinted in *Middle English Survey: Critical Essays*, edited by Edward Vasta (Notre Dame, 1965)

D. F. Hills, 'Gawain's Fault in *GGK*', *RES* N.S. 14 (1963), 124–31. See Howard and Zacher, 1968

Donald R. Howard, 'Structure and Symmetry in *Sir Gawain*', *Spec.* 39 (1964), 425–33. See Blanch, 1966; Fox, 1968; Howard and Zacher, 1968

Donald R. Howard and Christian K. Zacher, editors, *Critical Studies of Sir Gawain and the Green Knight* (Notre Dame and London, 1968). Contains, with other reprints, Loomis, 1959; Bloomfield, 1961; Bowers, 1963; M. Mills, 1965; Howard, 1964; Silverstein, 1964; Delany, 1965; Bercovitch, 1965; Hills, 1963; Burrow, 1964; and extracts from Benson, 1965; Borroff, 1962; Spearing, 1964

George Kane, *Middle English Literature: A Critical Study of the Romances, the Religious Lyrics and Piers Plowman* (London, 1951)

J. F. Kiteley, 'The *De Arte Honeste Amandi* of Andreas Capellanus and the Concept of Courtesy in *GGK*', *Anglia* 79 (1961–2), 7–16

Laura Hibbard Loomis, '*Gawain and the Green Knight*', in *Arthurian Literature in the Middle Ages: A Collaborative History*, edited by Roger S. Loomis (Oxford, 1959), 528–40. See Howard and Zacher, 1968

T. McAlindon, 'Magic, Fate, and Providence in Medieval Narrative and *GGK*', *RES* N.S. 16 (1965), 121–39

A. M. Markman, 'The Meaning of *GGK*', *PMLA* 72 (1957), 574–86. See Blanch, 1966

D. Mehl, ' "Point of View" in mittelenglischen Romanzen", *Germanisch-romanisch Monatsschrift* 45 (1964), 35–45

D. Mills, 'An Analysis of the Temptation Scenes in *GGK*', *JEGP* 67 (1968), 612–30

M. Mills, 'Christian Significance and Romance Tradition in *GGK*', *MLR* 60 (1965), 483–93. See Howard and Zacher, 1968

D. D. R. Owen, 'Burlesque Tradition and *GGK*', *FMLS* 4 (1968), 125–45

D. A. Pearsall, 'Rhetorical "Descriptio" in *GGK*', *MLR* 50 (1955), 129–34

A. Renoir, 'Descriptive Technique in *GGK*' *Orbis Litterarum* 13 (1958), 126–32

Henry L. Savage, 'The Significance of the Hunting Scenes in *GGK*', *JEGP* 27 (1928), 1–15

Henry L. Savage, *The Gawain-Poet: Studies in his Personality and Background* (Chapel Hill, N.C., 1956)

Hans Schnyder, '*Sir Gawain and the Green Knight*': An Essay in Interpretation (Berne, 1961)

G. M. Shedd, 'Knight in Tarnished Armour: The Meaning of *GGK*', *MLR* 62 (1967), 3–13

T. Silverstein, 'The Art of *GGK*', *UTQ* 33 (1963–64), 258–78. See Howard and Zacher, 1968

T. Silverstein, '*Sir Gawain*, Dear Brutus, etc.: A Study in Comedy and Convention', *MP* 62 (1964–65), 189–206

G. V. Smithers, 'What *GGK* is About', *Medium Ævum* 32 (1963), 171–89.

Anthony C. Spearing, *Criticism and Medieval Poetry* (London, 1964). See Howard and Zacher, 1968

Anthony C. Spearing, '*Patience* and the *Gawain*-poet', *Anglia* 84 (1966), 305–29. See Fox, 1968

J. Speirs, '*Sir Gawain and the Green Knight*', *Scrutiny* 16 (1949), 274–300. See Fox, 1968

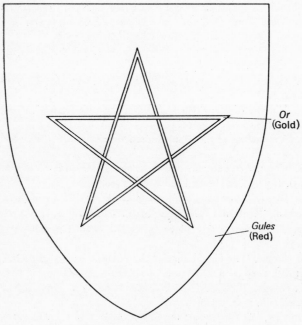

Gawain's shield (see lines 619–65)

Introduction

Sir Gawain and the Green Knight is our most accomplished example of medieval romance and a poem of rich psychological and moral interest. There are few students of medieval English literature who would not rank it beside Chaucer's *Canterbury Tales* and *Troilus and Criseyde* as one of the supreme achievements of fourteenth-century secular poetry in English. Yet the poem has achieved this assured place in the annals of our literature only comparatively recently and against great odds. B.M. MS Cotton Nero A.x., the single manuscript in which it survives (together with unique copies of three other poems very similar to it in language, metre, and style—though not in subject matter) is known to have belonged at about 1600 to a Yorkshire family; it later found its way into the library of Sir Robert Cotton and thence to the British Museum. The poem appeared in print for the first time in 1839 and it is only since about 1900 that a full measure of critical attention has been given, first to the investigation of the poem's sources and literary analogues (see now especially Loomis, 1959; Benson, 1965; Owen, 1968), and more recently (following a welcome change of direction in medieval literary studies) to the exploration of its poetic structure.[1]

Superficially the poem is an account of a typical chivalric *aventure*, an amalgam of a number of the best-known motifs of Arthurian romance—a challenge by a mysterious superhuman knight, a bargain which turns out to have unforeseen consequences, a lone quest, the attempted seduction of a Christian knight by a bewitching temptress. . . .

I The story begins in King Arthur's luxurious court at Camelot where Arthur, Gwenevere, and the knights of the Round Table are celebrating the full fifteen days of the combined medieval Christmas and New Year festival. On New Year's Day, in accordance with his custom, the youthful King Arthur will not touch food until he has been told the story of a true *aventure* (or has witnessed a joust between one of his knights and a challenger from outside the

---

[1] In view of the number and diversity of the interpretations of the poem put forward in the past two decades, nothing like a complete review can be attempted. In this Introduction the intention is to present a personal approach to the main substance of the poem which is yet (it is hoped) fairly close to the mainstream of critical opinion at the present time. The Select Bibliography (p. ix) is composed chiefly of items relevant to the themes discussed in the present essay.

court). In the event, the first act of the *aventure* takes place before his very eyes and it takes the form of a joust ('life against life in jeopardy'), but a grotesquely distorted one in which the rules of honourable combat are set aside in favour of those of a 'Christmas game'—a bout of pluck-buffet. The almost gigantic green knight who prances in on his green horse to deliver this challenge carries his own equipment for the game, an immense axe (his only weapon), together with a branch of holly to proclaim his Christmas goodwill. Ludicrously, he offers to submit to first blow from the savage blade on condition that the knight who delivers the blow will promise to accept a similar one from him in exactly a year's time. Stung by the stranger's insolence, King Arthur is first to seize the axe, but Sir Gawain eloquently pleads to be allowed to undertake the absurd performance, as it is beneath the king's dignity; after a whispered consultation among the courtiers, Gawain's request is granted. The Green Knight insists on a careful rehearsal of the terms of the agreement, and also upon Gawain's spoken affirmation that he will seek out the Green Knight in a year's time to receive the return blow, but withholds his own name and address until after Gawain has struck. The astonishing challenger has yet another, even more shattering surprise for the court of King Arthur, however. His head does indeed fall to the ground and roll under the courtiers' feet but instead of falling he jumps forward, groping for it wildly; he remounts his horse, holding the head up by the hair and directing the face towards the high table, and by its mouth he utters a grim admonition to Gawain to seek him at the Green Chapel. With a final fierce jerk on the reins he swings out of the hall, leaving uncertain amusement among the courtiers as they resume their celebration.

II   As the year rolls inexorably by, Gawain must prepare for his journey. At All Hallows Arthur gives a special farewell banquet in his honour, but all the revelry of the Round Table cannot mask the sadness which pervades the court at the prospect of Gawain's apparently certain death. The next day he is armed with ceremony, the poet taking the opportunity of explaining the spiritual and moral significance of the pentangle device (see p. xii) which he displays in his shield and coat-armour, and amid the courtiers' protests at the futility of it all he leaves the court. His journey takes him northwards from Camelot, through Wales and beyond the Wirral, and he encounters great perils from wild beasts, monsters, and (most of all) from the piercing cold; Christmas Eve finds him praying for shelter in the midst of a deep forest. As if in direct answer to his prayer, through the trees he immediately catches sight of a splendid castle and he is welcomed there with copy-book courtesy. Gawain can now briefly exchange his armour for silk and ermine, and foremost among the civilized delights which the castle has to offer him is the company of the host's lovely young wife, whose fresh beauty is set off to perfection against the wrinkled decrepitude of an old lady who is her companion. The host himself, a big jovial man, seems overjoyed to learn that he is entertaining the celebrated Gawain and when the other guests leave, two or three days after Christmas, he is able to dismiss Gawain's anxieties about reaching the Green Chapel; he need not leave the castle until New Year's Day, for it is not two miles away. Furthermore, the host proposes a pleasant amusement for the following day: while he himself is out hunting, Gawain can rest in bed late and spend the day in the company of the host's wife; in the evening they will exchange with each other whatever may have fallen to their lot during the day. The compact is sealed with a drink.

III   Next morning, soon after the host and his men have left the castle to hunt the deer in the surrounding woods, Gawain is astonished by the stealthy entry into his bedroom of the beautiful young wife. She sits on the edge of his bed and using both physical and intellectual means of persuasion—for the game is regulated by the endlessly debatable rules of courtly love—she attempts to seduce him. There ensues, in three stages on three successive mornings, a sustained battle of wits between the two—Gawain fighting all the time to preserve both his chastity and his host's honour while behaving with perfect courtesy towards his hostess; she using every appeal to his manhood and reputation to ensnare him. On the first day, the day of the deer-hunt, she succeeds only to the extent of making him kiss her at her command. The kiss is duly paid over to the host in the evening in exchange for an enormous quantity of venison but Gawain laughs off any suggestion that he should reveal the source of the kiss. The exchange agreement is renewed for the morrow. The next day, while the husband is chasing a ferocious boar, the lady kisses Gawain both at meeting and parting, and though she does not persuade him to teach her anything more of the art of true love, he parries so courteously that no offence is taken on either side. When the hunter returns, Gawain admires the boar—proof of the host's great accomplishment, for he has killed it with his own hand—and gives him two kisses in exchange for it. Once more they agree to the same terms for the following day, 31 December, the day of the fox-hunt. In the morning the lady once again comes to Gawain's room, jewels in her hair, her gown cut low. Now he politely submits to three kisses during the interview and, in addition, accepts from her a girdle made of green silk with gold ornaments, which she says has magic properties to protect the life of any man who wears it. It is only after he has accepted the belt that she begs him not to reveal her gift to her husband. He puts it away carefully, for it may be just the thing for his own predicament, and that evening, in exchange for the miserable fox-skin which the host apologetically hands over, Gawain gives him three kisses but says nothing about the belt. Before they go to bed he says goodbye to the lord of the castle, the two ladies, and to all their household.

IV   Before sunrise on New Year's Day, Gawain gets up and arms himself, wrapping the green belt around his waist on top of his surcoat. Accompanied only by the guide whom the host has assigned to him for the journey to the Green Chapel, he leaves the castle, full of gratitude for the generous hospitality he has received. The journey is a difficult and bewildering one over hills and moors and through woods but just after sunrise the guide stops Gawain and begs him to avoid the Green Chapel, for it is guarded by a huge, violent man who allows no one who passes there to escape with his life. When Gawain refuses, he points out the path to the Chapel and leaves him. Following the path down into a valley, Gawain sees no sign of a building, only a cave projecting from the side of the hill above a stream; from here he can hear a loud grinding noise coming from the cliff on the other side of the stream. In response to Gawain's call (and after a little more grinding), the Green Knight appears at the foot of the cliff and strides towards Gawain, as complete as when he first rode into Arthur's hall, and carrying another huge axe. The beheading 'game' proceeds, with Gawain this time bending his neck to the axe. The first time the Green Knight aims a blow at him, however, Gawain glances at the axe and flinches, and the Green Knight deliberately checks the stroke and taunts him with cowardice. Again he aims at Gawain but although the latter stands firm this time, the Green Knight again refrains from touching him with the axe in order to congratulate him on his resolution. Finally, at the third stroke, the Green Knight exacts some repayment, but instead of beheading Gawain he merely nicks him on the side of the neck. The Green Knight now reveals himself as Gawain's Christmas host and the true instigator of the temptations performed by his wife. The three strokes of the axe correspond to Gawain's conduct in the exchange of winnings game. Only on the last day did he practice deceit and retain the green belt, and then for no more heinous motive than that of saving his own life; such a little fault merited only a light tap by way of punishment. Nevertheless, Gawain blames himself bitterly for his lapse from virtue. Before they part, the Green Knight reveals his true name, Sir Bertilak de Hautdesert; the transformation and the original challenge were the work of Morgan le Fay, who is no other than the old lady of the castle. When he returns to Arthur's court, Gawain tells the story with self-reproach and resolves to wear the belt always to remind him of his fault; the other courtiers adopt the fashion too, but in token of the renown of the Round Table.

(ii)

The barest summary of the action of the poem reveals that it is concerned with the rights and wrongs of conduct, and some account must be given of the poem's viewpoint on the ethical problems raised. It must be made clear, however, that *GGK* is a poem which makes its moral statement largely by fictional means. It has the principal characteristics of medieval romance and many of its qualities are those of poetic narrative of any period.

In choosing to tell an Arthurian story, the poet is inviting his audience to re-enter the world of a quasi-historical society linked by genealogy to the realities of Troy and Rome, a world which generations of romance-writers had peopled with known characters whose deeds built a patterned chronicle of noble striving and noble failure. A number of advantages follow immediately from his pose that the story he has to tell is but one episode in this chronicle: a ready-made interest in the history of Britain and in the deeds of its earliest heroes, certain ready-made assumptions about the chief characters—the malevolence of Morgan, the great magnificence of Arthur—which would help the story along. At the same time, the period is a remote one and the atmosphere surrounding it is fabulous enough to enable him to introduce surprises and even miracles. Yet in spite of the solemn assurances, at beginning and end, of the truth of the *outtrage aventure*, the overall impression, into which even the element of the marvellous and supernatural seems finally to be absorbed, is one of everyday reality and genial common sense. Except, perhaps, for the beheading and its sequel, the writer himself will scarcely vouch for the genuineness of any apparent violation of natural law. The Green Knight, he believes, *may* have been *half* a giant on earth: it is certain, at least, that he was the biggest of men (140–1), taller than anyone in the house by the head and more (333); *the people there* thought he was of magical origin (240); and as for his miraculous survival after the beheading, well (even if there seems no doubt at all that the axe really does smash through his neck) the reader can, if he so wishes, take a hint from Arthur himself (470–5) and dismiss it all as an illusionist's trick. Where so much else in the romance is down to earth, where ironic detachment counts for so much in the analysis of character and situation, it would be contradictory to expect of the reader an attitude of naïve credulity towards the supernatural. To be sure, dragons, satyrs and giants appear beside wolves, bulls, bears, and boars in the list of adversaries Gawain had to fight on his journey, but none of them bothered him as much as the cold weather (720–6).[2] A similar point may be made in relation to the other element of

[2] *Cf.* Elizabeth M. Wright, 'Sir Gawain and the Green Knight', *JEGP* 34 (1935), 157*ff*; Loomis, 1959; Bowers, 1963.

unreality in the romance, the idealization: this is acceptable initially, because we are concerned with the past, when (as everyone knows) life came closer to the ideal (50–9); but it soon becomes apparent that within the poem itself ideal chivalry is being tested in situations which approximate, in complexity and indeterminateness, to those of real life. Again the abiding impression is one of authenticity in the depiction of character and action.

The poem has the twofold quality of all fiction which induces a high degree of imaginative realization in the mind of the reader—descriptive and dramatic power. The poet's descriptive art is many-sided. (See Kane, 1951; Everett, 1955; Renoir, 1958; Borroff, 1962; Benson, 1965.) Its visual aspect is that which has been most consistently singled out, but his poetry mediates an intense awareness of almost every sensory quality of experience; in particular, we are made to share the physical sensibilities of the hero, for instance when he lifts the axe:

> Gauan gripped to his ax and gederes hit on hyght;
> The kay fot on the folde he before sette,
> Let hit doun lyghtly lyght on the naked,
> That the scharp of the schalk schyndered the bones
> And schrank thurgh the schyire grece and schade hit in twynne,
> That the bit of the broun stel bot on the grounde.   (421–6)

or on his winter journey:

> When the colde cler water fro the cloudes schadde
> And fres er hit falle myght to the fale erthe.
> Ner slayn wyth the slete he sleped in his yrnes,
> Mo nyghtes then innoghe, in naked rokkes
> Theras claterande fro the crest the colde borne rennes
> And henged heghe over his hede in hard iisseikkles.   (727–32)

The alliterative requirements of the verse, and its strong beat, seem to have made poets of this school particularly alert to the plastic capabilities of words and to those correspondences in form and meaning which cause one word to reverberate to another. Nevertheless, 'sound symbolism' is not the whole explanation of effects like these. Obviously (in the first passage) sch- alliteration is deliberately chosen and continued through two lines to suggest the 'swish' of the axe as it falls and slices through the neck; but we should not overlook the more subtle imaginative reconstruction implicit in the first three lines, in the choice of gripped and gederes (both hands, strength, weight, slowness), in the account of the careful placing of the foot—the left foot—for balance, and in the multiple suggestions of lyghtly lyght (swiftness, ease, flashing descent). Action and gesture are recounted in terms of significant detail which admits the reader to a solid, full-bodied imaginative world.

Though this feeling for actuality is everywhere present in the descriptions, the poet's technique of presentation is very varied, ranging from the exhaustive picture, like that of the Green Knight and his horse, to the enlarged detail, like that of the lady's face, when Gawain opens his eyes to find his whole field of vision filled by her chin and cheek, her slender laughing lips (1204-7).

His most obvious method of description, and perhaps the least effective for the modern reader, is to saturate the text with detail. This is the rhetorical counterpart of the ornamental detail which was such a prominent feature of contemporary manuscript illustration, painting, architecture and the visual arts generally. (See Pearsall, 1955.) When he writes of clothing and armour, architecture, feasting, hunting or any other aspect of aristocratic life, he is particularly lavish, for he shares with other writers of courtly romance an unashamed delight in heightened descriptions of contemporary courtly life for their own sake. He has the advantage of a verse which can itself be readily clothed in 'tully and tars'—the rich, archaic diction of alliterative poetry. The method may be too slow, florid and decorative to appeal much to modern taste, but it is important to recognize that the style exemplified in these descriptions is an attribute of the medieval concept of courtesy itself; the wealth of minute descriptive detail helps to establish a sense of the civilized life of the two courts, with all its material adjuncts, *all the wele of the worlde*. Even such set pieces of description, however, are usually more than merely cumulative. That of the Green Knight and his horse, for instance (on the surface one of the most static of them), is in reality organized so as to trace not only the courtiers' visual construction of the image but also their bewilderment and their rudimentary conclusions about the significance of what they see. The very length of the description corresponds to the length of the pause which follows the entry and first bold enquiry of the Green Knight, when the courtiers

> al stouned at his steven and ston-stil seten
> In a swoghe sylence thurgh the sale riche.   (242*f*)

Though it actually precedes the overt reference to their stunned examination of the visitor, the course of the description is determined, as it were, by the movement of the eye and mind of an observer in Arthur's hall as he first (with some wonderment) registers the general size and shape of the Green Knight, then curiously investigates every further variation on the green-and-gold motif about his person, descends to his horse to establish the matching features there, and finally returns to the knight himself (with growing speculation about his intentions) to face the axe—for it can, indeed, no longer be ignored. In all this there is a dynamic aspect which is far removed from the mere systematic cataloguing of optical impressions, and it is noteworthy that each of the three bob-and-wheel sections which punctuate the description is a springboard for a new leap of surprised observation: *And overal enker grene* . . . (150); *A grene hors gret and thikke* . . . (175); *Hit semed as no mon myght Under his dynttes drye* . . . (201–2).

The 'point of view' technique, which thus involves the reader emotionally in the action at the beginning, becomes even more important in the second, third, and fourth fitts, where Gawain's is the dominating consciousness in the poem. (See Mehl, 1964; Benson, 1965.) Just as the Round Table's corporate reputation for bravery and honour is now entrusted to Gawain, to stand or fall by his achievement as an individual, so from the beginning of Fitt II the reader's hopes and fears are identified with the hero's; and so to some extent is his view of what happens. Certainly the reader's awareness of what is taking place must be presumed to be a little more comprehensive than that of Gawain (who, if he is over-modest to call himself *of wyt feblest*, nevertheless is required by the plot to be a trifle gullible): we are surely intended, for instance, to perceive the identity of Sir Bertilak and the Green Knight long before he does (see 844*n*, and consider also the significance of 908*f*, 1046*ff*, 1086*f*, 1679*ff*). On the whole, however, the evidence offered to us is limited to what Gawain might have been able to observe.[3] With the exception of the hunting episodes, which stand apart as a stylized and decorative border around the central psychological drama of the bedroom scenes, scarcely anything is recorded that does not take place in his presence, and at every important juncture we are aware of sharing in his perceptions and his emotional attitude towards the events and scenes described. An example is the description of the castle of Sir Bertilak, which Gawain first catches sight of in a frame made by the trunks and branches of the trees of the surrounding park. As he rides up and reins in on the edge of the moat we follow the movement of his eyes:

> The walle wod in the water wonderly depe
> Ande eft a ful huge heght hit haled upon lofte,
> Of harde hewen ston up to the tables, . . .   (787*ff*)

We are also aware of the wall as a barrier and can detect something of the mood which directs and colours his perceptions, the sense of isolation bred

---

[3] This is a strong argument for emendation at 1283*f*, where the reading of the MS appears to give us momentarily the lady's thoughts:

> 'Thagh I were burde bryghtest,' the burde in mynde hade,
> 'The lasse luf in his lode . . .' for lur that he soght . . .   (See 1283–5*n*)

We are not admitted to the private thoughts of Sir Bertilak until 2331–5, just before the dénouement.

in a man by weeks of privation and loneliness. As the description proceeds it becomes the vehicle of a complex blend of wonderment and anxiety. At first the castle might almost be a shimmering mirage—a creation of wishful thinking (772); upon closer examination it presents abundant evidence of human workmanship, but seems by that very token impregnable and forbidding.

Similarly, in 943–69 the comparison between the old and the young lady is made from no cold, dispassionate point of view but in such a way as strongly to suggest the natural preference of a vigorous young man for youth and beauty. Thus the reader is reminded of the pathos of his doomed situation and at the same time is prepared for the young lady's attempts to use her charms in the private interviews of Fitt III. Again, in the final fitt, at 2163–234, we share the hero's curiosity and misgivings in this last stage of his search for the Green Chapel and the Green Knight. In these, and other, passages, description which is ostensibly an objective visual record of scenes and actions becomes a means by which the central character's mental reaction is mediated to the reader, who thus participates in the inner psychological drama of the poem.

When we turn to the more conventionally 'dramatic' aspects of literary composition—depth and consistency of characterization, the creation of episodes involving people in conversation and conflict—we find a comparable skill and subtlety. The key to the poet's success here is his command of life-like speech:

> 'What, is this Arthures hous,' quoth the hathel thenne,
> 'That al the rous rennes of thurgh ryalmes so mony?
> Where is now your sourquydrye and your conquestes,
> Your gryndellayk and your greme and your grete wordes?
> Now is the revel and the renoun of the Rounde Table
> Overwalt wyth a worde of on wyes speche,
> For all dares for drede withoute dynt schewed!' (309–15)

The scornful tone of this is unmistakable; and so is the fierce resentment of Arthur's reply:

> 'Hathel, by heven thyn askyng is nys,
> And as thou foly has frayst, fynde the behoves. . . .' (324f)

Also remarkable is the extent to which the characters are individualized and differentiated through their linguistic mannerisms. Gawain's courtly deference is expressed in an involuted syntax, an exquisite deviousness of phrasing, which is noticeable as much in his public address to the king (343–61) as in his exchanges with the lady of the castle (e.g. 1218–21, 1263–7, 1535–48, 1801–12). The

Green Knight, by contrast, consistently uses a brusque, direct manner of speech, full of sharp statements and exclamations, and lacking in periphrasis (e.g. 448–56, 2239–49); though in Fitt IV his speech, appropriately, is somewhat modified by traits borrowed from that of his courtly other-self, while Gawain finds it impossible to sustain *his* elaborate politeness of address under the strain to which he is subjected. (See Spearing, 1964; Benson, 1965; Clark, 1966.)

(iii)

That the poet intends to use his considerable narrative and dramatic powers in the exploration of a moral theme first becomes unmistakable at the beginning of Fitt II. In a first reading of Fitt I we are aware most vividly of an atmosphere of Christmas festivity that is only temporarily interrupted by the grotesque spectacle of the beheading. Just a hint here and there of the inner moral turn the poem is going to take (the reference to *tresoun* and *tricherie* in the opening lines, the solemnity of the assurance—*bi thi trawthe*—which the Green Knight demands); otherwise all is startlingly entertaining, and reassuringly public. At the opening of Fitt II the sense of the inexorable drawing-on of time is conveyed superbly in the kaleidoscopic picture of the sequence of the seasons, and it is here that the more serious implications, for Gawain, of what had seemed (in the context of Christmas gaiety) only a macabre joke receive graver emphasis:

> Gawan was glad to begynne those gomnes in halle
> Bot thagh the ende be hevy haf ye no wonder,
> For thagh men ben mery in mynde when thay han mayn drynk,
> A yere yernes ful yerne and yeldes never lyke,
> The forme to the fynisment foldes ful selden. (495–9)

Gawain's performance in the return bout of the beheading game is all at once the focus of attention and it is apparent that the first fitt has merely been the dramatic prelude to a prolonged test of character.

This test is first and foremost one of honour in the face of death. Gawain must rise and go of his own volition and seek out his own destruction simply because he has given his word to do so. (In preventing him from binding himself to any religious oath—402–4—the Green Knight has ensured that he will be acting purely from motives of honour and not to avoid divine punishment.) At the same time it is a test of *deportment* in the face of death, because a courageous poise, a sustained gracefulness of life to the end, is part of Gawain's own ideal of conduct. So he preserves an attitude of *sangfroid* about his coming doom ('*never bot trifel*' 547) in the presence of the king and his companions in arms, and they abet him in this, covering their own anxiety with jests (540–2). His

> 'What schuld I wonde?
> Of Destinés derf and dere
> What may mon do bot fonde?' (563*ff*)

is a modest disavowal of heroism; and right up to the confrontation of the last fitt, Gawain's *manner* of facing death is more important, in the moral universe of the poem, than his mere legalistic fulfilling of the compact.

The manipulation of incident in order to set off the quality of conduct is particularly noticeable in the episode involving the guide (2089–159), which is more an opportunity for Gawain to demonstrate the correct attitude to duty and perfidy than a convincing further test of his courage. We can hardly expect the Gawain we know to accept the guide's suggestion that he should turn and run, when it is presented so baldly in the form of an invitation to deception and cowardice:

> 'And I schal hy me hom ayayn; and hete yow fyrre
> That I schal swere "Bi God and alle His gode halwes",
> "As help me God and the halydam", and othes innoghe,
> That I schal lelly yow layne and lauce never tale
> That ever ye fondet to fle for freke that I wyst.' (2121–5)

On the level of narrative, the episode raises a number of questions: why does the guide describe the guardian of the chapel as a simple giant who loves to kill? What is the reason for the frequent changes of tone in his speech, particularly the shift from the frustrated contempt of 2140*ff* :

> 'now thou so much spelles
> That thou wylt thyn awen nye nyme to thyselven
> And the lyst lese thy lyf, the lette I ne kepe.'

to the undisguised admiration of 2149:

> 'Now fares wel, on Godes half, Gawayn the noble!'

(where he even reverts momentarily to the respectful second person plural form of address in the imperative *fares*)? If the possibility that he is really the Green Knight in another disguise seems to be ruled out by 1971*ff*, is he, at least, in his master's confidence? The poet preserves a degree of narrative consistency by casting him as a blunt soldier of perhaps no great tact or intelligence (as is possibly suggested by the obscurities of expression in 2101*f* and 2109), but we are given no final explanation of his strange behaviour, and the most satisfactory solution is that the question of his identity and motive is here subordinate in the poet's intention. The guide's chief function is to act as a foil to Gawain, and as a stimulus to the correct response of dignified refusal.

The incident yields its full significance, however, only in relation to what has gone before. The poet is interested, where Gawain's actions are concerned, in the relation between publicly acknowledged principles and private motives, and it may be asserted that he has given the guide his role, and shaped it in this particular way, partly in order to show the imperfect identity between them in Gawain's case. The reader is uneasily conscious of the fact that, for all his aloof rectitude, Gawain is in possession of a belt which, he has been assured, has magical properties to protect his life. It is not, of course, certain how much trust in the lady's assurance we are to attribute to him, but the author's comment

That forgat not Gawayn, for gode of hymselven   (2031)

indicates at least a willingness to take no unnecessary chances. It will be remembered that Gawain has accepted that more subtle offer of escape without demur and has even agreed, at a moment when the moral issues are less clear,

for hir sake discever hit never
Bot to lelly layne fro hir lorde   (1862f)

—lelly layne is, significantly, the very formula which is used by the guide in the later episode (2124) and which Gawain himself on that other occasion somewhat scornfully rejects (2128). The implications are not to Gawain's credit, but they are not heavily underscored by the poet and hence do not detract greatly from his courage or nobility. There is no conscious duplicity on Gawain's part (his moral awakening comes later); there is just the hint, for the reader, of a performance which is slightly less perfect than it seems. (See also Delany, 1965.)

It is clear, however, despite the semi-exemplary nature of the poem, that the poet has no wish to hold an isolated virtue up for admiration in an otherwise rather inhuman character (as Chaucer, for instance, does in the Patient Griselda of The Clerk's Tale). On the contrary, he is concerned with a variety of virtues in interaction. (This is why he insists on the integrated pattern of the pentangle, the emblem of Gawain's character.) Whether he himself or some earlier writer was responsible for joining the various plots of the Beheading Game, Temptation, and Exchange of Winnings in their present form, their interlacement is cleverly exploited to show the difficulties which beset moral choice, and also moral judgement, in the complexities of real life.

Gawain's ordeal, then, is by no means a straightforward one. The poet knew that in life a genuine test of character always comes from the quarter from which it is least expected, and as if in demonstration of this truth he faces Gawain—and the reader—with a series of deceptive situations which always catch him on the wrong foot: *The forme to the fynisment foldes ful selden* (499). At a time when little courage appears to be demanded of him (*this note is so nys*: 'this affair is so foolish' 358), when social tact and rhetoric are all that is required to secure him the opportunity of ridding the court of the troublesome intruder on their Christmas revelries, he finds that he has taken on a real trial of nerve; after bracing himself for the return blow a year later, he finds that he has already been tested, on other terms, in the social warmth and security of Bertilak's castle. Just such an ambiguous reversal occurs with the initial, almost magical, appearance of the castle itself. Coming as it does on Christmas Eve, at the end of his *anious vyage* (with all the conventional challenges which that has presented to his knightly courage), the sudden materialization of the castle in the middle of the frozen forest is a rebirth of hope; at the same time it is to be the scene of a grave, because more insidious, threat to his honour. He is indeed to be given a second chance to save his life, yet may destroy his own integrity; and he is to act in ignorance of both possibilities.[4]

The moral danger to Gawain is complicated by the very mixture of demands made upon him by his own code of conduct. The ideal of *chevalry* to which he adheres is a composite code of behaviour which the later Middle Ages forged together from a number of disparate elements. The old Germanic attitudes of martial prowess, loyalty to one's lord, and generosity to one's followers formed the basis. Christianity contributed its moral absolutes—faith, charity, humility, chastity, etc.—and an emphasis on the use of power for the benefit of the weak; at the same time, the symbolism and ritual of the church set formal precedents which were followed in the investiture rites of the orders of chivalry. Finally, the various social accomplishments which flowered among

---

[4] McAlindon, 1965, argues persuasively that the poem's story-pattern is coloured by 'one of the oldest and most fundamental themes in Christian legend' the connection of magic with the devil, and the power of Providence to deliver the faithful from the false 'angel of light'. It is questionable, however, whether the logic of the plot allows us to see the castle—or Bertilak—as wholly evil ('The luminous and inviting appearance of the castle was of a piece with Gawain's whole experience, a characteristic product of the imitation angel of light. . . . The God-sent comfort and reassurance of Bertilak's (Morgan's?) castle was, in short, a dangerous illusion', p. 138). There is no evidence of any compulsion on Bertilak to spare Gawain's life, except his radical benevolence and admiration for Gawain's virtues (*cf.* 2341*ff*). One may wonder whether the poem is not closer to the pattern of a Providential testing, as in *The Clerk's Tale*. (See also M. Mills, 1965; Spearing, 1966.)

the feudal nobility of the high Middle Ages—the arts of music, poetry and elegant conversation, as much as horsemanship, jousting and hunting—all made their contribution to the complex idea of the perfect knight. The conglomerate was no doubt at first the accidental product of historical pressures but it became shaped, initially in response to the challenge of the crusades, into a fully conscious philosophy of conduct, codified in treatises such as Ramón Lull's *Le Libre del Orde de Cavayleria* and Christine de Pisan's *Le Livre des Faits d'Armes et de Chevalerie*.[5] Theorists such as these tend to stress the martial and religious side of chivalry. It is Ramón Lull's favourite theme that 'the offyce of preesthode & of chyvalry have grete concordaunce.' A somewhat different, and perhaps more generally influential, conception of knighthood—one in which social arts and refined manners are particularly prominent—was disseminated by the aristocratic literature of entertainment, the romances. In *GGK*, as in the French romances which the author knew, the ideal knight is an accomplished courtier, as much as a courageous man of battle and a devout Christian. Indeed, the terms *cortaysye*, *cortays(ly)* ('courtliness, courtly') take on the wider meanings of *chevalry*, *chevalrous* (in 263 the Green Knight equates *cortaysye* with 'knightly conduct, daring') while continuing to designate the narrower set of social qualities exemplified, for instance, in Gawain's address to the king or his behaviour towards the lady of Hautdesert. Moreover, in the romance conception of knighthood, love between the sexes (as an adjunct of social manners) plays a part of such importance that it can be regarded as the *sine qua non* of courtesy.

The possibility of a conflict between the religious and worldly demands of knighthood was too obvious to be ignored and one sees, in particular in the thirteenth-century treatment of the Grail legend, the emergence of the idea of 'two chivalries', *chevalerie seculer* and *chevalerie celestiel*, the one dedicated to worldly and the other to spiritual ends. (See Smithers, 1963.)

The author of *GGK* shows an awareness of the latent contradictions in the idea of chivalry. His intention, however, is surely not to stress them but to reconcile them as far as is logically possible and to present, in the character of

---

[5] The first was translated from a French version by Caxton and printed as *The Book of the Ordre of Chyvalry* (edited by A. T. P. Byles, London, EETS, 1926); the second was also printed in translation by Caxton as *The Book of Fayttes of Armes and of Chyvalrye* (edited by A. T. P. Byles, London, EETS, 1932). See also, for discussion of chivalry, Byles's chapter 'Medieval Courtesy Books and the Prose Romances of Chivalry' in *Chivalry: Its Historical Significance and Civilizing Influence*, edited by Edgar Prestage (London, 1928) and Gervase Mathew, 'Ideals of Knighthood in Late-Fourteenth-Century England' in *Studies in Medieval History Presented to F. M. Powicke*, edited by R. W. Hunt and others (Oxford, Clarendon Press, 1948; reprinted in part in Fox, 1968).

Gawain, a unity in diversity. The most explicit exposition of Gawain's charac-
ter, the discussion of the symbolism of his pentangle-device, with its blending
of Christian and courtly terminology, draws attention to the mixture of
religious and secular virtues in the chivalric code. (*Cf.* Ackerman, 1958; Green,
1962.) Through his somewhat strained allegory of the five lines and five
points, the poet declares Gawain's senses (*fyve wyttes*) and his actions (*fyve
fyngres*) to have been pure because of his trust in the salvation (*fyve woundes*)
of Christ; his supreme martial virtue of courage (*forsnes*) also has a religious
source in his devotion to the Virgin. The reference to the Five Wounds of
Christ and the Five Joys of Mary (see 645*n*) are intended to suggest not only
the general character of Gawain's piety but more specifically the devotional
quality of his personal religious life, which is later demonstrated by his anxiety
to carry out his Christian observances when Christmas Eve finds him still
searching for his rendezvous. The fifth pentad consists of moral virtues parti-
cularly associated with knighthood: *fraunchyse, felawschyp, clannes, cortaysye,*
and *pité*; upon examination, however, it will be seen that each of these terms
has both secular and religious connotations. *Fraunchyse* (literally 'freedom') is
primarily a social quality—that nobility of mind, generosity, and magnanimity
which was held to characterize the free-born man as opposed to the servile;
but it could also refer to the moral freedom which is the dignity of man (*al
that franches that I gave man in Paradis, Cursor Mundi, c.* 1300) and is Caxton's
word (in the translation of the *Golden Legend*) for the work of the Holy Spirit:
For where the holy ghoost is, there is fraunchyse and lyberté. Felawschyp is the spirit
of comradeship and could be applied equally to the brotherhood of knights or
the spiritual communion of the church. *Cortaysye* (also called *mensk* in other
parts of the poem, e.g. 2052) has a particularly wide range of meaning, em-
bracing the superficial graces of behaviour at one end of the spectrum and
theological Grace at the other (in *Pearl*, Mary is *Quene of cortaysye* 432 etc., and
Of courtaysye, as says Saynt Poule, Al arn we membres of Jesu Kryst 457*f*). *Pité* was
ambiguous between 'pity' and 'piety' at this time (see 654*n*). We are perhaps
in danger of overlooking, or taking for granted, the more literal sense of
clannes ('cleanness, purity') in relation to good manners, yet Guillaume de
Lorris thought it worth while to put some very practical advice on the subject
into his general plan of self-improvement for the courtly lover:

> Thyn hondis wassh, thy teeth make white,
> And let no filthe upon thee bee.[6]

and the author of *Sir Gawain* is by no means above such concerns himself.
(*Cf.* 72, 885, 956*n*.) However, it is purity of life that is most readily suggested

---

[6] From the ME translation of *The Romaunt of the Rose* (2280*f*).

by the word in this context, coming as it does after the statement about Gawain's devotion to the Virgin.

The juxtaposition of *clannes* with *cortaysye* is also of importance for the significance of *cortaysye*: whatever other people might mean by the word, the author wishes to portray the perfect knight as free from the taint of sinful love, though he will not reject anything from the traditional concept of *cortaysye* which can possibly be reconciled with Christian morality; his knight cannot be a prig or a prude. Thus, though Gawain does of course defend his chastity in the course of the action, he never once bases an argument on religious conviction or abstract morality. In order to tempt Gawain to have intercourse with her, the lady insists on discussing and acting out the conventional tenets of *fin amour* and, for fear of discourtesy, even the knight of Mary cannot refuse point-blank to take part in this elegant game. The lady's idea of the obligations of courtesy is obviously not the same as Gawain's, but he will parry her assaults on his virtue only by pretending to misunderstand her, or by protesting his own unworthiness—anything rather than openly criticize her conduct. The poet's intention is to place his knight in a situation in which the sides of the pentangle rub a little uncomfortably against one another. In this way the question of the compatibility of one element with another in this blend of manners, social obligations and high religious ideals is delicately explored. (*Cf.* Kiteley, 1961.) We are left in little doubt as to Gawain's view of the relative importance of the various aspects of chivalry; he has no yearnings for the *lel layk of luf* at a time when he is expecting to be called to give an account of his soul. Yet he would clearly like to achieve his spiritual victory without openly repudiating any of the demands which convention makes of the knight—not excepting that attitude of extravagant compliment and gallant courtship which knights were expected to maintain towards all ladies. (The courtly Gawain's first act towards both ladies, the sallow and repulsive as well as the young and attractive one, is to ask to be their *servaunt* (976), their loving admirer.)[7] Similarly, the poet, whose admiration for courtesy is almost unbounded, would like to bring it through the test which he has devised for it as complete as possible in all its aspects, the pattern of a well-integrated man.

It is this necessity of sustaining several roles at once that poses the most difficult problems for Gawain during his stay in the castle, as his tempters seem to know. It should not be supposed that the only moral area of any

[7] Here and there, for instance in the expectations of the courtiers of Hautdesert and of the lady herself (see 916–27, 1297–1301, 1508–34), the author appears to allow Gawain's 'other' reputation, as a seducer of women—see 919*n*—a peripheral role, though it is of course nowhere acknowledged explicitly. (See M. Mills, 1965; Brewer, 1966.)

interest to the author is the one in which Sir Gawain makes the wrong choice; the poet devotes almost the whole of the description of the three long interviews with the lady to demonstrating Gawain's success in balancing the demands of courtesy with those of chastity and of loyalty to his host—in showing that he is indeed

On the fautlest freke that ever on fote yede. (2363)

If it is true that his chastity is attacked through his courtesy, it is also true that he achieves his victory through that attribute of courtesy for which he is most famous, his skill in *the teccheles termes of talkyng noble* (917). To that extent his courtesy vindicates itself. (For a sensitive analysis of the conversations, see D. Mills, 1968.)

His single error of judgement occurs at the end of the third conversation (in a passage of great psychological subtlety, 1792–1869), when he agrees to conceal from the host his acceptance of the girdle, thus violating the agreement made between them on the night before the first hunt. His sole fault, then, is his lapse from the highest standards of honesty in the context of the exchange-of-winnings agreement. This temptation cannot, of course, be considered in complete isolation from the others, though it is of a different kind. There is an element of cunning in its placement just before the lady's final departure from his room, for his sustained success in resisting one type of inducement over three days would make him especially vulnerable to a superficially casual suggestion which contained no threat to his chastity. Nor can we discount the possible effect on his resolution of the all-pervading atmosphere of intimate gaiety, luxury and ease in the castle.[8] However, we can be sure (with the Green Knight—*cf.* 2367) that 'wooing' plays no direct part in his action, for he has previously had little difficulty in refusing the offer of a ring as a keepsake. Politeness, again, can be only a minor factor. It is true that the lady extracts from him the promise of concealment only after he has accepted the gift but we cannot infer (after his displays of skill in extricating himself from similar social traps) that he had no choice but to agree.[9] He agrees to the deception principally because he sees in the belt the possibility of saving his life.

[8] Note the emphasis, for instance, in 1310*ff*, 1468*ff*, 1560*ff*, 1729*ff*. In ME homiletic literature the sin of sloth comprises (among other things): *nessched of herte* (concern for creature comforts), *ydelnesse, untrewthe* (lack of resolution), *foryetfulnesse, grucchynge* (anger at being reproved), *sorwe* (touchiness), and *wanhope* (despair); see S. Wenzel, 'Sloth in Middle English Devotional Literature', *Anglia* 79 (1961–2), 287–318. The poet is content, however, with a mere ironic suggestion of self-indulgence.

[9] Nevertheless, somewhat contradictorily, the author relies upon the faint atmosphere of intrigue which he has built up around Sir Gawain and the lady

That we are supposed to see this in itself as an unworthy motive (or contrary to the beheading-agreement) is not, I think, implied in the poem. On the face of it, as long as he keeps his word by presenting himself at the appointed time and takes the return blow *withoute dabate* (2041), his moral duty in regard to his compact with the Green Knight is fulfilled; and he can hardly be blamed for taking the chance of magical protection against an adversary who so obviously has magic at his disposal. This appears to be the view which the Green Knight himself takes of the matter when, at the end of Fitt IV, he drops his terrifying pose and (without actually removing his disguise) merges in character once more with the genial Sir Bertilak. It is one of the most striking feats of the poet that in spite of the sympathy which has been so carefully nurtured for the sorely-tried Sir Gawain the reader so readily accepts this change of role from Green Knight to Sir Bertilak, from fiendish tormentor to kindly expositor of the morality. Sir Gawain is gently reproved for breaking his word in neglecting to yield up the whole of his winnings of the third day, but to Sir Bertilak (2368), as to the narrator (2037*ff*), it is a mitigating factor that his motive was one of self-preservation. Sir Bertilak, in other words, takes into account the gap in importance between the matter of life and death to which Gawain is committed at the Green Chapel and the exchange-of-winnings agreement. The levity with which the latter is proposed, and which accompanies its performance and reaffirmation each time, must indeed have given it the distinct character of a burlesque; the pledges are mock-solemn ones, made always *in bourde* 'in jest' (1409; *cf.* 1404: *in her bourdyng*; 1112*f*, 1681-5), and the incongruous 'winnings' are exchanged amid laughter and jokes (1392-9, 1623, 1644-7, 1932*ff*). To Gawain the whole thing is a hugely absurd *gomen*:

> 'And that yow lyst for to layke lef hit me thynkes.'   (1111)

The point has some bearing on the validity of the confession which he makes to the priest immediately after accepting the girdle, and in which he apparently makes no mention of his possession of it. At the time, to violate the rules of a parlour game in order to save his life must hardly have seemed a sin at all. Hence, when the narrator declares that he

> schrof hym schyrly and schewed his mysdedes,
> Of the more and the mynne, and merci beseches, ...   (1880*f*; *cf.* 1883*f*)

we can take it as a literal reflection of Gawain's state of mind and intentions.

(*cf.* especially 1010-19) to add plausibility to Gawain's ready acquiescence in her condition of secrecy. His complicity here is of a piece with his gallant refusal to disclose the source of the kisses to Bertilak (1395*ff*, 1940*f*).

It is only in retrospect, when he sees its connections, that it becomes a grave moral fault for him.

Gawain's bitter self-condemnation when he knows he has been found out is in sharp contrast to the 'plain man's' view of his fault taken by the narrator, by Sir Bertilak, and later by the knights of the Round Table (2513ff). He accuses himself repeatedly of *cowardyse* and *covetyse* (2374, 2379f, 2508), the first principally an offence against courage (the major virtue of chivalry), the second primarily a vice in the Christian code, the root of all evil and the antithesis of charity, but also in the poem the antithesis of *larges and lewté, that longes to knyghtes* (2381). (The deliberate crossing of the two terminologies is as noticeable in these passages as in the description of the pentangle, and serves a similar purpose.) Quite evidently he has never behaved as a coward in the literal sense, and nearly as much direct evidence is available to the reader that he has not literally acted out of covetousness.[10] The exaggerations of his outburst of self-reproach immediately after Bertilak's disclosure are wholly appropriate psychologically as the chagrined reaction of a humiliated man; a perfectionist who has failed by the merest margin, it is understandable that he was

> So agreved for greme he gryed withinne (2370)

and that he gave outlet to it in this form. It is when we hear him level these and similar charges against himself later in a tone of quieter remorse (both later in his conversation with Bertilak—2433ff—when the emotional temperature is a little lower, and at the very end when he is relating his story to Arthur and his knights, 2507ff) that we realize Gawain will never take his failure lightly. Perhaps it is psychologically consistent for a character like Gawain to behave in this way. Yet given the clear discrepancy of judgement, the reader is bound to wonder to what extent Gawain's self-condemnation and remorse are defined as excessive by the poem as a whole. Certainly the sentiments which he expresses about sin in the last stanza:

> 'For mon may hyden his harme bot unhap ne may hit,
> For ther hit ones is tachched twynne wil hit never,' (2511f)

appear to go counter to Catholic teaching on forgiveness, and to be tainted

[10] The very broad definition of covetousness in medieval theology (any action which puts self before God) must be borne in mind; also, he might technically plead guilty of covetousness in so far as he has retained something which was due to another (even though he did not want it for its material value). That he can use the term with any show at all of appropriateness depends on these considerations, but they only accentuate the discrepancy between Bertilak's view and his, and the difficulty of balancing the importance of intention against that of consequence. (See Hills, 1963; Burrow, 1964.)

by 'scrupulousness' and even 'despair'.[11] By contrast, the judgement of Bertilak in 2390–4:

> I halde the polysed of that plyght and pured as clene
> As thou hades never forfeted sythen thou was fyrst borne.

(if we may see the chivalric 'confession' as signifying confession generally) is positively orthodox.[12] Yet this 'criticism' of Gawain does not fully cancel out the note of admiration for youthful idealism which runs throughout the poem. Undoubtedly, too, Gawain makes *ernest of game*. Yet is it not a recurring theme of the poem that game and earnest are in continual alternation, the two faces of a single destiny (*cf.* 16–20, 495*ff*, 564*f*, 1681*f*) and that it is often impossible to foresee the consequences of trivial action?—

> Gawan was glad to begynne those gomnes in halle
> Bot thagh the ende be hevy haf ye no wonder, . . .   (495*f*)

[11] Absolution 'gives grace, removes guilt, and reconciles the sinner with God', *Catholic Dictionary*, by W. E. Adds and T. Arnold (revised edition, London, 1953), s.v. Absolution (p.5a). See also O. D. Watkins, *A History of Penance*, New York, reprinted 1961, I, 291. Fourteenth-century vernacular manuals of confession stress, on the one hand, the efficacy of shrift in removing sin and, on the other, the absolute necessity of faith in the sacrament on the part of the penitent; e.g. Robert Mannyng's *Handlyng Synne* (edited F. J. Furnivall, London, EETS, 1901–3):

> But yn every tyme that thou schryvest the,
> Of pyne shalt thou uncharged be;
> For the prest hath powere
> To asoyle the quyte and clere.   (11941*ff*)
> Here mowe ye se, that shryfte and sorowe
> Alle only may no man borowe
> But he have gode hope, whan he ys shryve,
> That hys synne shal be foryyve.   (12323*ff*)

Cf. Jacob's Well (edited A. Brandeis, London, EETS, 1900), 36; and Langland's discussion of the relation between inner disposition and oral confession in *Piers Plowman* B-text, XIV, 81–96. The emendation of *non* to *mon* in 2511 hardly affects the argument that these lines are unorthodox; on the other hand, the exact meaning of *harme* is important: I take it as particularized by *blame* 2506 and by its use in 2390.

[12] *Cf. Purity* 1129*ff*:

> So, if folk be defowled by unfre chaunce
> That he be sulped in sawle, seche to schryfte,
> And he may polyce hym at the prest, by penaunce taken,
> Wel bryghter then the beryl other browden perles.

This kind of inconclusiveness is by no means unparalleled in medieval poetry. Debate poems like *The Owl and the Nightingale* and *Winner and Waster* are more concerned to present opposed philosophies of life (as embodied in representative characters) with all their strengths and weaknesses, than to come to simple conclusions on one side or the other; and on a more specific topic— the nature of love and its relation to salvation—Chaucer's *The Parlement of Foules* is another example of a narrative poem whose train of dialectic is not resolved but merely broken off at the end. In *GGK* the balance is a very delicate one, for if Gawain's perfectionism is seen as impossible of attainment it remains to the end admirable as a noble ideal, and if his remorse appears excessive it nevertheless exposes as slightly superficial the cheerful readiness of the Arthurian courtiers to identify with his triumph rather than his shame.

(iv)

Thus ambiguity, which plays such an important part in the plot-structure and in the experience of the hero, is present at the heart of the moral significance of the poem, colouring the reader's evaluation of Gawain's action. It is present too in the texture of the poem, as a direct reflection, in the descriptive style, of the alternating gravity and gaiety of the incidents described, and also more indirectly. Frequently it is expressed in the antithetical balance of the alliterative line itself, as for instance in the equivocal opening stanzas:

> The tulk that the trammes of tresoun ther wroght
> Was tried for his tricherie, the trewest on erthe.
> Hit was Ennias the athel and his highe kynde, . . .   (3*ff*)

in the contrast, at the beginning of Fitt II, between burgeoning spring and barren winter:

> And al grayes the gres that grene was ere;
> Thenne al rypes and rotes that ros upon fyrst,
> And thus yirnes the yere in yisterdayes mony . . .   (527*ff*)

and in the counterpointed portraits of the two ladies:

> For if the yonge was yep, yolwe was that other; . . .   (951)

More diffusely, it appears in the contrast between the quiet, and apparently harmless, comedy of the bedroom episodes and the violent and bloody activities going on simultaneously in the surrounding woods and fields.

B

In all these antitheses the poet is interested not only in contrasts but also in the connections and affinities. The traitor is one with the illustrious founder of dynasties. (Silverstein, 1965.) The contrasting seasons merge into one another in the continuous cycle of the year. (Silverstein, 1964.) The old woman is what the young one will turn into. (Speirs, 1948.) In Fitt III, the structural formality directs attention to a number of different connections between the hunts out of doors and the stalking of Gawain within. (*Cf.* Savage, 1928, 1956.) On each of three days the poet first gets the host engaged in a fast and furious hunt in the open, then describes the bedroom-encounter in full, returns to the hunting-field for the kill, and finally brings the double narrative thread together in the hunters' return and the exchange of winnings. This structural patterning of bedroom and hunting episodes (with the interconnections provided by the husband-and-wife relationship of two of the participants and by the bargain made between the men) gives opportunity for subdued ironic contrast and comparison, rather in the way decorated initials and marginal illustrations in a medieval book can be used for apt (and sometimes ironic) comment upon the text.[13] We are made aware, for instance, that form and style are essential to both courtly hunting and courtly love-making. The play upon the word *gomen* (*game*) (see, e.g., 1314, 1319, 1532, 1536, 1894) links the boudoir battle of wits with the slaughter in the field and hints that the sort of *gomen* enjoyed by Gawain and the lady may possibly have bloody consequences too. The stylized alternation of the quarry—deer one day, boar the next, fox the next—suggests that another function of the hunts is to provide an oblique commentary on the features of the temptation which Gawain is undergoing at the time, and upon his expedients for escape. The cross-reference here is shadowy at first but becomes more directly focussed in the parallelisms of the third day, when Gawain shows some of the devious-ness of the cunning fox and falls, like the fox, into Bertilak's trap (*cf.* 1728*ff*, 1855*ff*, 1902, 2267). The company in the field make great joy over Reynard's destruction, and similarly Gawain is happier that day than he has been since he came to the castle, his trials over and his life apparently assured (1885–92), yet when the host returns, the *foule fox felle* is acknowledged to be a poor prize and the note of anticlimax recalls the tainted and equivocal nature of Gawain's victory.

The game of 'trivial or serious?' is played with the reader by the poet, as well as with Gawain by the Green Knight, for in dramatizing the action largely as it unfolds itself to Gawain's consciousness, the poet ensures that the reader too is kept continually guessing. The ambiguity is in part a device of dramatic

[13] Instances in D. W. Robertson, Jr., *A Preface to Chaucer* (Princeton, 1963)—for example, Fig. 39 (of a page of the Ormesby Psalter with the theme of harmony and discord) and discussion 129*f*.

suspense, though (as has been remarked) it penetrates to the deepest moral levels of the poem as well. In the outcome, the reader discovers that the end is not at all 'heavy', yet he is left with a sense that potentially grave issues have been in view throughout. It is significant that all the major passages of rhetorical amplification (prologues to Fitt I and Fitt II, pentangle passage, description of the ladies) while they each contain oppositions and ambiguities, have a universality that contributes, on balance, to the moral gravity of the poem. Through them the actions of Gawain are placed in a context successively of world history, the natural order, the moral law, and the mutability of human life and beauty. No precedent for these passages exists in any of the known analogues; they are evidently designed by the author to direct the reader's attention to the significance he wishes the story material to bear. His rhetorical aim in the portraits of the two ladies, for example, is to present a forceful illustration of the homiletic theme that age is a mirror of the frailty of the flesh. What Gawain is aware of is a raddled image against which the young lady's beauty shines the more lustrously; what else he might learn from the comparison is indicated obliquely by the poet in his description of the older one (on the surface a gratuitously cruel description) in terms reminiscent of religious lyrics of the 'Signs of Old Age' and 'Signs of Death' type:

> Wanne mine eyhnen misten
> And mine heren sissen   (*ears are stopped?*)
> And mi nose koldet   (*grows cold*)
> And mi tunge ffoldet
> And mi rude slaket   (*fresh complexion fades*)
> And mine lippes blaken   (*grow pale*)
> And mi muth grennet
> And mi spotel rennet . . .   (*spittle runs*)
> Al to late, al to late,
> Wanne the bere ys ate gate   (*bier*)[14]

Even in these passages, however, the poet prefers in general to avoid direct moralizing and to rely on the resonance of traditional religious language (as well as on the symbolism of the poem's structure and symmetry; *cf.* Howard,

---

[14] Trinity College, Cambridge MS 43, printed in *English Lyrics of the Thirteenth Century*, edited by Carleton Brown (Oxford, reprinted 1950), 130, 220*ff.* (*Cf.* GGK 951–69, especially 951, 961–3.) For discussion of the tradition, see Rosemary Woolf, *English Religious Lyric in the Middle Ages* (Oxford, 1968), 78*ff.*, 102*ff.* Grim irony, of the kind used here in

> A mensk lady on molde mon may hir calle,
>   For Gode!   (964*f.*)

is also characteristic of the genre.

1964) to bring home to the reader the more serious implications of the tale.[15] GGK is undoubtedly a romance told with the purpose of portraying ideal character in action. We have seen the poet's specific aim as a loving critique of courtesy. He wished to show that as the exemplar of a refined chivalry Gawain was also as nearly perfect a Christian as can ordinarily be expected in this imperfect world, and to demonstrate this without distorting the concept of true knighthood which he had learned from the most courtly romances. It is precisely his lightness of touch, his avoidance of overt didacticism, and his preference for irony, suggestion and implication, that enabled him to make his romance the vehicle of a wise morality without in the least disfiguring it as a romance.

Note on Language and Metre

The English of the poem is that of the north-west midland area in the late fourteenth century. Essential grammatical information (past forms of verbs, irregular plurals of nouns, etc.) will be found in the glossary and notes. The following additional features of language and style should be noticed:

1   The (polite) plural imperative of the verb usually ends in *-(e)s*: *Tas you* 1390 (*reflex.*), *Dos teches* 1533; occasionally in *-e*.

2   The present participle ends in *-ande*: *Talkkande* 108; the *-yng* forms are mostly verbal nouns: *talkyng* 'conversation' 917 (the two apparent exceptions, *sykyng* 753 and *gruchyng* 2126, are probably re-interpreted prepositional phrases: (*with*) *sykyng*, etc.).

3   Impersonal constructions are common: *hym wondered* 1201, *me byhoves* 1216.

4   Double negatives are equivalent to single negatives (also in indirect prohibitions, e.g. 1156*f*).

5   A main verb of motion is often omitted after an auxiliary or modal, e.g. 1959, 2132.

6   A subject relative pronoun may be omitted, e.g. 2072.

7   Relative clauses are often widely separated from their antecedents; see 145*n*.

---

[15] A number of striking parallels of phrase with the moral odes of the Vernon MS (edited by C. Horstmann and F. J. Furnivall, *Minor Poems of the Vernon MS*, London, EETS, 1892–1901, II, 658–746) gives some indication of the Gawain-poet's familiarity with contemporary didactic verse.

8   Prepositions often follow their nouns (pronouns): *you aboute* 351, *hym byforne* 1375.

9   Poetic inversion is frequent, e.g. 379*f*, 389 ('that you are to strike this blow').

10   Adjectives sometimes function as nouns: *the naked* 'the bare flesh' 423, *this wyly* (i.e. the fox) 1905.

11   In description, a 'catalogue' style (nominal, prepositional and participial phrases where finite verbs might be expected) is sometimes used, e.g. 571, 575, 582, 586.

12   Phrases like *in erde, that tyde, in londe*, are sometimes metrical expletives of very little (or only intensive) meaning; they can be used aptly on occasions, however, and allowance should always be made for the possibility of special significance; *cf.* 196*n*.

13   The alliterative poet needed synonyms of varying phonetic form for at least the most common concepts and is often compelled to use a word of specialized meaning in a generalized sense: *wale* 398 (normally 'choose', here 'find'); *cf.* 155*n*, 288*n*.

The principal characteristics of the metre of the poem can best be illustrated from some normal lines:

/ x x   x   / x ‖ x / x   x / x
Tic i us   to Tuskan   and teldes bigynnes   (11)

x / x   x / (x)‖ x /(x) x x   /(x)
Half-etayn in erde   I hope that he were   (140)

x x / x x x /(x) ‖ x   / x x / x
Ne no pysan ne no plate   that pented to armes   (204)

x   x /   x x / x ‖ x x x /   / x
For me think hit not semly — as hit is soth knawen   (348)

x   x x x   / x x / ‖ x   /   x / x x
And sythen this note is so nys   that noght hit yow falles   (358)

x   x / x x x x   / ‖ x / x x /
And he luflyly hit hym laft   and lyfte up his honde   (369)

Each line is divided by a caesura (‖) into two half-lines, containing two stresses (/) and linked by the repetition of the initial sounds of some of the stressed syllables (alliteration). There is no fixed number of unstressed syllables (x); the two stresses of the half-line may be separated by three or more (as in 369a) or by none (348b); unstressed syllables are likewise optional at the beginning and end of the half-line. The minimum half-line consists of four syllables, e.g.:

$$\text{x x / /}$$
as I tryst may   (380b)

Normal speech-rhythm obtains and there is no regular recurrence of stressed and unstressed syllables, as there is in accentual verse. Some rhythmical patterns are common, however (e.g. x / x x / x), and 358b shows that normal speech-emphasis (on *yow*) could be counterpointed with an expected ground-pattern (as in regular accentual verse). It was the rhythmical flexibility and adaptability of the alliterative metre that enabled it to survive the syntactical changes between OE and ME; hence, too, it is of little consequence that we are not certain whether the final unaccented *-e* of *plate* (204a) or *hope* (140b) was still pronounced in the Gawain poet's area at the time at which he was writing. (Elision may be assumed, in any case, in e.g. *note* 358, *lyfte* 369, before another vowel.) Probably the alliterative poet was aware not so much of metre in the abstract as of rhythm embodied in phrase patterns and syntactical patterns which were traditional to the style.

The alliterative requirements are similarly free. The general rule is that there should be one alliterating word in the first stressed position of the second half-line, and at least one, but usually two, in the first half-line (204, 358). The first half-line often contains more than two alliterating words, however—sometimes with an extra full or secondary stress (\):

$$\text{/   x   x   x   \\   /}$$
Braydes out a **bry**ght **br**ont   (1584a)

The rhythmical and syntactical patterns of these extended half-lines also occur without the extra alliteration:

$$\text{/ x x x   x   \\   (x) /}$$
Gederes up hys grymme tole   (2260a)[16]

Sometimes a line contains a double alliterative pattern:

And wyth a **c**ountenaunce **dr**ye he **dr**ow doun his **c**ote   (335)
Schaved wyth a **sch**arp **kn**yf, and the **sch**yre **kn**itten   (1331)

These lines also illustrate the fact that groups of sounds may alliterate (here *dr*- and *kn*-). A vowel may alliterate with any other vowel or with *h*-:

And **Y**wan, **U**ryn son, **e**tte with **h**ymselven   (113)

[16] The final *-e* of *tole* (direct object) is a spelling convention (indicating long medial *-o-*) and was never pronounced; *cf. honde* (369), above.

(*Cf.* 140 above.) Alliteration occasionally occurs in an unstressed word or syllable (*with* 987; *bi* 1571; *be* and *by-* 1216).

In *GGK* blocks of long lines are used to form stanzas of varying length, each of which is rounded off by a line of one stress (the 'bob') followed by a rhyming quatrain (the 'wheel') of three-stressed lines, the second and fourth of which rhyme with the bob.

NOTE TO THE TEXT

This edition of *GGK* is based on the *EETS* facsimile of the unique MS, B.M. Cotton Nero A.x. (on the MS itself in cases of doubt), and the text has been compared throughout with that of the editions listed in the Bibliography. New readings are proposed at 171, 1485 (word division), 1915 and 2440, and new emendations at 328, 1053, 1265*f*, 1440*f*, 1473 and 2177. Obvious errors are corrected, and abbreviations expanded, silently (where the -*us* abbreviation is apparently used for -*s* it is so rendered), and punctuation and capitalization are modern.

Obsolete characters are also modernized in accordance with the policy of the series: þ is replaced by *th*; ȝ (in origin two different characters) is replaced by *gh*, *y*, *w*, *s*, or *z*, as appropriate, though in the combination *yȝ* it is omitted in cases where a change to *gh* or *y* would be no advantage to the modern reader (*yȝen* 'eyes' 82: *yen*); the combination -*tȝ* is replaced by -*s*; *w*, when it is used in the MS for the diphthong /iu/, is replaced by *u* or *ew*; *qu*- and *wh*- spellings (to some extent interchangeable in the MS—*quy* 'why' 623, *Whene* 'Queen' 74) are normalized; and *u*/*v* and *i*/*j* are distinguished as vowel and consonant according to modern practice.

In replacing obsolete characters and uses of characters, the principle has been followed that alterations should, if possible, be a helpful step towards modern spelling; hence: *hwe* 'colour' 147 becomes *hue* (even though the scribe writes *hewe* for this word in 1471 and 1761), but *hwen* '(they) cut' 1346 becomes *hewen*; *hyȝe* 'high' 1033 becomes *hyghe*, but *hyȝe* 'hie, hasten' 299 becomes *hye*; *loȝe* 'laughed' 2389 becomes *loghe*, but *loȝe* 'low' 1170 becomes *lowe* (even though the scribe spells the word *loghe* in 1373). In the case of completely obsolete words the fourteenth-century pronunciation is given most weight (*haȝerer* 'more valiant' 352: *hawerer*).

Sir Gawain and the Green Knight

I

Sithen the sege and the assaut was sesed at Troye,
The borgh brittened and brent to brondes and askes,
The tulk that the trammes of tresoun ther wroght
Was tried for his tricherie, the trewest on erthe.
Hit was Ennias the athel and his highe kynde,   5
That sithen depreced provinces, and patrounes bicome
Welneghe of al the wele in the west iles.
Fro riche Romulus to Rome ricchis hym swythe,
With gret bobbaunce that burghe he biges upon fyrst
And nevenes hit his aune nome, as hit now hat;   10
Ticius to Tuskan and teldes bigynnes,

3. 'the man who framed the treasonable plots there was tried (and 'became famous', a pun) for his treachery, the most authentic example on earth.' Medieval legend associated Aeneas with the traitor Antenor in plotting with the Greeks (see, for instance, the ME alliterative *Destruction of Troy* (edited D. Donaldson and G. A. Panton, London, EETS, 1869–74), based on Guido del Colonna). It has been argued that Antenor is the traitor referred to here, but it seems likely that the poet is enunciating the motif of 'shame and success' (or *blysse and blunder*) which is dominant in the present adventure of Gawain, a descendant of Aeneas, and which can be discerned in the lives of other members of this *highe kynde*, Brutus and Arthur (see notes to 13, 2465*f*). The account in the *Laud Troy Book* (*c.* 1400), which does not attempt to exonerate Aeneas, relates the trial and exile of Aeneas and Antenor with their kin, after the departure of the Greeks; note especially

> And yit afftirward hit schop so
> That the traytoures bothe two
> For here ffalsnesse were afftir demed (*sentenced*)
> To be exiled & afftir flemed (*banished*)
> With al here kyn & here lynage. (edited J. E. Wülfing, London,
> EETS, 1902–3, 18599–603)

7. *the west iles:* 'lands of the west'; *iles* here follows the *OT* (and Hebrew) usage, signifying 'lands across the sea'.

11. While Langaberde and Brutus are well known in medieval legend as eponymous founders of Lombardy and Britain respectively, the name Ticius

Langaberde in Lumbardie lyftes up homes,
And fer over the French flod, Felix Brutus
On mony bonkkes ful brode Bretayn he settes
        Wyth wynne,   15
        Where werre and wrake and wonder
    Bi sythes has wont therinne
        And oft bothe blysse and blunder
        Ful skete has skyfted synne.

Ande when this Bretayn was bigged bi this burn rych   20
Bolde bredden therinne, baret that lofden,
In mony turned tyme tene that wroghten.
Mo ferlyes on this folde han fallen here oft
Then in any other that I wot, syn that ilk tyme.
Bot of alle that here bult of Bretaygne kynges   25
Ay was Arthur the hendest, as I haf herde telle.
Forthi an aunter in erde I attle to schawe,
That a selly in sight summe men hit holden
And an outtrage awenture of Arthures wonderes.
If ye wyl lysten this laye bot on littel while,   30

---

is not recorded elsewhere. Recognized 'founders' of Tuscany include a Tuscus and a Tirius; the form Ticius may be either an adaptation of, or a scribal error for, the latter. (See Silverstein, 1965.)

13. *Felix:* this is unique as a praenomen of Brutus (great-grandson of Aeneas), though the epithet ('happy') is associated in Roman tradition with founders of cities, etc., and in the EME form *sæl*, it is applied to him by the poet Layamon in his chronicle-poem *Brut*. It is appropriately used of Brutus, who is said to have been fated to early misfortune (his mother died giving birth to him and he later killed his father by accident) but upon exile from Italy successfully founded Britain; the name is echoed by *Wyth wynne* 'with joy' 15.

25. *of Bretaygne kynges:* inverted construction: 'kings of Britain' (in apposition to *alle*).

27, 28. *in erde, in sight:* poetic tags, but see glossary.

28. *That . . . hit:* relative construction (= 'which').

30. *laye:* an OF word used by Marie de France (twelfth century) to designate the short Breton tales which she versified; originally 'a short narrative poem intended to be sung or recited', it had come to mean simply 'poem' or 'song' by the fourteenth century, though perhaps with some 'Celtic' associations of magic and love; the present context suggests that it was still associated with minstrelsy.

I schal telle hit astit, as I in toun herde,
    With tonge.
      As hit is stad and stoken
      In stori stif and stronge,
      With lel letteres loken,   35
      In londe so has ben longe.

This kyng lay at Camylot upon Krystmasse
With mony luflych lorde, ledes of the best—
Rekenly of the Rounde Table alle tho rich brether—
With rych revel oryght and rechles merthes.   40
Ther tournayed tulkes by tymes ful mony,
Justed ful jolilé thise gentyle knightes,
Sythen kayred to the court, caroles to make;
For ther the fest was ilyche ful fiften dayes,
With alle the mete and the mirthe that men couthe avyse: 45
Such glaum ande gle glorious to here,
Dere dyn upon day, daunsyng on nyghtes—
Al was hap upon heghe in halles and chambres
With lordes and ladies, as levest him thoght.
With all the wele of the worlde thay woned ther samen,   50
The most kyd knyghtes under Krystes selven

31*ff.* 'I shall tell it at once, aloud, as I have heard it in the court. The form in which it is (here) set down and fixed, in a brave and powerful story enshrined in true syllables, is that in which it has long existed.' 33–5 are evidently a reference to the text of the present poem, which the reciter would have in front of him. Other interpretations of the passage are possible with different punctuation. 35 can also be read 'linked with true letters' and the ambiguity may be deliberate; while asserting the authenticity of his version, the poet may be making oblique reference to the accuracy of the metre in which it is embodied. 36 may also be an allusion to the antiquity of the alliterative style ('as has long been the custom in the land'). See also Frankis, *NQ* 206 (1961), 329.

37. According to French romance, Arthur held court five times a year on the great Christian festivals, Easter, Ascension, Whitsun, All Saints (*cf.* 536–7), and Christmas. In the *Livre de Carados*, possibly the poet's source for the story of the Beheading Game, the challenger enters Arthur's court at Carduel at the Whitsuntide feast.

43. *caroles:* courtly ring dances with singing; *cf.* the description in Chaucer's translation of the *Roman de la Rose* 743*ff.*

51. *under Krystes selven:* 'except Christ himself'.

And the lovelokkest ladies that ever lif haden,
And he the comlokest kyng, that the court haldes;
For al was this fayre folk in her first age,
      On sille,   55
    The hapnest under heven,
    Kyng hyghest mon of wylle—
    Hit were now gret nye to neven
    So hardy a here on hille.

Wyle New Yer was so yep that hit was newe cummen,   60
That day doubble on the dece was the douth served.
Fro the kyng was cummen with knyghtes into the halle,
The chauntré of the chapel cheved to an ende,
Loude crye was ther kest of clerkes and other,   ⌐
Nowel nayted onewe, nevened ful ofte.   65
And sythen riche forth runnen to reche hondeselle,
Yeyed 'Yeres yiftes!' on high, yelde hem bi hond,
Debated busyly aboute tho giftes;
Ladies laghed ful loude thogh thay lost haden
And he that wan was not wrothe—that may ye wel trawe.   70
Alle this mirthe thay maden to the mete tyme.
When thay had waschen worthyly, thay wenten to sete,
The best burne ay abof, as hit best semed;

54. Arthur and his courtiers were all in their youth(*first age*); by implication
this was also the golden age of Arthur's court and reign, before the appearance
of the treachery which brought about the downfall of the Round Table—the
theme of the first stanza (the rise and fall of kingdoms) is heard faintly in the
background.

60. The whole line is a periphrasis for 'On New Year's Day'.

63. *cheved to an ende:* a participial phrase, 'having ended'.

64. *Loude crye:* the greeting *Nowel* ('Merry Christmas') of the next line
(*cf. nevened ful ofte*).

65. *onewe:* i.e. the festive spirit of Christmas Day was renewed on New
Year's Day.

66ff. *hondeselle* probably designates gifts to subordinates (Christmas boxes),
yeres yiftes those given to equals. The giving of the latter takes the form of a
guessing game like Handy Dandy (*cf. bi hond* 67) with forfeits: if the lady fails
to guess which hand the present is in, the knight wins a kiss (hence the somewhat
arch comment of 69*f*).

73. i.e. 'in order of degree throughout, as was most fitting.'

Quene Guenore ful gay graythed in the myddes,
Dressed on the dere des, dubbed al aboute: 75
Smal sendal bisides, a selure hir over
Of tryed tolouse, of tars tapites innoghe
That were enbrawded and beten wyth the best gemmes
That myght be preved of prys wyth penyes to bye
      In daye. 80
    The comlokest to discrye
    Ther glent with yen gray;
    A semloker that ever he sye
    Soth moght no mon say.

Bot Arthure wolde not ete til al were served; 85
He was so joly of his joyfnes, and sumwhat childgered,
His lif liked hym lyght; he lovied the lasse
Auther to longe lye or to longe sitte,
So bisied him his yonge blod and his brayn wylde.
And also another maner meved him eke, 90
That he thurgh nobelay had nomen: he wolde never ete
Upon such a dere day, er hym devised were
Of sum aventurus thyng, an uncouthe tale
Of sum mayn mervayle that he myght trawe,
Of alderes, of armes, of other aventurus; 95

79f. 'whose value could ever (In daye) be tested by buying them with money', i.e. 'that money could buy'.

81. comlokest: 'gem' is understood, a metaphor which is picked up in glent: 'glanced' or 'sparkled'; Guenevere is meant, of course, a jewel beyond price in comparison with those of 78-80.

82. yen gray: heroines of medieval romance often have grey eyes; it is possible, however, that ME gray (and OF vaire) designated a colour in eyes which we would call 'blue'.

86-9. 'He was so lively in his youthfulness (and somewhat boyish), he loved an active life; he didn't much care for lying in bed or sitting long, he was so agitated by his young blood and his restless mind.'

91. That he . . . nomen: probably a relative clause, 'which he had undertaken as a matter of honour'.

92ff. er . . . mervayle: 'until he had been told of some daring enterprise, a strange tale of some great wonder'.

95. alderes: either 'princes' (OE aldor) or 'ancestors' (OE ældra); the two are, indeed, confused in ME in some contexts. Morte Arthure 13: Off elders of alde

Other sum segg hym bisoght of sum siker knyght
To joyne wyth hym in justyng, in jopardé to lay,
Lede, lif for lyf, leve uchon other,
As fortune wolde fulsun hom, the fayrer to have.
This was kynges countenaunce where he in court were,   100
At uch farand fest among his fre meny
            In halle.
        Therfore of face so fere
        He stightles stif in stalle;
        Ful yep in that New Yere,   105
        Much mirthe he mas with alle.

Thus ther stondes in stale the stif kyng hisselven,
Talkkande bifore the hyghe table of trifles ful hende.
There gode Gawan was graythed Gwenore bisyde,
And Agravayn a la Dure Mayn on that other syde sittes—   110
Bothe the kynges sister-sunes and ful siker knightes;
Bischop Bawdewyn abof bigines the table,

---

tyme and of theire awke dedys appears to support the meaning 'elders, ancestors'
here; on the other hand it could be argued that the phrase *elders of alde tyme* is
redundant and is therefore probably an adaptation or a scribal corruption of a
poorly understood *alderes* ('princes') *of alde tyme*.

96-9. 'or else some man entreated him for a true knight to engage in
jousting with him, for a man (*lede*) to lay life against life in jeopardy, either
one to concede victory to the other, as fortune saw fit to help (*fulsun*) them.'
97-9 summarize the terms of honourable combat.

110. *a la Dure Mayn:* 'of the hard hand'. Agravain and Gawain were sons of
Lot, King of Orkney; their mother was Arthur's half-sister, Anna, (sometimes
known as Belisent). Another half-sister of Arthur was Morgan, *cf.* 2463 *ff.*
on that other syde: i.e. of Gawain. Guenevere sits on Arthur's left, at the
centre of the table; Gawain and Agravain are to the left of her. On Arthur's
right are Bishop Baldwin and Iwain.

112. *abof bigines the table:* an idiomatic expression meaning 'sits in the place
of honour' (at the right of the host, *cf.* 1001). When the host sat at the end of
the table the guest of honour would occupy the first place on his right at the
'top' of the long side. The poet does not introduce the Round Table, though
he uses the phrase for the abstract 'Arthur's court'; in general the background
details of the romance are drawn from contemporary aristocratic life.

And Ywan, Uryn son, ette with hymselven.
Thise were dight on the des and derworthly served,
And sithen mony siker segge at the sidbordes.   115
Then the first cors come with crakkyng of trumpes
Wyth mony baner ful bryght, that therbi henged;
Newe nakryn noyse with the noble pipes,
Wylde werbles and wyght wakned lote,
That mony hert ful highe hef at her towches.   120
Dayntés dryven therwyth of ful dere metes,
Foysoun of the fresche, and on so fele disches
That pine to fynde the place the peple biforne
For to sette the sylveren that sere sewes halden
> On clothe.   125
>> Iche lede as he loved hymselve
>> Ther laght withouten lothe;
>> Ay two had disches twelve,
>> Good ber and bryght wyn bothe.

Now wyl I of hor servise say yow no more,   130
For uch wye may wel wit no wont that ther were.
Another noyse ful newe neghed bilive,
That the lude myght haf leve liflode to cach;
For unethe was the noyce not a whyle sesed,

113. *ette with hymselven:* 'shared dishes with him' (i.e. with Baldwin), *cf.*
128. At the end of a line, *hymselven* is frequently used for *him*, with no special
emphasis.

116. *cors:* A 'course' comprised a variety of dishes (enough to constitute a
complete meal by any modern standard). A medieval banquet consisted of a
number of these courses. For instance, at the marriage of Henry IV in 1403,
there were three meat courses and three fish courses, each course consisting of
between seven and fourteen separate dishes and ending in its own *sotelté*
(sweetmeat). *Cf.* 128.

117. *Wyth . . . bryght:* 'resplendent with many a banner'.

119. 'Spirited, piercing trills roused echoes'.

126. *as . . . hymselve:* 'as he himself liked'.

132f. 'Another, quite new, noise drew near suddenly, so that the prince
might have leave (i.e. which was to give the prince leave) to take food (*liflode*)';
cf. 90ff.

134. 'For scarcely a moment after the music had finished . . .' (*cf.* 116ff).
The double negative is merely emphatic.

And the fyrst cource in the court kyndely served,   135
Ther hales in at the halle dor an aghlich mayster,
On the most on the molde on mesure hyghe;
Fro the swyre to the swange so sware and so thik,
And his lyndes and his lymes so longe and so grete,
Half-etayn in erde I hope that he were,   140
Bot mon most I algate mynn hym to bene,
And that the myriest in his muckel that myght ride;
For of bak and of brest al were his bodi sturne,
Both his wombe and his wast were worthily smale,
And alle his fetures folwande in forme, that he hade,   145
      Ful clene.
        For wonder of his hue men hade,
        Set in his semblaunt sene;
        He ferde as freke were fade,
        And overal enker grene.   150

Ande al graythed in grene this gome and his wedes:
A strayt cote ful streght that stek on his sides,
A meré mantile abof, mensked withinne
With pelure pured apert—the pane ful clene—
With blythe blaunner ful bryght, and his hod bothe,   155

135. *served: was* is understood from the previous line.
137. 'The very biggest man on earth in height'. *On the most*, 'one the biggest' is an idiomatic superlative, not yet confused with the weaker 'one of the biggest'.
141f. '(that) I think he was half-giant on earth, but at any rate I suppose (declare?) him to be the biggest man (on earth) and moreover the most elegant for his size who could ride a horse'.
145f. 'And every part of him agreeing in proportion completely.' Possibly, however, *folwande in forme* is an oblique reference to his colour (to be revealed in the subsequent lines): 'matching in outward appearance (colour)'. This would enable us to understand *for* (147) in its usual sense. In either case, *that he hade* qualifies *fetures*, repeating the force of *his* (cf. 327), rather than *forme* (note the absence of definite article). For other such separated relative clauses cf. 429, 785, 1456, 1914, etc.
151. *graythed:* 'adorned'. But he is not merely dressed in green; he is green himself.
154. *the pane ful clene:* 'the whole of the garment (material)'.
155. *blaunner:* probably 'ermine' (OF *blanc* 'white' + *neir* 'black'); however,

That was laght fro his lokkes and layde on his schulderes;
Heme wel-haled hose of that same grene,
That spenet on his sparlyr, and clene spures under
Of bryght golde, upon silk bordes barred ful ryche,
And scholes under schankes there the schalk rides.   160
And alle his vesture verayly was clene verdure,
Bothe the barres of his belt and other blythe stones
That were richely rayled in his aray clene
Aboutte hymself and his sadel, upon silk werkes;
That were to tor for to telle of tryfles the halve   165
That were enbrauded abof, wyth bryddes and flyes,
With gay gaudi of grene, the golde ay inmyddes.
The pendauntes of his payttrure, the proude cropure,
His molaynes and alle the metail anamayld was thenne,
The steropes that he stod on stayned of the same,   170
And his arsouns al after, and his athel scurtes,
That ever glemered and glent al of grene stones.
The fole that he ferkkes on fyn of that ilke,
          Sertayn:
      A grene hors gret and thikke,   175
      A stede ful stif to strayne,
      In brawden brydel quik;
      To the gome he was ful gayn.

---

since the poet insists throughout the description on the greenness of the new-comer, it seems better to take the word in the more general sense 'fur' here. (*Cf.* Note on Language and Metre, *n.* 13.) *ful bryght:* may either qualify *blaunner* or *mantile* (parallel to *mensked*); for a similar inversion *cf.* 117, where the antecedent is almost certainly *trumpes*.

160. 'and the man rides there without any shoes on his feet (lit. 'under legs').' I.e. he wore only stockings or soft socks—considered appropriate wear for peaceful pursuits (e.g. hunting) in the fourteenth century. Knights in armour, on the other hand, wore steel shoes (*sabatouns, cf.* 574); the expression 'shoeless', therefore, accords with the assurance (203 *ff*) that the Green Knight had no piece of armour about him. See Cecily Clark, *RES* N.S. 6 (1955) and Marjorie Rigby *RES* N.S. 7 (1956).

165 *ff*. The first *that* is a demonstrative pronoun (*cf.* 719): 'It would be too difficult to relate half the details that were embroidered on it (i.e. *his aray clene*) —including birds and butterflies (*flyes*)—with lovely green beadwork every-where amongst the gold.'

Wel gay was this gome gered in grene
And the here of his hed of his hors suete: 180
Fayre fannand fax umbefoldes his schulderes.
A much berd as a busk over his brest henges,
That wyth his highlich here that of his hed reches
Was evesed al umbetorne abof his elbowes,
That half his armes therunder were halched in the wyse   185
Of a kynges capados that closes his swyre;
The mane of that mayn hors much to hit lyke,
Wel cresped and cemmed, wyth knottes ful mony
Folden in wyth fildore aboute the fayre grene,
Ay a herle of the here, another of golde;   190
The tayl and his toppyng twynnen of a sute
And bounden bothe wyth a bande of a bryght grene
Dubbed wyth ful dere stones, as the dok lasted,
Sythen thrawen wyth a thwong; a thwarle knot alofte,
Ther mony belles ful bryght of brende golde rungen.   195
Such a fole upon folde, ne freke that hym rydes,
Was never sene in that sale wyth syght er that tyme
        With ye.
        He loked as layt so lyght—
        So sayd al that hym sye.   200
        Hit semed as no mon myght
        Under his dynttes drye.

181. *fannand:* lit. 'fanning'; usually understood as 'waving, floating', but perhaps the sense is rather 'spreading out like a fan'. In *The Miller's Tale*, Absolon the fop (admittedly a different type of character) has curly, golden hair which *strouted* (spread out) *as a fanne large and brode* (*CT* I (A)3315). *Cf.* also *MED: fannen* 2(*c*).

185f. 'So that his upper arms were enclosed beneath it in the manner of a king's cape, which encircles (wraps round) his neck.' A *capados* was a short leather cape with a hood, *cf.* 572.

193. *as the dok lasted:* 'to the end of the tuft (*dok*)'.

194f. 'then drawn up with a thong; (there was) an intricate knot at the top, on which many glittering bells of pure gold were ringing.'

196ff. The redundancy of *upon folde . . . in that sale . . . er that tyme*, and of *sene . . . wyth syght . . . With ye*, aptly conveys the stupefaction of the courtiers.

199. 'His glance was as swift as lightning (*layt*)'; *loked* means 'glanced a look' rather than the passive 'appeared'.

Whether, hade he no helme ne hawbergh nauther
Ne no pysan ne no plate that pented to armes
Ne no schafte ne no schelde to schuve ne to smyte;   205
Bot in his on honde he hade a holyn bobbe
(That is grattest in grene when greves ar bare)
And an ax in his other, a hoge and unmete,
A spetos sparthe to expoun in spelle whoso myght.
The hede of an elnyerde the large lenkthe hade,   210
The grayn al of grene stele and of golde hewen,
The bit burnyst bryght, wyth a brod egge
As wel schapen to schere as scharp rasores.
The stele of a stif staf the sturne hit bi grypte,
That was wounden wyth yrn to the wandes ende   215
And al bigraven with grene in gracios werkes;
A lace lapped aboute that louked at the hede
And so after the halme halched ful ofte,
Wyth tryed tasseles therto tacched innoghe
On botouns of the bryght grene brayden ful ryche.   220
This hathel heldes hym in and the halle entres,
Drivande to the heghe dece—dut he no wothe.

203. *Whether:* 'Yet'. Note the dramatic nature of the description; the speculation that 'it seemed as if no man might survive his blows' (201–2) leads the observer (as it were) to look more closely for armour and weapons.

206f. A branch carried in the hand was a sign of peace (*cf.* 265f). Messengers in the Middle Ages often carried an olive branch; it is entirely in keeping with the enigmatical humour of the Green Knight that he should carry a Christmas evergreen, like some wassailer wishing peace and joy to the house, while showing them an enormous weapon of war in the other hand.

209. 'A cruel battle-axe for anyone to describe in words.'

210. 'The axe-head was as long as an ell-rod' (i.e. 45 inches); *cf.* the second axe, 2225. Both axes evidently had half-moon shaped blades measuring about four feet from upper to lower extremity. In addition, the poet appears to describe this one, at least, as having a spike (*grayn*) sticking out at the back of the blade.

213. *rasores:* 'razor's (edge)'.

214ff. 'The grim knight gripped it by the handle (*stele*), consisting of a strong staff which was bound with iron to the end of the shaft and carved all over with pleasing designs in green.'

Haylsed he never one bot heghe he overloked.
The fyrst word that he warp, 'Wher is,' he sayd,
'The governour of this gyng? Gladly I wolde   225
Se that segg in syght and with hymself speke
         Raysoun.'
       To knyghtes he kest his ye
       And reled hym up and doun.
       He stemmed and con studie   230
       Who walt ther most renoun.

Ther was lokyng on lenthe the lude to beholde,
For uch mon had mervayle what hit mene myght
That a hathel and a horse myght such a hue lach
As growe grene as the gres and grener hit semed,   235
Then grene aumayl on golde glowande bryghter.
Al studied that ther stod and stalked hym nerre
Wyth al the wonder of the worlde what he worch schulde.
For fele sellyes had thay sen bot such never are;
Forthi for fantoum and fayrye the folk there hit demed.   240
Therfore to answare was arwe mony athel freke
And al stouned at his steven and ston-stil seten
In a swoghe sylence thurgh the sale riche.
As al were slypped upon slepe so slaked hor lotes
         In hye—   245
       I deme hit not al for doute

---

224. *The fyrst word that he warp:* a traditional formula for introducing a speech.

229. *reled hym:* possibly 'rolled them (his eyes)', cf. 304; but in view of *He stemmed* ('stopped') in the next line it is perhaps better to read 'swaggered up and down' or 'turned (rode) to and fro'.

230. *con studie:* a metrical past tense ('did gaze'); the construction, a development of *gan* + infin. 'began to', is most often used in this poem in the concluding quatrain, cf. 275, 340, 362, etc. In 2273 the pa.t. *cowthe* appears to be used in the same way.

236. Poetic inversion: 'shining brighter than green enamel on gold'.

237. 'All who were standing there stared and cautiously approached him'. These are presumably the servants, whose naïve curiosity is thus suitably differentiated from the stunned silence of the courtiers (241*ff*).

244*f*. 'Their voices died away as suddenly as if they had all fallen asleep.'

Bot sum for cortaysye—
Bot let hym that al schulde loute
Cast unto that wye.

Thenn Arthour, bifore the high dece, that aventure byholdes 250
operly And rekenly hym reverenced, for rad was he never,
And sayde, 'Wye, welcum iwys to this place.
The hede of this ostel, Arthour I hat.
Light luflych adoun and lenge, I the praye,
And whatso thy wylle is we schal wyt after.'   255
'Nay, as help me,' quoth the hathel, 'He that on hyghe syttes,
To wone any whyle in this won hit was not myn ernde;
Bot for the los of the, lede, is lyft up so hyghe
And thy burgh and thy burnes best ar holden,
Stifest under stel-gere on stedes to ryde,   260
The wyghtest and the worthyest of the worldes kynde,
Preue for to play wyth in other pure laykes,
And here is kydde cortaysye, as I haf herd carp—
And that has wayned me hider, iwyis, at this tyme.
Ye may be seker bi this braunch that I bere here   265
That I passe as in pes and no plyght seche;
For had I founded in fere, in feghtyng wyse,
I have a hauberghe at home and a helme bothe,
A schelde and a scharp spere, schinande bryght,
Ande other weppenes to welde, I wene wel, als;   270

248f. 'But allowed him to whom all were duty bound to defer (i.e. Arthur) to address that man.' Possibly, however, *let* is to be read as imperative, addressed to the audience, as in 1994.

253. 'I, the head of this house, am called Arthur.'

254. *I the praye*: as king, Arthur properly uses the singular pronoun to everyone except Guenevere; his general manner towards the Green Knight is courteous and hospitable in the extreme. The latter's use of *thou* to Arthur, however, is a mark of disrespect (contrast Gawain's manner of addressing the king in 343ff).

256. *He that on hyghe syttes*: a periphrasis for 'God'.

258. 'But because your renown, sir, is built up to such a height'.

262. *other pure laykes*: sc. 'than jousting'. He alludes to the beheading game.

267. *in fere*: probably 'in martial fashion, array' from a phrase such as *in fere* (i.e. 'show, array') *of war*.

Bot for I wolde no were, my wedes ar softer.
Bot if thou be so bold as alle burnes tellen,
Thou wyl grant me godly the gomen that I ask
        Bi ryght.'
            Arthour con onsware   275
            And sayd, 'Sir cortays knyght,
            If thou crave batayl bare,
            Here fayles thou not to fyght.'

'Nay, frayst I no fyght, in fayth I the telle;
Hit arn aboute on this bench bot berdles chylder.   280
If I were hasped in armes on a heghe stede,
Here is no mon me to mach, for myghtes so wayke.
Forthy I crave in this court a Crystemas gomen,
For hit is Yol and Newe Yer, and here ar yep mony.
If any so hardy in this hous holdes hymselven,   285
Be so bolde in his blod, brayn in hys hede,
That dar stifly strike a strok for another,
I schal gif hym of my gyft thys giserne ryche,
This ax, that is hevé innogh, to hondele as hym lykes,
And I schal bide the fyrst bur as bare as I sitte.   290
If any freke be so felle to fonde that I telle,
Lepe lyghtly me to and lach this weppen—
I quit-clayme hit for ever, kepe hit as his auen—
And I schal stonde hym a strok, stif on this flet,

274. I.e. 'by prerogative of the Christmas season'.
278. 'You will not be short of fighting here.'
280. Hit arn ... bot: 'there are only ...'.
285ff. 'If anyone in this house considers himself so brave, (to) be so bold-spirited, so reckless (brayn adj.) of mind, that (he) dares ...'.
288. giserne: the term gisarm was usually applied to a battle-axe with a long blade in line with the shaft, sharpened on both sides and ending in a point, though the description in 209ff appears to distinguish the greyn (spike) from the blade. However, there is little doubt that the variations ax, giserne, denes ax, and sparthe are introduced mainly for the sake of alliteration and that they are all used as synonyms for 'battle-axe'.
291. 'If any warrior be so daring (as) to put to the test what I propose'.
292f. Lepe ... lach ... kepe: subjunctives, 'let him run, seize, keep'.

Elles thou wyl dight me the dom to dele hym another   295
      Barlay,
    And yet gif hym respite
    A twelmonyth and a day.
    Now hye, and let se tite
    Dar any herinne oght say.'   300

If he hem stowned upon fyrst, stiller were thanne
Alle the heredmen in halle, the hygh and the lowe.
The renk on his rouncé hym ruched in his sadel
And runischly his rede yen he reled aboute,
Bende his bresed browes, blycande grene,   305
Wayved his berde for to wayte whoso wolde ryse.
When non wolde kepe hym with carp he coghed ful hyghe
Ande rimed hym ful richely and ryght hym to speke.
'What, is this Arthures hous,' quoth the hathel thenne,
'That al the rous rennes of thurgh ryalmes so mony?   310
Where is now your sourquydrye and your conquestes,
Your gryndellayk and your greme and your grete wordes?
Now is the revel and the renoun of the Rounde Table
Overwalt wyth a worde of on wyes speche,
For al dares for drede withoute dynt schewed!'   315

---

296. *Barlay:* usually identified with the dialect word *barley,* used in children's games to call a truce or to lay first claim to something ('bags I'); perhaps 'I claim first blow'. A suggested etymology is OF *par loi, par lei* 'by law', which would agree with the regular stress pattern in the bob: $\mathbf{x} \, / \, (\mathbf{x})$. Another explanation is that the word is a noun meaning 'blow'. (See B. M. White, *Neophil.* 37 (1953), 113-5.)

298. A traditional expression meaning 'until the same day a year hence'. In the present case, from 1 January 'a twelvemonth' would extend to 31 December, and the extra day is mentioned to make it clear that the term expires on the following day, 1 January.

306. 'Turned his head from side to side (lit. 'waved his beard') to see if anyone would rise.'

307. *kepe hym with carp:* the preposition governs *hym:* 'hold speech with him'.

310. *That ... of:* 'of which'.

315. 'for everyone is cowering in fear without a blow being offered.' The ambiguity of the last phrase (i.e. offered to them, or offered to him, in response to his request) is no doubt deliberate.

Wyth this he laghes so loude that the lorde greved;
The blod schot for scham into his schyre face
> And lere;
>> He wex as wroth as wynde;
>> So did alle that ther were.   320
>> The kyng, as kene bi kynde,
>> Then stod that stif mon nere,

Ande sayde, 'Hathel, by heven thyn askyng is nys,
And as thou foly has frayst, fynde the behoves.
I know no gome that is gast of thy grete wordes.   325
Gif me now thy geserne, upon Godes halve,
And I schal baythen thy bone that thou boden habbes.'
Lyghtly lepes he hym to and laght hit at his honde.
Then feersly that other freke upon fote lyghtis.
Now has Arthure his axe and the halme grypes   330
And sturnely stures hit aboute, that stryke wyth hit thoght.
The stif mon hym bifore stod upon hyght,
Herre then ani in the hous by the hede and more.
Wyth sturne schere ther he stod he stroked his berde
And wyth a countenaunce drye he drow doun his cote,   335
No more mate ne dismayd for hys mayn dintes
Then any burne upon bench hade broght hym to drynk

328. hit: *supplied (cf. 827).*

---

316. *the lorde greved:* 'the lord (Arthur) was offended'.

320. *that ther were:* 'who were there'.

321. *as kene bi kynde:* 'like the brave man he was by nature', *cf.* 1104.

322. *nere:* strictly comparative of *negh,* i.e. 'nearer'.

324. 'And as you have asked for foolishness it behoves you to find it.'

328. 'Swiftly he springs towards him and seized it from his hand.'

331. 'And fiercely brandishes it about (like one) who intended to strike with it.'

335. *drow doun his cote:* i.e. from the back of his neck.

336. *for hys mayn dintes:* 'for his mighty blows'—i.e. either the ones he seemed prepared to deliver, or the blows he was practising at that moment; there is no implication (as has been supposed) that Arthur is actually attempting to behead the Green Knight at this point.

337f. *to drynk Of wyne:* 'some wine to drink'; this use of *of* is probably an imitation of Fr *de (du,* etc.), *cf.* 854.

Of wyne.
Gawan, that sate bi the quene,
To the kyng he can enclyne,   340
'I beseche now with sawes sene
This melly mot be myne.'

'Wolde ye, worthilych lorde,' quoth Wawan to the kyng,
'Bid me bowe fro this benche and stonde by yow there,
That I wythoute vylanye myght voyde this table,   345
And that my legge lady lyked not ille,
I wolde com to your counseyl bifore your cort ryche.
For me think hit not semly—as hit is soth knawen—
Ther such an askyng is hevened so hyghe in your sale,
Thagh ye yourself be talenttyf, to take hit to yourselven, 350
Whil mony so bolde yow aboute upon bench sytten
That under heven I hope non hawerer of wylle
Ne better bodyes on bent ther baret is rered.
I am the wakkest, I wot, and of wyt feblest,
And lest lur of my lyf, who laytes the sothe.   355
Bot for as much as ye ar myn em I am only to prayse;

---

340. *can enclyne:* 'bowed'; see 230*n.*

341*f.* These two lines are probably to be understood as a brief summary of
Gawain's speech to the king, which is given in its full elaboration in the next
stanza; for the same device (*transitio*), *cf.* 387–9, 734–9, 2185–8, 2237*f.*

343. *Wolde ye:* 'If you would . . . (bid me)'. *Wawan* (MS *Gawan*): the poet
several times uses the alternative form with initial *W-*, when he wishes to
alliterate on *w* (as in 559, 906, etc.). The Celtic form of the name (like that of
Guenever, which appears as *Wenore* in 945) began with *Gw-*, which alternated
with *W-* in certain positions.

345. *wythoute vylanye:* 'without discourtesy'. Gawain's *cortaysye* shows in
this stanza as an elaborate politeness of manner and speech.

346. 'And if that did not displease my sovereign lady (Guenevere)'; *that* is
subject.

347. *com to your counseyl:* 'give you advice'; *cf.* 'come to someone's help.'

348. *me think:* a conflation of *I think* and *me thinketh* ('it seems to me').

350. *to take hit:* sc. 'for you . . .'.

352. 'that I think none on earth (to be) more resourceful (*hawerer*) in
courage'.

353. *on bent . . . rered:* 'on the field of battle'.

356. 'I am only praiseworthy in that you are my uncle'; (*only* repeats *Bot*).

No bounté bot your blod I in my bodé knowe.
And sythen this note is so nys that noght hit yow falles,
And I have frayned hit at yow fyrst, foldes hit to me.
And if I carp not comlyly let alle this cort rych   360
          Bout blame.'
          Ryche togeder con roun;
          And sythen thay redden alle same
          To ryd the kyng wyth croun
          And gif Gawan the game.   365

Then comaunded the kyng the knyght for to ryse;
And he ful radly upros and ruchched hym fayre,
Kneled doun bifore the kyng and caches that weppen.
And he luflyly hit hym laft and lyfte up his honde
And gef hym Goddes blessyng, and gladly hym biddes   370
That his hert and his honde schulde hardi be bothe.
'Kepe the, cosyn,' quoth the kyng, 'that thou on kyrf sette,
And if thou redes hym ryght, redly I trowe
That thou schal byden the bur that he schal bede after.'
Gawan gos to the gome with giserne in honde   375
And he baldly hym bydes—he bayst never the helder.
Then carppes to Sir Gawan the knyght in the grene,
'Refourme we oure forwardes, er we fyrre passe.
Fyrst I ethe the, hathel, how that thou hattes
That thou me telle truly, as I tryst may.'   380

---

358. *this note is so nys:* 'this matter is so foolish'.

360f. 'and if *I* speak unfittingly let all this noble court (speak) without offence.' Other interpretations are possible, however: 'let all this noble court be free from blame' (see *TG–Davis n.*), or (taking *rych* as a verb, meaning 'decide'): 'let all this court decide without reproach whether I speak fittingly or not.'

372. *Kepe the:* 'Take care'. *that . . . sette:* 'that you strik eone blow' (*cf.* 287, 294, and Gawain's words in 2252). For this use of *set*, see *OED set* v. III 20.

373f. 'and if you deal with him properly, I fully believe that you will stand the blow that he is to offer afterwards.' In addition to the humorous implication 'because he'll be dead', there may well be a pun on *byden*, which can mean 'endure' or 'wait for'.

376. *he bayst never the helder:* 'he was dismayed no more for that'.

379f. *how that . . . truly:* 'that you tell me truly what you are called'.

'In god fayth,' quoth the goode knyght, 'Gawan I hatte
That bede the this buffet (whatso bifalles after)
And at this tyme twelmonyth take at the another
Wyth what weppen so thou wylt—and wyth no wy elles
      On lyve.'   385
       That other onswares agayn,
       'Sir Gawan, so mot I thryve
       As I am ferly fayn
       This dint that thou schal dryve.'

'Bigog,' quoth the grene knyght, 'Sir Gawan, me lykes   390
That I schal fange at thy fust that I haf frayst here.
And thou has redily rehersed, bi resoun ful true,
Clanly al the covenaunt that I the kynge asked,
Saf that thou schal siker me, segge, bi thi trawthe,
That thou schal seche me thiself, whereso thou hopes   395
I may be funde upon folde, and foch the such wages
As thou deles me today bifore this douthe ryche.'
'Where schulde I wale the?' quoth Gauan. 'Where is thy place?
I wot never where thou wonyes, bi Hym that me wroght,
Ne I know not the, knyght, thy cort ne thi name.   400
Bot teche me truly therto and telle me howe thou hattes,
And I schal ware alle my wyt to wynne me theder—
And that I swere the for sothe and by my seker traweth.'
'That is innogh in Newe Yer—hit nedes no more,'

---

384 f. *and wyth . . . lyve:* If this means 'with no one else present' it was not included in the challenge, unless in the obscure *barlay*, though Gawain does meet the Green Knight alone (*cf.* especially 2149*ff*, 2242–6). However, the meaning is almost certainly 'at the hands of no other living person' (for *wyth:* 'at the hands of' *cf.* 681); Gawain might be expected to insist on this point, which appears to give him a good chance of escaping the return blow (*cf.* 373*f*, 410).

389. There is a suggestion of special stress on *thou*, which is echoed in the next stanza and at 908*ff*, and 2239*ff*.

391. *that I haf frayst:* 'that which I have asked'.

401. 'but direct me faithfully to it and tell me what you are called'.

404. The New Year is still a time for making solemn resolutions. The Green Knight discourages Gawain from taking a stronger oath. (*Cf.* Introduction, p. 10.)

Quoth the gome in the grene to Gawan the hende.   405
'Yif I the telle truly when I the tape have
And thou me smothely has smyten, smartly I the teche
Of my hous and my home and myn owen nome,
Then may thou frayst my fare and forwardes holde;
And if I spende no speche thenne spedes thou the better,   410
For thou may leng in thy londe and layt no fyrre.
            Bot slokes!
        Ta now thy grymme tole to the
        And let se how thou cnokes.'
        'Gladly, sir, forsothe,'   415
        Quoth Gawan; his ax he strokes.

The grene knyght upon grounde graythely hym dresses;
A littel lut with the hede, the lere he discoveres;
His longe lovelych lokkes he layd over his croun,
Let the naked nec to the note schewe.   420
Gauan gripped to his ax and gederes hit on hyght;
The kay fot on the folde he before sette,
Let hit doun lyghtly lyght on the naked,
That the scharp of the schalk schyndered the bones
And schrank thurgh the schyire grece and schade hit in twynne,
That the bit of the broun stel bot on the grounde.   426
The fayre hede fro the halce hit to the erthe,
That fele hit foyned wyth her fete there hit forth roled;
The blod brayd fro the body, that blykked on the grene.
And nawther faltered ne fel the freke never the helder   430
Bot stythly he start forth upon styf schonkes
And runyschly he raght out thereas renkkes stoden,

---

409. *frayst my fare:* an idiom meaning 'call on me'; *cf.* also 2494.

410. *spedes thou the better:* 'it will be all the better for you'.

412. *slokes:* probably a verb connected with OE *slacian* 'to slacken' (see *OED slake* v. and *cf. slaked* 244) or OIcel. *slokna* 'to be extinguished'; but several interpretations are possible: e.g. 'let us stop' (1 pl. imperat.), 'stop' (2 pl. imperat.), 'you are dawdling' (2 sing. indic.); the last is perhaps to be preferred.

416. *his ax he strokes:* i.e. to test its edge.

424. 'so that the man's sharp blade cut through the bones'.

429. *that blykked:* qualifies *blod*.

Laght to his lufly hed and lyft hit up sone,
And sythen bowes to his blonk, the brydel he cachches,
Steppes into stel-bawe and strydes alofte,   435
And his hede by the here in his honde haldes;
And as sadly the segge hym in his sadel sette
As non unhap had hym ayled, thagh hedles nowe
        In stedde.
    He brayde his bluk aboute,   440
    That ugly bodi that bledde.
    Moni on of hym had doute,
    Bi that his resouns were redde.

For the hede in his honde he haldes up even,
Toward the derrest on the dece he dresses the face   445
And hit lyfte up the ye-lyddes and loked ful brode
And meled thus much with his muthe as ye may now here:
'Loke, Gawan, thou be graythe to go as thou hettes
And layte as lelly til thou me, lude, fynde
As thou has hette in this halle, herande thise knyghtes.   450
To the Grene Chapel thou chose, I charge the, to fotte
Such a dunt as thou has dalt—disserved thou habbes—
To be yederly yolden on New Yeres morn.
The Knight of the Grene Chapel men knowen me mony;
Forthi me for to fynde, if thou fraystes, fayles thou never.   455
Therfore com, other recreaunt be calde the behoves.'
With a runisch rout the raynes he tornes,
Halled out at the hal dor, his hed in his hande,

438. nowe: MS howe (Cawley)

442f. 'Many a one was frightened of him by the time he had finished speaking' (*redde*: declared). A good instance of the poet's use of the *wheel* for surprise and suspense.

445. *the derrest*: probably 'the nobles'. It is suggested that Guenevere ('the noblest') is meant—Arthur is not yet seated—but, in spite of the motive revealed belatedly in 2460, this is not a very likely reading, since the words are addressed to Gawain.

447. *his* is neuter possessive at this time: 'with its mouth'.

450. *herande*: absolute use of the present participle: '(while) these knights (were) listening'.

454. *men knowen me mony*: 'I am widely known as'.

That the fyr of the flynt flawe fro fole hoves.
To what kyth he becom knewe non there,   460
Never more then thay wyste fram whethen he was wonnen.
         What thenne?
     The kyng and Gawen thare
     At that grene thay laghe and grenne,
     Yet breved was hit ful bare   465
     A mervayl among tho menne.

Thagh Arther the hende kyng at hert hade wonder,
He let no semblaunt be sene bot sayde ful hyghe
To the comlych quene wyth cortays speche,
'Dere dame, today demay yow never.   470
Wel bycommes such craft upon Cristmasse—
Laykyng of enterludes, to laghe and to syng—
Among thise kynde caroles of knyghtes and ladyes.
Neverthelece to my mete I may me wel dres,
For I haf sen a selly I may not forsake.'   475
He glent upon Sir Gawen and gaynly he sayde,
'Now sir, heng up thyn ax, that has innogh hewen.'

460f. A 'fairy' formula. Cf. Sir Orfeo (edited A. J. Bliss, Oxford, 1954) 288:
No never he nist whider thai bicome and 296: Ac never he nist whider thai wold; cf.
also 2477f below.

470. 'Dear lady, do not be perturbed (reflex.) on a day like this.'

472f. 'playing of interludes, laughing and singing—among the courtly
carols performed by knights and ladies.' The term enterludes (L interludium,
lit. 'between play') was possibly first used of short dramatic or mimic enter-
tainments between courses at a banquet. Though by the fourteenth century it
seems to have designated simply 'plays' (sometimes 'miracle plays'), the word
may have retained a derogatory association with minstrelsy or mumming.
Robert Mannyng of Brunne, in his Handlyng Synne (a translation of William
of Wadington's Manuel de Pechiez made about 1303), condemns together

              entyrludes, or syngynge,
         Or tabure bete, or other pypynge

if they take place in the church or churchyard. In contrasting what they have
just seen with the courtiers' own caroles, King Arthur conveys an aristocratic
disdain for professional entertainment and at the same time contrives to suggest
that the beheading may have been no more than an illusionist's trick (craft).

477. Arthur aptly (gaynly) quotes a proverbial expression meaning 'cease
from strife'.

And hit was don abof the dece on doser to henge,
Ther alle men for mervayl myght on hit loke
And, bi true tytel, therof to telle the wonder.   480
Thenne thay bowed to a borde thise burnes togeder,
The kyng and the gode knyght, and kene men hem served
Of alle dayntyes double, as derrest myght falle,
With alle maner of mete and mynstralcie bothe.
Wyth wele walt thay that day, til worthed an ende   485
        In londe.
        Now thenk wel, Sir Gawan,
        For wothe that thou ne wonde
        This aventure for to frayn
        That thou has tan on honde.   490

479f. 'where everyone could look at it in amazement and relate the wonder
of it by true right.' Possibly, however, *to telle* is grammatically parallel to *to
henge*: the axe would tell its own wonderful story (*cf.* 626); in this case we
should read *therof* with *tytel* rather than with *wonder*.

483. *as derrest myght falle:* either 'in the noblest fashion possible' or 'as might
be fitting to nobles'.

485f. 'They spent that day in enjoyment until it came to an end (lit. 'an
end came').'

488f. 'that you do not shrink because of the danger from making trial of
this exploit which you have undertaken.'

II

This hanselle has Arthur of aventurus on fyrst
In yonge yer for he yerned yelpyng to here.
Thagh hym wordes were wane when thay to sete wenten,
Now ar thay stoken of sturne werk, staf-ful her hond.
Gawan was glad to begynne those gomnes in halle   495
Bot thagh the ende be hevy haf ye no wonder,
For thagh men ben mery in mynde when thay han mayn drynk,
A yere yernes ful yerne and yeldes never lyke,
The forme to the fynisment foldes ful selden.
Forthi this Yol overyede, and the yere after,   500
And uche sesoun serlepes sued after other:
After Crystenmasse com the crabbed Lentoun,
That fraystes flesch wyth the fysche and fode more symple,
Bot thenne the weder of the worlde wyth wynter hit threpes,
Colde clenges adoun, cloudes uplyften,   505
Schyre schedes the rayn in schowres ful warme,
Falles upon fayre flat, flowres there schewen,
Bothe groundes and the greves grene ar her wedes,
Bryddes busken to bylde and bremlych syngen
For solace of the softe somer that sues therafter   510
     Bi bonk,
       And blossumes bolne to blowe
       Bi rawes rych and ronk,

491. *has:* 'has received'.

493. 'Though (such) speeches (i.e. the *yelpyng* of 492) were not forthcoming for him when they sat down'—an allusion to the beginning of the feast, 72–102. *hym* may mean 'them' with little change of sense: 'Though they lacked such speeches. . . .'.

494. *staf-ful:* A word of obscure origin; if it is understood to mean 'as full as one's hand is when holding a staff' it contains an oblique ironical reference to the axe. *Cf.* also *OED staff-full*.

503. 'Which tests the body with fish and plainer food'.

504. 'but then nature's weather (i.e. the coming of spring) contends (*threpes*) with winter'. The changing of the seasons was traditionally imagined as a battle between Summer and Winter which manifested itself particularly in the equinoctial storms (*cf.* 523ff). In 2000, however, the phrase *wederes of the worlde* refers to the storms of winter.

505. *Colde clenges adoun:* 'frost shrinks into the earth (dies)'.

Then notes noble innowe
Ar herde in wod so wlonk. 515

After, the sesoun of somer wyth the soft wyndes,
When Zeferus syfles hymself on sedes and erbes;
Wela wynne is the wort that waxes theroute,
When the donkande dewe dropes of the leves,
To bide a blysful blusch of the bryght sunne. 520
Bot then hyes Hervest and hardenes hym sone,
Warnes hym for the wynter to wax ful rype;
He dryves wyth droght the dust for to ryse,
Fro the face of the folde to flye ful hyghe;
Wrothe wynde of the welkyn wrasteles with the sunne, 525
The leves laucen fro the lynde and lyghten on the grounde,
And al grayes the gres that grene was ere;
Thenne al rypes and rotes that ros upon fyrst,
And thus yirnes the yere in yisterdayes mony
And wynter wyndes ayayn, as the worlde askes, 530
    No fage,

531. fage: MS sage (Onions)

---

516. *After:* best taken as the adverb 'afterwards'; this implies a partial recapitulation of 510*ff*, but overlapping of stanzas is not uncommon (see note to 341*f*) and it is particularly appropriate here, where the poet seeks to suggest the merging of the seasons.

518. *theroute:* possibly 'outside, out of doors' (as in 2000) but better 'out of it (the seed)'.

520. *To bide:* the subject is *the wort* (518).

521. *hardenes hym:* as the next line makes clear, this is a play upon words: 'encourages him' (i.e. the *wort*) and 'makes him hard with fruit'; we might render 'puts heart into him'.

522. *for the wynter:* 'against (the coming of) the winter'.

523. *He:* i.e. *Hervest:* 'with drought he (Autumn) makes the dust rise'.

525. The reference is to the equinoctial gales (*cf.* 504*n*).

528*ff.* 'Then everything that grew in the beginning ripens and rots, and thus the year runs by in many yesterdays and winter comes back, as nature demands, in truth'. This use of 'yesterday' to suggest the mutability of earthly life (*cf.* Macbeth's 'All our yesterdays have lighted fools the way to dusty death'), is no doubt reminiscent of texts such as *Job* VIII, 9 and *Psalm* XC, 4, where early English versions invariably have 'yesterday' (*dæg gystran, yhistre-dai,* etc.) for *dies hesterna.*

C

> Til Meghelmas mone
> Was cumen wyth wynter wage.
> Then thenkkes Gawan ful sone
> Of his anious vyage.   535

Yet whyl Al Hal Day with Arther he lenges;
And he made a fare on that fest for the frekes sake,
With much revel and ryche of the Rounde Table.
Knyghtes ful cortays and comlych ladies
Al for luf of that lede in longynge thay were;   540
Bot never the lece ne the later thay nevened bot merthe.
Mony joyles for that jentyle japes ther maden.
For aftter mete with mournyng he meles to his eme
And spekes of his passage, and pertly he sayde,
'Now, lege lorde of my lyf, leve I yow ask.   545
Ye knowe the cost of this cace; kepe I no more
To telle yow tenes therof—never bot trifel—
Bot I am boun to the bur barely tomorne
To sech the gome of the grene, as God wyl me wysse.'
Thenne the best of the burgh bowed togeder,   550
Aywan and Errik and other ful mony—
Sir Doddinaual de Savage, the Duk of Clarence,
Launcelot, and Lyonel, and Lucan the gode,
Sir Boos and Sir Bydver, big men bothe,
And mony other menskful, with Mador de la Port.   555

533. *wyth wynter wage:* 'with pledge of winter'.

536. *Al Hal Day:* 'All Saints' Day', 1 November.

541. *never ... the later:* a parallel expression to *never the lece.*

542. 'Many who were joyless on account of that noble knight made jokes there.'

546f. 'You know the nature of this affair; I do not care to relate the troubles of it any more to you—it is only a minor matter'.

549. *wyl me wysse:* 'sees fit to guide me'.

551ff. Some of the knights mentioned here (e.g. Eric, Lancelot, Bedevere) play an important part in other Arthurian romances. Here their names are introduced (like those of 110ff) in order to invest the story with authenticity for readers conversant with the Arthurian background. *Aywan* is the Ywain of 113; *Sir Doddinaual de Savage* was so named for his love of hunting (OF *salvage*, L *silvāticus* 'of the woods'); *the Duk of Clarence* is a cousin (or brother) of Sir Dodinal. *Mador de la Port:* 'Mador the doorkeeper'.

Alle this compayny of court com the kyng nerre
For to counseyl the kynght, with care at her hert.
There was much derve doel driven in the sale
That so worthé as Wawan schulde wende on that ernde
To drye a delful dynt and dele no more   560
        Wyth bronde.
      The knyght mad ay god chere
      And sayde, 'What schuld I wonde?
      Of Destinés derf and dere
      What may mon do bot fonde?'   565

He dowelles ther al that day and dresses on the morn,
Askes erly hys armes and alle were thay broght.
Fyrst a tulé tapit tyght over the flet,
And miche was the gyld gere that glent theralofte.
The stif mon steppes theron and the stel hondeles,   570
Dubbed in a dublet of a dere tars,
And sythen a crafty capados, closed aloft,
That wyth a bryght blaunner was bounden withinne.
Thenne set thay the sabatouns upon the segge fotes,
His leges lapped in stel with luflych greves,   575
With polaynes piched therto, policed ful clene,
Aboute his knes knaged wyth knotes of golde;
Queme quyssewes then, that coyntlych closed
His thik thrawen thyghes, with thwonges to tachched;
And sythen the brawden bryné of bryght stel rynges   580

558. *derve:* may be read as *derne* 'secret' (*cf.* 540-2).
559. *schulde wende:* 'should have to go'.
560*f. dele . . . bronde:* 'give none (i.e. blows) in return with his sword'—
perhaps also 'never use his sword again'.
564*f.* 'What can a man do but make trial of that which Destiny offers,
whether painful or pleasant?' (*Destinés* is possessive.)
571. The armour was put on over the knight's clothes (the doublet and
capados); *cf.* 2015.
574*ff.* 'Then they placed the steel shoes (*sabatouns*) upon the man's feet; his
legs (were) enclosed in steel by beautiful greaves to which were attached
brightly polished knee pieces (*polaynes*), fastened (*knaged*) about his knees
with gold knots'.
579. *with . . . tachched:* 'tied on with laces'.

Umbeweved that wy, upon wlonk stuffe,
And wel bornyst brace upon his bothe armes,
With gode cowters and gay and gloves of plate,
And alle the godlych gere that hym gayn schulde
            That tyde;   585
      Wyth ryche cote-armure,
      His gold spores spend with pryde,
      Gurde wyth a bront ful sure
      With silk sayn umbe his syde.

When he was hasped in armes his harnays was ryche: 590
The lest lachet other loupe lemed of golde.
So harnayst as he was he herknes his masse
Offred and honoured at the heghe auter.
Sythen he comes to the kyng and to his cort-feres,
Laches lufly his leve at lordes and ladyes,   595
And thay hym kyst and conveyed, bikende hym to Kryst.
Bi that was Gryngolet grayth and gurde with a sadel
That glemed ful gayly with mony golde frenges,
Aywhere naylet ful newe, for that note ryched,
The brydel barred aboute, with bryght golde bounden.   600
The apparayl of the payttrure and of the proude skyrtes,
The cropore, and the covertor, acorded wyth the arsounes.
And al was, rayled on red, ryche golde nayles,
That al glytered and glent as glem of the sunne.
Thenne hentes he the helme and hastily hit kysses,   605
That was stapled stifly and stoffed wythinne.
Hit was hyghe on his hede, hasped bihynde,
Wyth a lyghtly urysoun over the aventayle,

581. *upon wlonk stuffe:* qualifies *rynges.*

586. *cote-armure:* a knight's surcoat, or coat of arms, i.e. a cloth tunic worn over the armour and embroidered with his heraldic device (which hence itself receives the name 'coat-of-arms').

592f. *he herknes . . . honoured:* 'he hears his Mass offered and celebrated' (past participles).

603. 'And it was all costly gold studs, set upon a red background'.

606. *stapled:* i.e. at the joints.

608. The *urysoun* (OF *hourson*) was a band of embroidered silk which

Enbrawden and bounden wyth the best gemmes
On brode sylkyn borde, and bryddes on semes, 610
As papjayes paynted perving bitwene,
Tortors and trulofes entayled so thyk
As mony burde theraboute had ben seven wynter
    In toune.
    The cercle was more o prys 615
    That umbeclypped hys croun,
    Of diamauntes a devys
    That bothe were bryght and broun.

Then thay schewed hym the schelde, that was of schyr goules
Wyth the pentangel depaynt of pure golde hues; 620
He braydes hit by the bauderyk, aboute the hals kestes.
That bisemed the segge semlyly fayre
And why the pentangel apendes to that prynce noble
I am in tent yow to telle, thof tary hyt me schulde.
Hit is a syngne that Salamon set sumwhyle 625
In bytoknyng of trawthe, bi tytle that hit habbes;

---

attached the *aventayle* (or *camail*), a piece of chain mail for the protection of the neck, to the bottom of the helmet.

611. 'such as parrots depicted between periwinkles (*perving*)'; the word may alternatively be read *perning* 'preening themselves', or perhaps 'flitting' (see *NQ* 206 (1961), 9); however, the present participle usually ends in *-ande* in this poem (see *TG-Davis n*). As 'periwinkle' it must be understood collectively here, unless it is a corruption of *pervinkes*.

615–8. 'The circlet (band of gold) which ringed his head was (even) more valuable with perfect (*a devys*) diamonds which were both clear and brown (i.e. of all tints).'

625. In the Middle Ages the idea developed that Solomon's magic seal bore a six-pointed star made of two interlaced triangles; in course of time this became identified with the five-pointed star (*pentangle*, *pentacle*, *pentalpha*, or *pentagramma*) which was used by the Pythagoreans and other sects as a symbol of health or perfection. In Christian eyes it was associated with black magic, but was sometimes made symbolic, instead, of the name Jesus or Maria (each of five letters), or of the five wounds of Christ. (See Green, 1962.)

626. *bi tytle that hit habbes:* 'by its intrinsic right'. The complex unity of the figure makes it a 'natural' symbol of moral integrity, in the manner expounded in the lines which follow.

For hit is a figure that haldes fyve poyntes
And uche lyne umbelappes and loukes in other
And aywhere hit is endeles (and Englych hit callen
Overal, as I here, 'the endeles knot').   630
Forthy hit acordes to this knyght and to his cler armes,
For ay faythful in fyve and sere fyve sythes,
Gawan was for gode knawen and, as golde pured,
Voyded of uche vylany, wyth vertues ennourned
        In mote.   635
      Forthy the pentangel newe
      He ber in schelde and cote,
      As tulk of tale most true
      And gentylest knyght of lote.

Fyrst he was funden fautles in his fyve wyttes.   640
And efte fayled never the freke in his fyve fyngres.
And alle his afyaunce upon folde was in the fyve woundes
That Cryst kaght on the croys, as the Crede telles.
And wheresoever thys mon in melly was stad,
His thro thoght was in that, thurgh alle other thynges,   645

627. *poyntes*: a significant pun, in as much as the word can mean 'virtue, quality' in ME (*cf*. 654). Perhaps it is also to be understood after *ay faythful in fyve* in 632.

628. 'and each line interlaces with (*umbelappes*) and joins on to the others' (*cf*. 657). Each line of the pentangle passes over one, and under one, and joins the other two at its ends; see illustration, p. xii.

630. *as I here*: to be read with *Overal*: 'English people in all parts, I am told'. In fact, the phrase is not elsewhere recorded.

632f. 'for, always trustworthy in five ways, and five times in each way, Gawain was known as a virtuous knight...'. The five pentads of virtues are detailed in the next stanza.

636. *newe*: i.e. 'newly painted'; *cf*. 620.

641. *in his fyve fyngres*: i.e. 'in his deeds' (?) The symbolism is strained and uneven in parts.

643. *Crede*: 'the Apostle's Creed' (*crucifixus, mortuus, et sepultus*).

645f. 'his earnest intent was on this above all else: that he should get all his courage from the five joys . . .' (*fong* is pres. subj.; for similar examples of pres. subj. after pa.t. see 738, 739.) The Five Joys of Mary were the Annunciation, Nativity, Resurrection, Ascension, and Assumption; with the Five Wounds of Christ they form subjects of popular devotions in the Middle Ages.

That alle his forsnes he fong at the fyve joyes
That the hende Heven Quene had of hir Chylde.
(At this cause the knyght comlyche hade
In the inore half of his schelde hir ymage depaynted,
That when he blusched therto his belde never payred.)   650
The fyft fyve that I finde that the frek used
Was fraunchyse and felawschyp forbe al thyng,
His clannes and his cortaysye croked were never,
And pité, that passes alle poyntes—thyse pure fyve
Were harder happed on that hathel then on any other.   655
Now alle these fyve sythes forsothe were fetled on this knyght
And uchone halched in other, that non ende hade,
And fyched upon fyve poyntes that fayld never,
Ne samned never in no syde, ne sundred nouther,
Withouten ende at any noke I owhere fynde,   660
Whereever the gomen bygan or glod to an ende.
Therfore on his schene schelde schapen was the knot,
Ryally wyth red golde upon rede gowles,
That is the pure 'pentaungel' wyth the peple called
With lore.   660
Now graythed is Gawan gay
And laght his launce ryght thore
And gef hem alle goud day—

---

660. I owhere: MS jquere (o *written above* u?); see *TG-Davis n.*

648f. Earlier related of Arthur.

651-5. The five virtues of chivalry are to be seen as forming a single group
on a par with the other pentads of 640, 641, 642, and 646.

653. *croked:* 'crooked, out of true'—an allusion to the symbolism of the
lines of the pentangle; *cf. poyntes* 654.

654. *Pity* and *piety* are not completely differentiated in meaning at this
date (both forms of the word go back, through OF, to L *pietas*). Here, among
the virtues of chivalry, the sense is primarily 'compassion' (*cf.* Chaucer's *For
pitee renneth soone in gentil herte*), but 'devotion to duty' is also of obvious
importance in Gawain's story (as in that of his ancestor Aeneas).

657. *that . . . hade:* 'so that none (of them) came to an end'.

660. 'without end at any angle that I can find anywhere (*owhere*)'.

664f. 'which is called the noble "pentangle" by learned people'; *cf.* 629f.
This 'learned' name is an adaptation of the Fr *pentacle* (L *pentaculum*).

He wende for ever more.

He sperred the sted with the spures and sprong on his way   670
So stif that the ston-fyr stroke out therafter.
Al that segh that semly syked in hert
And sayde sothly al same segges til other,
Carande for that comly, 'Bi Kryst, hit is scathe
That thou, leude, schal be lost, that art of lyf noble!   675
To fynde hys fere upon folde, in fayth, is not ethe.
Warloker to haf wroght had more wyt bene
And haf dyght yonder dere a duk to have worthed.
A lowande leder of ledes in londe hym wel semes,
And so had better haf ben then britned to noght,   680
Hadet wyth an alvisch mon, for angardes pryde.
Who knew ever any kyng such counsel to take
As knyghtes in cavelaciouns on Crystmasse gomnes?'
Wel much was the warme water that waltered of yen
When that semly syre soght fro tho wones   685
            Thad daye.
        He made non abode
        Bot wyghtly went hys way.
        Mony wylsum way he rode,
        The bok as I herde say.   690

Now rides this renk thurgh the ryalme of Logres,
Sir Gauan, on Godes halve, thagh hym no gomen thoght—
Oft leudles alone he lenges on nyghtes

669. 'he thought (he was saying goodbye) for ever.'

673. *sothly:* Gollancz notes that the context here requires the (now dialectal) word, meaning 'softly, quietly' and compares Keats's 'jellies soother than the creamy curd' (*Eve of St. Agnes*) and the verb *to soothe.*

675. *that ... noble:* '(you) who are (so) noble of life'.

677. *had more wyt bene:* 'would have made more sense'.

680. 'and it would have been better so than (for him to be) utterly destroyed'.

683. 'as that of knights in trivial arguments about Christmas games?'

690. 'as I learned from the book'; a conventional reference to the romance-writer's source, real or imaginary.

691. *Logres:* Geoffrey of Monmouth's name for Arthur's Britain (Welsh *Lloegyr*).

692. *on Godes halve:* an exclamation, or perhaps lit. 'in the cause of God'.

Ther he fonde noght hym byfore the fare that he lyked;
Hade he no fere bot his fole bi frythes and dounes,   695
Ne no gome bot God bi gate wyth to karp—
Til that he neghed ful neghe into the Northe Wales.
Alle the iles of Anglesay on lyft half he haldes
And fares over the fordes by the forlondes;
Over at the Holy Hede, til he hade eft bonk   700
In the wyldrenesse of Wyrale. Wonde ther bot lyte
That auther God other gome wyth goud hert lovied.
And ay he frayned, as he ferde, at frekes that he met
If thay hade herde any karp of a knyght grene
In any grounde theraboute, of the Grene Chapel.   705
And al nykked hym wyth nay that never in her lyve
Thay seghe never no segge that was of suche hues
       Of grene.
    The knyght tok gates straunge

698ff. *the iles of Anglesay:* i.e. Anglesey itself and the neighbouring small islands (including Holy I. and Puffin I.). Gawain's journey takes him to Caernarvon and eastwards along the north coast of Wales. A fourteenth-century map in the Bodleian Library shows the usual route as passing through Bangor, Conway, Abergele, Rhuddlan, and Flint (see E. J. S. Parsons, *The Map of Great Britain Circa 1360, Known as The Gough Map: An Introduction to the Facsimile*, with 'The Roads of the Gough Map' by Sir Frank Stenton, Oxford, 1958). With its geographical particularity, the description of this part of his journey contrasts with that of the beginning and end, which (appropriately enough) are clouded in a romantic vagueness. The poet, writing in the north-west midlands, probably knew, and expected his original audience to know, this part of the journey.

699. Apparently a reference to his crossing of the Conway and Clwyd. *Holy Hede* (700) may then be identifiable as Holywell, near Basingwerk Abbey, where the Roman road reaches the Dee. The lowest identifiable medieval fording place was at Shotwick, some eight miles up river, where the Dee is much narrower; the poet may have had a boat-crossing in mind here, however, as the phrase *hade eft bonk* perhaps suggests. The name has been much discussed; the only real certainty is that it does not refer to Holyhead in Anglesey (*cf.* 698).

701f. 'in the wild country of Wirral. Very few lived there whom either God or a good-hearted man loved.' The forest of Wirral was a notorious refuge for outlaws in the fourteenth century.

706. *nikked him with nay:* nikke 'to say no to' (from *ne ic* 'not I'?); *with nay* is therefore redundant; *cf.* 2471.

C*

In mony a bonk unbene.   710
His cher ful oft con chaunge,
That chapel er he myght sene.

Mony klyf he overclambe in contrayes straunge.
Fer floten fro his frendes, fremedly he rydes.
At uche warthe other water ther the wye passed   715
He fonde a foo hym byfore, bot ferly hit were,
And that so foule and so felle that feght hym byhode.
So mony mervayl bi mount ther the mon fyndes
Hit were to tore for to telle of the tenthe dole.
Sumwhyle wyth wormes he werres and with wolves als,   720
Sumwhyle wyth wodwos that woned in the knarres,
Bothe wyth bulles and beres, and bores otherwhyle,
And etaynes that hym anelede of the heghe felle.
Nade he ben dughty and drye and Dryghtyn had served,
Douteles he hade ben ded and dreped ful ofte.   725
For werre wrathed hym not so much that wynter nas wors,
When the colde cler water fro the cloudes schadde
And fres er hit falle myght to the fale erthe.
Ner slayn wyth the slete he sleped in his yrnes,
Mo nyghtes then innoghe, in naked rokkes   730
Theras claterande fro the crest the colde borne rennes
And henged heghe over his hede in hard iisseikkles.
Thus in peryl and payne and plytes ful harde
Bi contray caryes this knyght tyl Krystmasse Even,
          Alone.   735
     The knyght wel that tyde

726. nas: MS was (Davis)

---

711. A play upon words (*significatio*): 'he looked this way and that' and 'his mood changed many times'; cf. 2169.

721. *wodwos:* pl. (OE *wudu wasa* 'wood man'); hairy woodland monsters of medieval imagination; they were often portrayed in medieval art and civic pageantry and seem to have appealed to alliterative writers particularly; see, e.g., *Wars of Alexander* (edited W. W. Skeat, London, EETS, 1886) 1540, *Winner and Waster* (edited Sir Israel Gollancz, London, 1931) 7of.

725. 'there were many occasions when he would doubtless have been killed (*ded and dreped*)'.

To Mary made his mone
That ho hym red to ryde
And wysse hym to sum wone.

Bi a mounte on the morne meryly he rydes   740
Into a forest ful dep, that ferly was wylde,
Highe hilles on uche a halve and holtwodes under
Of hore okes ful hoge, a hundreth togeder.
The hasel and the hawthorne were harled al samen,
With roghe raged mosse rayled aywhere,   745
With mony bryddes unblythe upon bare twyges,
That pitosly ther piped for pyne of the colde.
The gome upon Gryngolet glydes hem under
Thurgh mony misy and myre, mon al hym one,
Carande for his costes, lest he ne kever schulde   750
To se the servyse of that Syre that on that self nyght
Of a burde was borne oure baret to quelle.
And therfore sykyng he sayde, 'I beseche The, Lorde,
And Mary, that is myldest moder so dere,
Of sum herber ther heghly I myght here masse   755
Ande Thy matynes tomorne, mekely I ask,
And therto prestly I pray my Pater and Ave
                    And Crede.'
            He rode in his prayere
            And cryed for his mysdede.
            He sayned hym in sythes sere   760
            And sayde, 'Cros Kryst me spede.'

Nade he sayned hymself, segge, bot thrye
Er he was war in the wod of a won in a mote,
Abof a launde, on a lawe, loken under boghes   765

738. 'that she would direct his course'.
740. *on the morne:* i.e. of Christmas Eve (*cf.* 755*f*). The stanza amplifies the
preceding wheel. *meryly:* at first sight a singularly inappropriate adv.; but
mery (like *gay*) often has the sense 'elegant, splendid', *cf.* 142, 153.
756. *Thy matynes:* i.e. Matins of Christmas Day.
761. *in sythes sere:* each time he said one of the prayers, *cf.* 763.
762. *Cros Kryst:* 'Christ's Cross'; the word order is French.

Of mony borelych bole aboute bi the diches,
A castel the comlokest that ever knyght aghte,
Pyched on a prayere, a park al aboute,
With a pyked palays pyned ful thik,
That umbeteye mony tre mo then two myle.   770
That holde on that on syde the hathel avysed,
As hit schemered and schon thurgh the schyre okes.
Thenne has he hendly of his helme and heghly he thonkes
Jesus and Sayn Gilyan, that gentyle ar bothe,
That cortaysly had hym kydde and his cry herkened.   775
'Now bone hostel,' cothe the burne, 'I beseche yow yette!'
Thenne gederes he to Gryngolet with the gilt heles
And he ful chauncely has chosen to the chef gate,
That broght bremly the burne to the bryge ende
          In haste.   780
      The bryge was breme upbrayde,
      The yates wer stoken faste,
      The walles were wel arayed—
      Hit dut no wyndes blaste.

The burne bode on bonk, that on blonk hoved,   785

769. 'fenced in by a close palisade of spikes'. In the thirteenth-century
French romance *La Mule Sans Frein*, in which a version of the Beheading
Game occurs (as also in the German *Diu Krône*, apparently derived from it),
Gawain arrives at a castle surrounded by a circle of stakes on each of which
(with one exception!) is a human head. The *piked palays* plays no such role in
the English poem but its presence may be due to reminiscence of this version
of the story.

770. *mo then two myle*: presumably in diameter.

773. 'Then he respectfully takes off his helmet and solemnly he thanks . . .'.

774. *Sayn Gilyan*: St. Julian, the patron saint of travellers.

776. *bone hostel*: a Fr phrase meaning 'good lodging', a standard invocation
to St. Julian; *cf*. the eagle in Chaucer's *House of Fame*, 1021-2:

          Now up the hed, for al ys wel;
          Seynt Julyan, loo, bon hostel!

781f. 'The drawbridge was firmly raised (*upbrayde*); the gates were securely
shut (*stoken*)'; (a description of state, not action, of course).

785f. 'The horseman tarried, waiting on the bank of the deep double ditch
which surrounded the house.' The description in 787-93 is of the outer
fortification (barbican).

Of the depe double dich that drof to the place.
The walle wod in the water wonderly depe
Ande eft a ful huge heght hit haled upon lofte,
Of harde hewen ston up to the tables,
Enbaned under the abataylment, in the best lawe;   790
And sythen garytes ful gaye gered bitwene,
Wyth mony luflych loupe that louked ful clene;
A better barbican that burne blusched upon never.
And innermore he behelde that halle ful hyghe,
Towres telded bytwene, trochet ful thik,   795
Fayre fylyoles that fyed, and ferlyly long,
With corvon coprounes, craftyly sleye.
Chalk-whyt chymnées ther ches he innoghe,
Upon bastel roves that blenked ful whyte.
So mony pynakle payntet was poudred aywhere   800
Among the castel carneles, clambred so thik,
That pared out of papure purely hit semed.   .
The fre freke on the fole hit fayr innoghe thoght
If he myght kever to com the cloyster wythinne,

790. 'fortified under the battlements in the best style' (*enbaned:* 'defended by horizontal projecting courses').

796. *fylyoles:* 'pinnacles', apparently in quasi-apposition to *trochet.*

799. 'which shone very white upon roofs of towers' (qualifying *chymnées*).

800. *pynacle payntet:* Fr word order.

802. 'that it looked as if it were all completely cut out of paper.' The castle is compared to the paper cut-outs which sometimes decorated food brought to table in fourteenth-century banquets. Chaucer's Parson speaks disapprovingly of *pride of the table . . . in . . . swich manere bake-metes and dissh-metes, brennynge of wilde fir and peynted and castelled with papir. (CT* X (I), 440–5.) *Cf.* also the description of Belshazzar's feast in the companion poem *Purity* (especially 1408) and see Ackerman, *JEGP* 56 (1957), 410–7. The same comparison occurs later to the Renaissance Italian architect Giorgio Vasari (1511–74), but for him it exposes the illogicality of Gothic architecture: 'in the same way on the façades and other decorated parts they made a malediction of little tabernacles one above another, with so many pyramids and points and leaves that it seems impossible for it to support itself, let alone other weights. They look more as if they were made of paper than of stone or marble.' *Le vite,* Introduzione, Dell'architettura, Cap. III; cited by E. H. Gombrich, *Norm and Form* (London, 1966), 84.

804. 'if only he might manage to get inside the bailey (*cloyster*).'

To herber in that hostel whyl halyday lested,   805
    Avinant.
    He calde, and sone ther com
    A porter pure plesaunt;
    On the wal his ernd he nome
    And haylsed the knyght erraunt.   810

'Gode sir,' quoth Gawan, 'woldes thou go myn ernde
To the hegh lorde of this hous, herber to crave?'
'Ye, Peter!' quoth the porter, 'and purely I trowee
That ye be, wye, welcum to won whyle you lykes.'
Then yede the wye yerne and com ayayn swythe   815
And folke frely hym wyth to fonge the knyght.
Thay let doun the grete draght and derely out yeden
And kneled doun on her knes upon the colde erthe
To welcum this ilk wy as worthy hom thoght.
Thay yolden hym the brode yate, yarked up wyde,   820
And he hem raysed rekenly and rod over the brygge.
Sere segges hym sesed by sadel whel he lyght
And sythen stabeled his stede stif men innoghe.
Knyghtes and swyeres comen doun thenne
For to bryng this buurne wyth blys into halle.   825
When he hef up his helme ther hied innoghe
For to hent hit at his honde, the hende to serven;
His bronde and his blasoun bothe thay token.
Then haylsed he ful hendly tho hatheles uchone
And mony proud mon ther presed that prynce to honour.   830
Alle hasped in his hegh wede to halle thay hym wonnen,
Ther fayre fyre upon flet fersly brenned.

815. yerne and com: *supplied* (Davis); Gollancz: yare . . .

---

    806. *Avinant:* 'pleasantly', or adj. 'pleasant' qualifying *hostel.*
    813. *Peter:* 'by St. Peter'—an appropriate oath for a porter (the half-line appears to be an adaptation of (*St.*) *Peter the porter*—i.e. 'of heaven'—which occurs in *Piers Plowman,* B-text XV. 18).
    819. *as . . . thoght:* 'in the way which seemed proper to them'.
    821. *raysed:* i.e. he asked them to rise from their knees.

Thenne the lorde of the lede loutes fro his chambre
For to mete wyth menske the mon on the flor.
He sayde, 'Ye are welcum to welde, as yow lykes,   835
That here is; al is yowre awen to have at yowre wylle
        And welde.'
        'Graunt mercy,' quoth Gawayn.
        'Ther Kryst hit yow foryelde.'
        As frekes that semed fayn   840
        Ayther other in armes con felde.

Gawayn glyght on the gome that godly hym gret,
And thught hit a bolde burne that the burgh aghte,
A hoge hathel for the nones and of hyghe eldee.
Brode, bryght was his berde and al bever-hued,   845
Sturne, stif on the stryththe on stalworth schonkes,
Felle face as the fyre, and fre of hys speche;
And wel hym semed forsothe, as the segge thught,
To lede a lortschyp in lee of leudes ful gode.
The lorde hym charred to a chambre and chefly cumaundes 850
To delyver hym a leude hym lowly to serve;
And there were boun at his bode burnes innoghe

---

833. The lord's chamber is to be imagined as a small room leading off a gallery, from which he comes down to greet Gawain in the hall. Later Gawain's bedroom is referred to as a *lofte* (1096, 1676).

835f. 'You are welcome to enjoy whatever is here, as you please; it is all your own to have and use as you wish.' The repetition suggests that some dramatic irony is intended; *cf.* 1237f.

839. 'May Christ recompense you for it.' *Ther(e)* is used idiomatically in ME to introduce blessings and curses.

840. 'In the manner of joyful men'.

844. *of hyghe eldee:* 'of mature age'. The portrait echoes, in muted tones, features of the description of the Green Knight (*cf.*, e.g., 844 and 137*ff*, 845 and 182, 846 and 431).

847. *fre of hys speche:* 'courteous in speech', *cf.* 1031*ff* and contrast the arrogance of the Green Knight in Fitt I.

848f. 'and it appeared to Gawain that he was certainly a suitable person to exercise sovereignty in the castle over excellent knights.'

851. *To delyver:* passive use of the infinitive: 'that a man should be assigned to him'.

That broght hym to a bryght boure ther beddyng was noble:
Of cortynes of clene sylk wyth cler golde hemmes
And covertores ful curious with comlych panes   855
Of bryght blaunmer above, enbrawded bisydes,
Rudeles rennande on ropes, red golde rynges,
Tapytes tyght to the wowe, of tuly and tars,
And under fete, on the flet, of folwande sute.
Ther he was dispoyled, wyth speches of myerthe,   860
The burn of his bruny and of his bryght wedes;
Ryche robes ful rad renkkes hym broghten
For to charge and to chaunge and chose of the best.
Sone as he on hent and happed therinne,
That sete on hym semly, wyth saylande skyrtes,   865
The ver by his visage verayly hit semed
Welnegh to uche hathel, alle on hues,
Lowande and lufly alle his lymmes under;
That a comloker knyght never Kryst made,
          Hem thoght.   870
             Whethen in worlde he were,
             Hit semed as he moght
             Be prynce withouten pere
             In felde ther felle men foght.

A cheyer byfore the chemné, ther charcole brenned,   875
Was graythed for Sir Gawan graythely with clothes:
Quyssynes upon queldepoyntes, that koynt wer bothe;
And thenne a meré mantyle was on that mon cast,
Of a broun bleeaunt, enbrauded ful ryche
And fayre furred wythinne with felles of the best,   880
Alle of ermyn in erde, his hode of the same.
And he sete in that settel semlych ryche
And achaufed hym chefly, and thenne his cher mended.

---

854. *Of cortynes:* cf. 337n.
864-8. 'As soon as he had taken one and had it on, one which looked well on him with flowing skirts, truly it seemed to everyone from his appearance, almost as if spring (*ver*) had come in all its colours, his limbs under the garment shining and beautiful'.

Sone was telded up a tabil on trestes ful fayre,
Clad wyth a clene clothe that cler whyt schewed, 885
Sanap and salure and sylverin spones.
The wye wesche at his wylle and went to his mete.
Segges hym served semly innoghe
Wyth sere sewes and sete, sesounde of the best,
Doublefelde, as hit falles, and fele kyn fisches— 890
Summe baken in bred, summe brad on the gledes,
Summe sothen, summe in sewe savered with spyces—
And ay sawses so sleye that the segge lyked.
The freke calde hit a fest ful frely and ofte
Ful hendely, when alle the hatheles rehayted hym at ones 895
        As hende,
        'This penaunce now ye take
        And eft hit schal amende.'
        That mon much merthe con make,
        For wyn in his hed that wende. 900

Thenne was spyed and spured upon spare wyse,
Bi prevé poyntes of that prynce put to hymselven,
That he beknew cortaysly of the court that he were
That athel Arthure the hende haldes hym one,
That is the ryche ryal kyng of the Rounde Table, 905
And hit was Wawen hymself that in that won syttes,
Comen to that Krystmasse, as case hym then lymped.
When the lorde hade lerned that he the leude hade,
Loude laghed he therat, so lef hit hym thoght,

893. sawses: MS sawes; sleye: MS sleyes (Napier)

---

884. Gawain is, of course, dining alone in his bedroom, not in the main hall; but temporary tables on trestles were quite usual in the Middle Ages (*cf.* 1648—apparently in the hall).

894–8. 'The knight very courteously and graciously called it a feast again and again when all together the men, equally courteously (*As hende*), pressed him (with the words), . . .' *As* may, however, introduce a polite imperative in ME: 'Do, gracious sir, accept this penance for the time being . . .'.

897f. They modestly refer to the meal as a 'penance' (Christmas Eve being a day of abstinence) and promise him better fare later (i.e. on Christmas Day).

900. 'Because of the wine, which went to his head.'

And alle the men in that mote maden much joye   910
To apere in his presense prestly that tyme
That alle prys and prowes and pured thewes
Apendes to hys persoun and praysed is ever,
Byfore alle men upon molde his mensk is the most.
Uch segge ful softly sayde to his fere,   915
'Now schal we semlych se sleghtes of thewes
And the teccheles termes of talkyng noble.
Wich spede is in speche unspurd may we lerne,
Syn we haf fonged that fyne fader of nurture.
God has geven us His grace godly forsothe,   920
That such a gest as Gawan grauntes us to have
When burnes blythe of His burthe schal sitte
          And synge.
      In menyng of maneres mere
      This burne now schal us bryng.   925
      I hope that may hym here
      Schal lerne of luf-talkyng.'

Bi that the diner was done and the dere up
Hit was negh at the niyght neghed the tyme.
Chaplaynes to the chapeles chosen the gate,   930
Rungen ful rychely, ryght as thay schulden,
To the hersum evensong of the hyghe tyde.

912f. *That ... to hys:* a form of the relative, 'to whose'.

918f. 'Now we can learn, without asking, what sort of thing success in conversation is.'

919. *that fyne fader of nurture:* in many medieval romances Gawain is the *beau idéal* of courtesy, though not of chastity; from the thirteenth century onwards, however, his character tends to be denigrated by writers whose chief aim is to idealize other knights (e.g. Lancelot or Tristram). This development accounts for the contradiction in Malory's treatment of Gawain and for Tennyson's unsympathetic attitude towards him. (See B. J. Whiting, *Mediaeval Studies* 9 (1947), 189; excerpts in Fox, 1968; also Owen, 1968.)

921. 'Who allows us to receive such a guest as Gawain'.

926f. 'I believe anyone who has the opportunity of listening to him will learn something of the art of conversation for lovers.'

928. 'By the time dinner was over and the noble knight had risen'.

930. *the chapeles:* the poet has in mind a large castle with several chapels, like Caernarvon.

The lorde loutes therto and the lady als;
Into a cumly closet coyntly ho entres.
Gawan glydes ful gay and gos theder sone.   935
The lorde laches hym by the lappe and ledes hym to sytte
And couthly hym knowes and calles hym his nome
And sayde he was the welcomest wye of the worlde.
And he hym thonkked throly; and ayther halched other
And seten soberly samen the servise whyle.   940
Thenne lyst the lady to loke on the knyght;
Thenne com ho of hir closet with mony cler burdes.
Ho was the fayrest in felle, of flesche and of lyre
And of compas and colour and costes, of alle other,
And wener then Wenore, as the wye thoght.   945
Ho ches thurgh the chaunsel to cheryche that hende.
Another lady hir lad bi the lyft honde
That was alder then ho, an auncian hit semed,
And heghly honowred with hatheles aboute.
Bot unlyke on to loke tho ladyes were: 950
For if the yonge was yep, yolwe was that other;
Riche red on that on rayled aywhere,
Rugh ronkled chekes that other on rolled;
Kerchofes of that on, wyth mony cler perles,
Hir brest and hir bryght throte bare displayed,   955
Schon schyrer then snawe that schedes on hilles;

946. Ho: MS he (Wright; *cf.* 971)

---

934. Her closed pew (*closet*) is evidently in the chancel; *cf.* 942–6.
937. *hym knowes:* 'acknowledges him'.
943f. 'She was the most beautiful creature alive (*fayrest in felle . . . of alle other*) in respect of flesh, face, figure (*compas*), complexion, and deportment (*costes*)'; *in felle* (lit. 'in skin') is best taken as a tag ('creature, person'); note the change of construction from *in . . .* to *of . . . of . . . of . . . .*
950. *unlyke on to loke:* 'dissimilar in appearance (lit. 'to look upon')'.
952. 'a glowing pink everywhere adorned the first one'.
953. *that other on rolled:* 'sagged on the other'.
956. The subject of *schon* is apparently *kerchofes* (which left her neck bare and shone brighter than snow) and this reading is supported by the simile of *hilles* for *brest*; but the whiteness of *hir brest and hir bryght throte* is also suggested by the line (especially in contrast to 958, 961).

That other wyth a gorger was gered over the swyre,
Chymbled over hir blake chyn with chalk-whyte vayles,
Hir frount folden in sylk, enfoubled aywhere,
Toret and treleted with tryfles aboute,   960
That noght was bare of that burde bot the blake browes,
The tweyne yen and the nase, the naked lyppes,
And those were soure to se and sellyly blered.
A mensk lady on molde mon may hir calle,
                For Gode!   965
        Hir body was schort and thik,
        Hir buttokes balw and brode;
        More lykkerwys on to lyk
        Was that scho hade on lode.

When Gawayn glyght on that gay that graciously loked,   970
Wyth leve laght of the lorde, he lent hem ayaynes.
The alder he haylses, heldande ful lowe,
The loveloker he lappes a lyttel in armes.
He kysses hir comlyly and knyghtly he meles.
Thay kallen hym of aquoyntaunce and he hit quyk askes   975
To be her servaunt sothly, if hemself lyked.
Thay tan hym bytwene hem, wyth talkyng hym leden
To chambre, to chemné, and chefly thay asken
Spyces, that unsparely men speded hom to bryng,
And the wynnelych wyne therwith uche tyme.   980

958. chalk-whyte: MS mylkquyte (Onions)
967. balw: MS bay (Tolkien and Gordon)
971. lent: MS went (Andrew)

---

960. '(her forehead) framed by embroidered hems (*toret: toret-ed*, pp.) and veiled in lattice work (*treleted*), covered in fine stitching' (all in fuller description of the *sylk* of 959).

969. *that:* 'that which' (i.e. the younger lady).

975f. 'They ask to be better acquainted with him and he swiftly asks to be their servant truly, if it pleased them' (*hit* anticipates the next phrase; *servaunt* has its courtly connotation, 'admirer').

979. *hom to bryng:* 'to bring to them'.

The lorde luflych aloft lepes ful ofte,
Mynned merthe to be made upon mony sythes,
Hent heghly of his hode and on a spere henged
And wayned hom to wynne the worchip therof
That most myrthe myght meve that Crystenmas whyle.   985
'And I schal fonde, bi my fayth, to fylter wyth the best,
Er me wont the wede, with help of my frendes.'
Thus wyth laghande lotes the lorde hit tayt makes
For to glade Sir Gawayn with gomnes in halle
        That nyght,   990
    Til that hit was tyme
    The lord comaundet lyght.
    Sir Gawen his leve con nyme
    And to his bed hym dight.

On the morne, as uch mon mynes that tyme   995
That Dryghtyn for oure destyné to deye was borne,
Wele waxes in uche a won in worlde for His sake.
So did hit there on that day, thurgh dayntés mony:
Bothe at mes and at mele messes ful quaynt
Derf men upon dece drest of the best.   1000
The olde auncian wyf heghest ho syttes;
The lorde lufly her by lent as I trowe.
Gawan and the gay burde togeder thay seten
Even inmyddes, as the messe metely come,

992. lord: MS kyng (Tolkien and Gordon)

981-7. 'The lord often leaps to his feet in friendly manner, reminded them
over and over again to make merry, ceremoniously took off his hood and
hung it on a spear and directed that those who devised most amusement
during Christmas were to win it as a trophy: "And, on my honour, I shall try
with the help of my friends to contend with the best, before I lose the garment."'

995. *On the morne:* 'On the morrow'. The two lines are a periphrasis for
'On Christmas Day'; *cf.* 60.

999. *messes ful quaynt:* direct object of (*derf men*) *drest*.

1001. *heghest:* 'in place of honour'; *cf.* 112.

1002. *lufly her by lent:* 'courteously took his place beside her'.

1004 *ff.* 'right in the centre, where the food properly came and afterwards
(went) around the whole hall, as seemed most fitting to them, until each man
in order of his degree was duly served.'

And sythen thurgh al the sale, as hem best semed,   1005
Bi uche grome at his degré graythely was served.
Ther was mete, there was myrthe, ther was much joye,
That for to telle therof hit me tene were,
And to poynte hit yet I pyned me paraventure.
Bot yet I wot that Wawen and the wale burde   1010
Such comfort of her compaynye caghten togeder
Thurgh her dere dalyaunce of her derne wordes,
Wyth clene cortays carp closed fro fylthe,
That hor play was passande uche prynce gomen,
                    In vayres.   1015
            Trumpes and nakerys,
            Much pypyng ther repayres.
            Uche mon tented hys
            And thay two tented thayres.

Much dut was ther dryven that day and that other,   1020
And the thryd as thro thronge in therafter—
The joye of Sayn Jones day was gentyle to here
And was the last of the layk leudes ther thoghten.
Ther were gestes to go upon the gray morne;
Forthy wonderly thay woke and the wyn dronken,   1025
Daunsed ful dreyly wyth dere caroles.
At the last, when hit was late, thay lachen her leve,
Uchon to wende on his way that was wye stronge.

1009. 'Even if, perchance, I were to take pains to describe it in detail.'
1011. 'found such pleasure in each other's company'.
1014f. 'that their pleasant occupation surpassed any royal (*prynce*) sport, in truth.'
1016–9. 'There were trumpets, kettledrums and much piping present. Each man attended to his own pleasure (understood from *play*, 1014) and those two attended to theirs.'
1021ff. *the thryd* (St. John's Day) is 27 December; but the hunting (which begins on the morning when the guests leave) occupies the last three days of December. So 28 December—Holy Innocents' Day—is unaccounted for. Perhaps, as Gollancz suggested, it was referred to in a line between 1022 and 1023, now lost.
1027ff. The guests who are leaving early next morning take their leave before going to bed (*cf.* 1120, 1126f). The situation is repeated in 1960ff.

Gawan gef hym god day; the godmon hym lachches,
Ledes hym to his awen chambre, the chymné bysyde,   1030
And there he drawes hym on drye and derely hym thonkkes
Of the wynne worschip that he hym wayned hade
As to honour his hous on that hyghe tyde
And enbelyse his burgh with his bele chere.
'Iwysse, sir, whyl I leve me worthes the better   1035
That Gawayn has ben my gest at Goddes awen fest.'
'Grant merci, sir,' quoth Gawayn, 'in god fayth hit is yowres,
Al the honour is your awen—the Heghe Kyng yow yelde—
And I am, wye, at your wylle to worch youre hest,
As I am halden therto in hyghe and in lowe   1040
        Bi right.'
        The lorde fast can hym payne
        To holde lenger the knyght;
        To hym answres Gawayn
        Bi non way that he myght.   1045

Then frayned the freke ful fayre at himselven
What derve dede had hym dryven at that dere tyme
So kenly fro the kynges kourt to kayre al his one,
Er the halidayes holly were halet out of toun.
'Forsothe, sir,' quoth the segge, 'ye sayn bot the trawthe.   1050
A heghe ernde and a hasty me hade fro tho wones,
For I am sumned myselfe to sech to a place

1029. 'Gawain said goodbye to him (but) the host seizes him'.
1033f. Though in indirect speech, the words are chosen to suggest the
Host's *frenkysch fare* (1116), which is evident not only in his generous choice of
the French terms *honour*, *enbelyse* and *bele cher* in reference to Gawain, but also
in his modest use of the homely *hous* and *burgh* of his own castle.
1035. 'Indeed, sir, it will be the better for me as long as I live'.
1042f. 'The lord earnestly endeavoured to keep the knight longer (i.e. in
the castle)'.
1045. 'that he could by no means (stay longer).' *Cf.* 2471.
1047ff. Perhaps a humorous covert allusion to the beheading: 'What crime
had you committed that you had to leave Arthur's court so hastily?'
1049. 'Before the holidays were completely over.' *out of toun* (lit. 'from the
homestead') is a conventional tag here, 'away'.

I not in worlde whederwarde to wende hit to fynde.
I nolde bot if I hit negh myght on New Yeres morne
For alle the londe inwyth Logres, so me Oure Lorde help!   1055
Forthy, sir, this enquest I require yow here:
That ye me telle with trawthe, if ever ye tale herde
Of the Grene Chapel, where hit on grounde stondes,
And of the knyght that hit kepes, of colour of grene.
Ther was stabled bi statut a steven us bytwene   1060
To mete that mon at that mere, yif I myght last;
And of that ilk New Yere bot neked now wontes,
And I wolde loke on that lede, if God me let wolde,
Gladloker, bi Goddes Sun, then any god welde!
Forthi, iwysse, bi yowre wylle, wende me bihoves;   1065
Naf I now to busy bot bare thre dayes,
And me als fayn to falle feye as fayly of myyn ernde.'
Thenne laghande quoth the lorde, 'Now leng the byhoves,
For I schal teche yow to that terme bi the tymes ende.
The Grene Chapayle upon grounde greve yow no more   1070
Bot ye schal be in yowre bed, burne, at thyn ese
Whyle forth dayes and ferk on the fyrst of the yere
And cum to that merk at mydmorn, to make what yow likes
        In spenne.
            Dowelles whyle New Yeres daye   1075
            And rys and raykes thenne.
            Mon schal yow sette in waye;
            Hit is not two myle henne.'

1053. not: MS wot; *cf.* 726

1054. 'I would not fail to reach it on New Year's morning' (lit. 'I would not wish otherwise than that I might . . .').

1061. *yif I myght last:* 'if I happened to live so long'.

1064. *bi Goddes Sun:* i.e. 'by Christ'.

1070. 'Let the whereabouts of the Green Chapel bother you no more'. In view of the actual nature of the Green Chapel (2170*ff*) the repetition of *upon grounde* (*cf.* 1058) may be ironical.

1072. *whyle forth dayes:* 'until late in the day'; presumably the Host here means 'on the day you leave', emphasizing the nearness of the Green Chapel. He later suggests a lie-in for Gawain on the next day (1093*ff*).

1074. A tag of obscure origin, meaning 'there'.

1077. 'You shall be put on the right road'.

Thenne was Gawan ful glad and gomenly he laghed:
'Now I thonk yow thryvandely thurgh alle other thynge.   1080
Now acheved is my chaunce, I schal at your wylle
Dowelle and elles do what ye demen.'
Thenne sesed hym the syre and set hym bysyde,
Let the ladies be fette to lyke hem the better.
Ther was seme solace by hemself stille;   1085
The lorde let for luf lotes so myry
As wy that wolde of his wyte, ne wyst what he myght.
Thenne he carped to the knyght, criande loude,
'Ye han demed to do the dede that I bidde—
Wyl ye halde this hes here at thys ones?'   1090
'Ye, sir, forsothe,' sayd the segge true,
'Whyl I byde in yowre borghe be bayn to yowre hest,'
'For ye haf travayled,' quoth the tulk, 'towen fro ferre,
And sythen waked me wyth, ye arn not wel waryst
Nauther of sostnaunce ne of slepe, sothly I knowe.   1095
Ye schal lenge in your lofte and lye in your ese
Tomorn whyle the messewhyle and to mete wende
When ye wyl wyth my wyf, that wyth yow schal sitte
And comfort yow with compayny til I to cort torne.
                    Ye lende   1100
               And I schal erly ryse;
               On huntyng wyl I wende.'
               Gauayn grantes alle thyse,
               Hym heldande, as the hende.

'Yet firre,' quoth the freke, 'a forwarde we make: 1105

1080. *thurgh . . . thynge:* i.e. 'beyond all your other kindnesses'.
1083. *set hym bysyde:* 'seated Gawain beside himself'.
1087. '(he seemed) like a man who was about to go off his head, who didn't know what he might (do).' The last expression has an idiomatic appearance: *cf.* the OE poem *Judith* 68–9, *swa he nyste ræda nanne|on gewitlocan*, of the drunken Holofernes (who appears to have been actually unconscious, however).
1104. 'Bowing (*Hym heldande* reflex.), like the courteous man he was.'
1105. *we make:* 'let us make'.

Whatsoever I wynne in the wod hit worthes to youres
And what chek so ye acheve chaunge me therforne.
Swete, swap we so: sware with trawthe,
Whether leude so lymp lere other better.'
'Bi God,' quoth Gawayn the gode, 'I grant thertylle;   1110
And that yow lyst for to layke lef hit me thynkes.'
'Who brynges us this beverage, this bargayn is maked,'
So sayde the lorde of that lede; thay laghed uchone.
Thay dronken and daylyeden and dalten untyghtel,
Thise lordes and ladyes, whyle that hem lyked,   1115
And sythen with frenkysch fare and fele fayre lotes
Thay stoden and stemed and stylly speken,
Kysten ful comlyly and kaghten her leve.
With mony leude ful lyght and lemande torches
Uche burne to his bed was broght at the laste   1120
        Ful softe.
    To bed yet er thay yede,
    Recorded covenauntes ofte;
    The olde lorde of that leude
    Cowthe wel halde layk alofte.   1125

1106*f.* 'Whatever I win in the forest becomes yours and you give me in
exchange for it whatever bad luck you have.' The antithetical *chek* is outwardly
expressive of the host's courtly generosity (*cf. lere* 1109) but has sinister over-
tones: in chess, it is 'check(mate)' (suggestive of the battle of wits in the
bedroom episodes), and in hawking 'A false stoop, when a hawk forsakes her
quarry for baser game' (*OED*), (suggesting Gawain's lapse from the pursuit of
the highest ideals). The word has an unequivocally negative sense at 1857 and
2195.

1108*f.* 'My dear man, let us strike a bargain (*swap*) on these terms: to
answer honourably, to whichever man may fall the worse lot or the better.'
Whether . . . so: 'whichever (of two)' (*cf. what . . . so*); *lere:* quasi-compar. adj.
'worse'(?) (*cf. lur* 'loss').

1112. 'If someone will bring us the drink (to pledge our word), this bargain
is made'; *beverage* became a technical term in this sense in ME and was also
used for 'bargain' itself (*cf.* also 1409, 1684).

1124*f.* 'He who had long been lord of that people certainly knew how to
keep up the fun.'

III

Ful erly bifore the day the folk uprysen.
Gestes that go wolde hor gromes thay calden
And thay busken up bilyve blonkkes to sadel,
Tyffen her takles, trussen her males;
Richen hem the rychest, to ryde alle arayde,   1130
Lepen up lyghtly, lachen her brydeles,
Uche wye on his way ther hym wel lyked.
The leve lorde of the londe was not the last
Arayed for the rydyng with renkkes ful mony;
Ete a sop hastyly, when he hade herde masse,   1135
With bugle to bent-felde he buskes bylyve.
By that any daylyght lemed upon erthe,
He with his hatheles on hyghe horsses weren.
Thenne thise cacheres that couthe cowpled hor houndes,
Unclosed the kenel dore and calde hem theroute,   1140
Blewe bygly in bugles three bare mote.
Braches bayed therfore and breme noyse maked;
And thay chastysed and charred on chasyng that went,
A hundreth of hunteres, as I haf herde telle,
       Of the best.   1145
    To trystors vewters yod,
    Couples huntes of kest;
    Ther ros for blastes gode
    Gret rurd in that forest.

1128. *And thay:* i.e. 'the servants'. In 1130 the subject changes back to 'the nobles' (*the rychest*).

1129. 'prepare their gear and pack their bags'.

1139. 'Then hunters who were expert leashed their hounds in pairs'; *this* and *thise* ('these') are used idiomatically to refer to something familiar to the listener though not necessarily present, *cf.* 473, 1112, 1514, 1914, 2423.

1141. *three bare mote:* 'three single notes of the horn' (the signal for unleashing the hounds).

1143. 'And they scolded and turned back (the hounds) that chased false scents'.

1146f. 'Keepers of hounds (*vewters*) went to their hunting-stations (*trystors*), huntsmen took off the leashes (*couples*)'.

At the fyrst quethe of the quest quaked the wylde.   1150
Der drof in the dale, doted for drede,
Hied to the hyghe, bot heterly thay were
Restayed with the stablye, that stoutly ascryed.
Thay let the herttes haf the gate, with the hyghe hedes,
The breme bukkes also, with hor brode paumes;   1155
For the fre lorde hade defende in fermysoun tyme
That ther schulde no mon meve to the male dere.
The hindes were halden in with 'Hay!' and 'War!'
The does dryven with gret dyn to the depe slades.
Ther myght mon se, as thay slypte, slentyng of arwes;   1160
At uche wende under wande wapped a flone,
That bigly bote on the broun with ful brode hedes.
What! thay brayen and bleden, bi bonkkes thay deyen,
And ay rachches in a res radly hem folwes,
Hunteres wyth hyghe horne hasted hem after   1165
Wyth such a crakkande kry as klyffes haden brusten.
What wylde so atwaped wyes that schotten

1150. 'At the first sound of the baying of hounds on the scent the wild animal trembled.'

1153. 'turned back by the ring of beaters, who shouted loudly.' The purpose of the ring of beaters (*stablye*) which encircled the hunting area was to drive the quarry towards the arrows of the huntsmen (1160). Those which were not killed outright were pulled down by hounds at the *resayt:* (collective) 'receiving stations' (1168).

1154–9. The close-season (*fermysoun*) for the male deer, harts (*herttes*) and bucks (*bukkes*), was 14 September–24 June; these the beaters allow to pass. The females, hinds and does, could be hunted during the winter, however, and were therefore prevented from escaping and driven back (1158–9).

1159. *dryven* could be pa.t.pl. (as in 121; *cf.* 1151), 'ran (poured) with great clamour . . .'; but if 1158 is a parallel, it seems better to take it as pp., '(were) driven by loud shouting'.

1160ff. 'There could be seen the slanting flight of arrows as they slipped (from the bow); at every turning in the wood an arrow swished (*wapped*), burying their broad heads deep in the brown flesh.'

1166. *as . . . brusten:* 'as if rocks were splitting'.

1167–73. 'Any animal that escaped (*atwaped*) the archers was pulled down (*al toraced*) and slaughtered (with the knife) at the receiving line, when they had been harrassed on the heights and driven (*taysed*) down to the streams, so skilful were the men at the low stations; and so huge were the greyhounds that (they)

Was al toraced and rent at the resayt,
Bi thay were tened at the hyghe and taysed to the wattres,
The ledes were so lerned at the lowe trysteres;   1170
And the grehoundes so grete that geten hem bylyve
And hem tofylched as fast as frekes myght loke
          Ther ryght.
      The lorde, for blys abloy,
      Ful oft con launce and lyght   1175
      And drof that day wyth joy
      Thus to the derk nyght.

Thus laykes this lorde by lynde-wodes eves
And Gawayn the god mon in gay bed lyges,
Lurkkes whyl the daylyght lemed on the wowes,   1180
Under covertour ful clere, cortyned aboute.
And as in slomeryng he slode, sleyly he herde
A littel dyn at his dor and derfly upon;
And he heves up his hed out of the clothes,
A corner of the cortyn he caght up a lyttel,   1185
And waytes warly thiderwarde what hit be myght.
Hit was the ladi, loflyest to beholde,
That drow the dor after hir ful dernly and stylle
And bowed towarde the bed. And the burne schamed
And layde hym doun lystyly and let as he slepte.   1190
And ho stepped stilly and stel to his bedde,
Kest up the cortyn and creped withinne
And set hir ful softly on the bed-syde
And lenged there selly longe to loke when he wakened.

quickly seized them and pulled them down as fast as men could turn and look (lit. 'look right there').'

   1174f. 'The lord, transported (*abloy*) with delight, galloped forward and dismounted again and again'.

   1178. *by lynde-wodes eves:* 'along the edges of the forest'.

   1182f. 'And as he drifted in sleep (dozed) he heard a little stealthy sound at his door and (heard it) quickly open (*upon* v.)'; *sleyly* is to be loosely construed with the next line, rather than with *herde*. It has been plausibly suggested that *derfly* (here translated 'quickly') is a scribal error for *dernly* 'secretly' (*n* misread as *u*, and written *f*); *cf.* 1188.

The lede lay lurked a ful longe whyle,   1195
Compast in his concience to what that cace myght
Meve other amount. To mervayle hym thoght;
Bot yet he sayde in hymself, 'More semly hit were
To aspye wyth my spelle in space what ho wolde.'
Then he wakenede and wroth and to hir-warde torned   1200
And unlouked his ye-lyddes and let as hym wondered
And sayned hym, as bi his sawe the saver to worthe,
        With hande.
    Wyth chynne and cheke ful swete,
    Bothe whit and red in blande,   *Medieval Picture of* 1205
                    Ideal Beauty
    Ful lufly con ho lete
    Wyth lyppes smal laghande:

'God moroun, Sir Gawayn,' sayde that gay lady,
'Ye ar a sleper unslye, that mon may slyde hider.
Now ar ye tan astyt! Bot true us may schape,   1210
I schal bynde yow in your bedde—that be ye trayst.'
Al laghande the lady lauced tho bourdes.
'Goud moroun, gay,' quoth Gawayn the blythe,
'Me schal worthe at your wille and that me wel lykes,
For I yelde me yederly and yeye after grace;   1215
And that is the best, be my dome, for me byhoves nede!'
(And thus he bourded ayayn with mony a blythe laghter).
'Bot wolde ye, lady lovely, then, leve me grante
And deprece your prysoun and pray hym to ryse,
I wolde bowe of this bed and busk me better;   1220
I schulde kever the more comfort to karp yow wyth.'

1208. gay: MS fayr (Tolkien and Gordon)

1196*f.* 'Pondered in his mind what that circumstance could portend or signify. It seemed amazing to him; . . .'.
1199. 'by talking to her, to discover (*aspye*) in due course what she wants.'
1202. *as . . . worthe:* 'as if to become the safer by his prayer'.
1206*f.* 'she spoke very amiably with slender laughing lips' (for *lete* 'speak', *cf.* 1086).
1210. *Bot . . . schape:* 'Unless we can arrange a truce (*true*) between ourselves'. The subject *we* is omitted.
1214. *me . . . wille:* 'my fate shall be as you determine'.

'Nay forsothe, beau sir,' sayd that swete,
'Ye schal not rise of your bedde. I rych yow better:
I schal happe yow here that other half als
And sythen karp wyth my knyght that I kaght have.   1225
For I wene wel, iwysse, Sir Wowen ye are,
That alle the worlde worchipes; whereso ye ride,
Your honour, your hendelayk is hendely praysed
With lordes, with ladyes, with alle that lyf bere.
And now ye ar here, iwysse, and we bot oure one;   1230
My lorde and his ledes ar on lenthe faren,
Other burnes in her bedde, and my burdes als,
The dor drawen and dit with a derf haspe;
And sythen I have in this hous hym that al lykes,
I schal ware my whyle wel, whyl hit lastes,   1235
      With tale.
            Ye ar welcum to my cors,
            Yowre awen won to wale,
            Me behoves of fyne force
            Your servaunt be, and schale.'   1240

'In god fayth,' quoth Gawayn, 'gayn hit me thynkkes.
Thagh I be not now he that ye of speken—
To reche to such reverence as ye reherce here
I am wye unworthy, I wot wel myselven—
Bi God, I were glad and yow god thoght   1245

1230. *bot oure one:* 'quite by ourselves'.

1237*f.* The lady's declaration is not as unequivocal as it appears to the modern reader: *my cors* is used in ME as a periphrasis for 'me'; the line can therefore be understood as 'I am pleased to have you here', and this is how Gawain chooses to take it (*cf.* 1241). The bolder suggestion, is, however, apparent in the next line: 'to take your own pleasure'. (See *TG-Davis n.*)

1239*f.* 'I must of necessity be your servant, and shall be.' Basing her argument on Gawain's illustrious reputation as a courtier (borne out, she says, by his behaviour in her house) the lady attempts to reverse the usual roles and become *his* 'servant' (*cf.* 1214–6); *of fyne force* implies 'by the logic of the situation'.

1243. 'To attain to such an honour as you have just mentioned'—i.e. at 1240.

1245*ff.* 'by God, I should be glad if you saw fit that I should devote myself, by word or deed, to obliging your worthy self; it would be a sheer joy.'

At sawe other at servyce that I sette myght
To the plesaunce of your prys; hit were a pure joye.'
'In god fayth, Sir Gawayn,' quoth the gay lady,
'The prys and the prowes that pleses al other,
If I hit lakked other set at lyght, hit were littel daynté.   1250
Bot hit ar ladyes innoghe that lever wer nowthe
Haf the, hende, in hor holde, as I the habbe here,
To daly with derely your daynté wordes,
Kever hem comfort and colen her cares,
Then much of the garysoun other golde that thay haven.   1255
Bot I louve that ilk Lorde that the lyfte haldes
I haf hit holly in my honde that al desyres,
       Thurghe grace.'
      Scho made hym so gret chere,
      That was so fayr of face.
      The knyght with speches skere   1260
      Answared to uche a cace.

'Madame,' quoth the myry mon, 'Mary yow yelde,
For I haf founden, in god fayth, yowre fraunchis nobele;
And other ful much of other folk fongen for hor dedes;   1265
Bot the daynté that thay delen my disert nys ever—
Hit is the worchyp of yourself, that noght bot wel connes.'
'Bi Mary,' quoth the menskful, 'me thynk hit an other;
For were I worth al the wone of wymmen alyve,

1265. for: *supplied from* 1266
1266. my: MS for my (*cf.* 1265); nys ever: MS nyseu (er. *abbr. omitted*)

1253*f.* 'to make courtly play with your charming words, to find solace for themselves and assuage their longings'.

1257. *that al desyres:* 'that which (i.e. him whom) everyone wants'.

1265*ff.* 'and some people win a great deal of respect from others for their achievements; but the honour which they bestow is not at all my deserving— it does credit to yourself, revealing the goodness of your own heart (lit. 'who can only behave generously')'. The passage is somewhat elliptical, perhaps reflecting Gawain's tact; he wants to dismiss his reputation (especially among women—*cf.* 1249*ff*) as mere tittle-tattle, without implying too strongly that *she* is over-credulous.

1268. *me thynk: cf.* 348*n.*

And al the wele of the worlde were in my honde,   1270
And I schulde chepen and chose to cheve me a lorde,
For the costes that I haf knowen upon the, knyght, here
Of bewté and debonerté and blythe semblaunt—
And that I haf er herkkened and halde hit here truee—
Ther schulde no freke upon folde bifore yow be chosen.'   1275
'Iwysse, worthy,' quoth the wye, 'ye haf waled wel better;
Bot I am proude of the prys that ye put on me
And, soberly your servaunt, my soverayn I holde yow
And yowre knyght I becom, and Kryst yow foryelde.'
Thus thay meled of muchwhat til mydmorn paste   1280
And ay the lady let lyk a hym loved mych.
The freke ferde with defence and feted ful fayre;
Thagh ho were burde bryghtest the burne in mynde hade,
The lasse luf in his lode for lur that he soght
          Boute hone—   1285
      The dunte that schulde hym deve,
      And nedes hit most be done.
      The lady thenn spek of leve;
      He graunted hir ful sone.

Thenne ho gef hym god day and wyth a glent laghed;   1290
And as ho stod ho stonyed hym wyth ful stor wordes:
'Now He that spedes uche spech this disport yelde yow,
Bot that ye be Gawan hit gos in mynde!'
'Wherfore?' quoth the freke, and freschly he askes,

1283. ho: MS I; burne: MS burde (Morris)

1274. '—for this is what I have heard before and now believe it to be true—'.
The lady is rebutting Gawain's modest denial at 1266.
1281f. 'And all the time the lady behaved as if (*lyk*) she loved him a great
deal. The man acted guardedly and behaved most politely'.
1283ff. 'Though she was the loveliest lady the warrior had ever known
(lit. 'remembered'—*cf.* 943*ff*), he had brought with him so much the less love
because of the penalty he was going to meet forthwith'. Morris's emendations
to 1283, which are adopted here (though with different punctuation), avoid
the difficulty of the repeated *burde* as well as the momentary inconsistency of
narrative point of view (see Introduction, p. 8). The error could have arisen
through misunderstanding of *in mynde hade*.
D

Ferde lest he hade fayled in fourme of his castes.   1295
Bot the burde hym blessed and 'Bi this skyl:' sayde,
'So god as Gawayn gaynly is halden,
And cortaysye is closed so clene in hymselven,
Couth not lyghtly haf lenged so long wyth a lady
Bot he had craved a cosse bi his courtaysye,   1300
Bi sum towch of summe tryfle at sum tales ende.'
Then quoth Wowen: 'Iwysse, worthe as yow lykes;
I schal kysse at your comaundement, as a knyght falles,
And fire, lest he displese yow, so plede hit no more.'
Ho comes nerre with that and caches hym in armes,   1305
Loutes luflych adoun and the leude kysses.
Thay comly bykennen to Kryst ayther other;
Ho dos hir forth at the dore withouten dyn more,
And he ryches hym to ryse and rapes hym sone,
Clepes to his chamberlayn, choses his wede,   1310
Bowes forth, when he was boun, blythely to masse;
And thenne he meved to his mete, that menskly hym keped,
And made myry al day til the mone rysed,
          With game.
          Was never freke fayrer fonge   1315
          Bitwene two so dyngne dame,
          The alder and the yonge;
          Much solace set thay same.

And ay the lorde of the londe is lent on his gamnes,
To hunt in holtes and hethe at hyndes barayne;   1320
Such a sowme he ther slowe bi that the sunne heldet,
Of dos and of other dere, to deme were wonder.

1296. *him blessed* here seems to mean 'exclaimed "God bless you"' (see
OED *bless*); *Bi this skyl:* 'For this reason'.

1297f. 'Anyone as good as Gawain is rightly (*gaynly*) considered to be and
in whom courtesy is so completely embodied'.

1301. 'by some trifling hint at the end of a speech'.

1304. *And fire:* 'and further'. Gawain appears to be saying that it would be
his duty as a knight to go even further than kissing at her command, for fear
of displeasing her. The speech is not as acquiescent as it appears at first, however,
for it implies a firm refusal to act on his own initiative.

Thenne fersly thay flokked in, folk, at the laste,
And quykly of the quelled dere a querré thay maked.
The best bowed therto with burnes innoghe,   1325
Gedered the grattest of gres that ther were
And didden hem derely undo as the dede askes.
Serched hem at the asay summe that ther were;
Two fyngeres thay fonde of the fowlest of alle.
Sythen thay slyt the slot, sesed the erber,   1330
Schaved wyth a scharp knyf, and the schyre knitten.
Sythen rytte thay the foure lymmes and rent of the hyde;
Then brek thay the balé, the boweles out token,

1327. 'And had them gracefully cut open, in the prescribed manner.' The breaking of only one deer is described but the description is evidently meant to be representative. The breaking (or brittling) of the deer is a romance convention (cf., e.g., *The Parlement of the Thre Ages* (edited M. Y. Offord, London, EETS, 1959) 66ff., for a similar alliterative description, and the *Tristan* of Gottfried von Strassburg (fl. 1210), English translation by A. T. Hatto (Penguin Books, 1960, chapter 4) which reflects the importance attached to hunting skills as aristocratic accomplishments.

1328f. 'Some who were there examined them at the "assay"; they found two fingers' breadth of flesh on the poorest of them all.' The 'assay' was a ceremonious testing of the quality of the game; the word was also used of the part of the breast where the cut was made (cf. *The Parlement of the Thre Ages* 70).

1330-52. 'Then they slit the hollow at the base of the throat (*slot*), took hold of the first stomach (*erber*—cf. 1360), scraped it with a sharp knife and tied up the flesh. Then they cut off the four legs and stripped off the skin; then they opened the belly, drew the bowels carefully to avoid undoing (*for laucyng*) the ligature (*lere*) of the knot (cf. 1331). (1335:) They seized the throat (*gargulun*) and properly separated the gullet (*wesaunt*) from the wind-pipe and tossed (*walt*) out the guts. Then they cut out the shoulder-joints with their sharp knives, drawing them through a small hole so as to keep the sides intact; then they cut open the breast and divided it in two. (1340:) And then one of them (*on*) begins once again (*eft*) at the neck, quickly cuts the carcase open right to the fork (*byght*), removes the neck offal (*avanters*) and truly after that they promptly loosen all the membranes (*rymes*) on the ribs; (1344:) thus they correctly clear out the offal along the bones of the back right down (*evenden*) to the haunch, so that it all hung together, and they lift it up quite intact and cut it off there—and that, I believe, they naturally (*bi kynde*) designate the "numbles". They then loosen the folds of skin (*lappes*) behind the fork of the thighs; they make haste to cut the carcase in two, dividing it along the backbone.'

Lystily for laucyng the lere of the knot.
Thay gryped to the gargulun and graythely departed   1335
The wesaunt fro the wynt-hole and walt out the guttes.
Then scher thay out the schulderes with her scharp knyves,
Haled hem by a lyttel hole to have hole sydes;
Sithen britned thay the brest and brayden hit in twynne.
And eft at the gargulun bigynes on thenne,   1340
Ryves hit up radly ryght to the byght,
Voydes out the avanters and verayly therafter
Alle the rymes by the rybbes radly thay lauce;
So ryde thay of by resoun bi the rygge bones
Evenden to the haunche, that henged alle samen,   1345
And heven hit up al hole and hewen hit of there—
And that thay neme for the 'noumbles' bi nome, as I trowe,
          Bi kynde.
     Bi the byght al of the thyghes
     The lappes thay lauce bihynde;   1350
     To hewe hit in two thay hyes,
     Bi the bakbon to unbynde.

Bothe the hede and the hals thay hewen of thenne
And sythen sunder thay the sydes swyft fro the chyne
And the corbeles fee thay kest in a greve.   1355
Thenn thurled thay ayther thik side thurgh bi the rybbe
And henged thenne ayther bi hoghes of the fourches,
Uche freke for his fee as falles for to have.
Upon a felle of the fayre best fede thay thayr houndes
Wyth the lyver and the lyghtes, the lether of the paunches, 1360
And bred bathed in blod blende theramonges.
Baldely thay blew prys, bayed thayr rachches,
Sythen fonge thay her flesche, folden to home,

1334. the (1st): MS & (Gollancz)

1355. *corbeles fee:* 'raven's fee'; a piece of gristle from the end of the breast-bone, traditionally thrown to the crows or ravens.
1358. 'each man receiving what befits him for his fee (prize)'.
1360. *lether of the paunches:* 'lining of the stomachs'.
1362. *bayed thayr rachches:* 'their hounds barked (bayed)'.

Strakande ful stoutly mony stif motes.
Bi that the daylyght was done the douthe was al wonen   1365
Into the comly castel, ther the knyght bides
    Ful stille,
      Wyth blys and bryght fyr bette.
      The lorde is comen thertylle;
      When Gawayn wyth hym mette   1370
      Ther was bot wele at wylle.

Thenne comaunded the lorde in that sale to samen alle the meny,
Bothe the ladyes on loghe to lyght with her burdes.
Bifore alle the folk on the flette frekes he beddes
Verayly his venysoun to fech hym byforne;   1375
And al godly in gomen Gawayn he called,
Teches hym to the tayles of ful tayt bestes,
Schewes hym the schyree grece schorne upon rybbes:
'How payes yow this play? Haf I prys wonnen?
Have I thryvandely thonk thurgh my craft served?'   1380
'Ye iwysse,' quoth that other wye, 'here is wayth fayrest
That I segh this seven yere in sesoun of wynter.'
'And al I gif yow, Gawayn,' quoth the gome thenne,
'For by acorde of covenaunt ye crave hit as your awen.'
'This is soth,' quoth the segge, 'I say yow that ilke: 1385
That I haf worthyly wonnen this wones wythinne
Iwysse with as god wylle hit worthes to youres.'
He hasppes his fayre hals his armes wythinne
And kysses hym as comlyly as he couthe awyse:
'Tas yow there my chevicaunce; I cheved no more.   1390
I wowche hit saf fynly, thagh feler hit were.'

1371. 'there was all the happiness that could be desired.'

1377. 'Directs his attention to the numbers (tails) of extremely well-grown beasts'. The parallel structure of 401 and 1069 suggests that *to* governs *the tayles* rather than *hym*. *Tayles* appears to contain a deliberate pun ('tails' and 'tallies'); the tails were left on the carcases and would serve as tallies.

1379. *play:* 'sport'; but implying the product rather than the activity (*cf. gomen* 1635, and the modern *game*).

1382. *this seven year:* i.e. 'for many a year'.

1391. 'I bestow (vouchsafe) it completely (and would do so) even if there were more.'

'Hit is god,' quoth the godmon, 'grant mercy therfore.
Hit may be such hit is the better, and ye me breve wolde
Where ye wan this ilk wele bi wytte of yorselven.'
'That was not forward,' quoth he; 'frayst me no more,   1395
For ye haf tan that yow tydes; trawe ye non other
          Ye mowe.'
                    Thay laghed and made hem blythe
                    Wyth lotes that were to lowe.
                    To soper thay yede asswythe,   1400
                    Wyth dayntés newe innowe.

And sythen by the chymné in chamber thay seten,
Wyes the walle wyn weghed to hem oft,
And efte in her bourdyng thay baythen in the morn
To fylle the same forwardes that thay byfore maden: 1405
Wat chaunce so bytydes hor chevysaunce to chaunge,
What newes so thay nome, at naght when thay metten.
Thay acorded of the covenauntes byfore the court alle—
The beverage was broght forth in bourde at that tyme—
Thenne thay lovelych leghten leve at the last;   1410
Uche burne to his bedde busked bylyve.
Bi that the coke hade crowen and cakled bot thryse,
The lorde was lopen of his bedde, the leudes uchone,
So that the mete and the masse was metely delyvered,
The douthe dressed to the wod, er any day sprenged,   1415

1406. Wat: MS that (Tolkien and Gordon)

1393f. 'It may be of such a nature that it would turn out to be the better
prize, if only you would tell me from whom . . .'

1396f. For . . . tydes: 'for you have received what is due to you'. Gawain
may be conscious that the kisses were Bertilak's by right of a husband as well as
of the game. It may be noted here that there would be no need of concealment
of their source if the kisses were entirely innocent (cf. Introduction, p. 17 n. 9).
trawe . . . mowe: 'rest assured you cannot (have) anything else.'

1401. 'with many (innowe) new delicacies'.

1407. What newes so: partitive genitive, lit. 'whatever of new'—i.e. 'what-
ever new thing'.

1409. beverage: see 1112n, 1684.

1412-5. See 2008n.

To chace.
Hegh with hunte and hornes,
Thurgh playnes thay passe in space,
Uncoupled among tho thornes
Raches that ran on race.   1420

Sone thay calle of a quest in a ker syde;
The hunt rehayted the houndes that hit fyrst mynged,
Wylde wordes hym warp wyth a wrast noyce.
The howndes that hit herde hastid thider swythe
And fellen as fast to the fuyt, fourty at ones.   1425
Thenne such a glaver ande glam of gedered rachches
Ros that the rocheres rungen aboute.
Hunteres hem hardened with horne and wyth muthe;
Then al in a semblé sweyed togeder
Bitwene a flosche in that fryth and a foo cragge.   1430
In a knot bi a clyffe at the kerre syde,
Theras the rogh rocher unrydely was fallen,
Thay ferden to the fyndyng, and frekes hem after.
Thay umbekesten the knarre and the knot bothe,
Wyes, whyl thay wysten wel wythinne hem hit were   1435
The best that ther breved was wyth the blodhoundes.
Thenne thay beten on the buskes and bede hym upryse;
And he unsoundyly out soght, segges overthwert.

1419. *Uncoupled: cf.* 1139*n; among tho thornes:* an indication that they are to
hunt the boar, which lived among thorns and thick bushes.
1421ff. 'Soon the hounds signal (by baying) that they have a scent at the
edge of a wooded marsh (*cf.* 1150); the huntsman urged on the hounds who
had first drawn attention to the scent, uttered excited words to them with a
loud noise.'
1431–6. 'In the middle of a wooded mound beside a high rock at the edge
of the marsh, where the rough hillside had fallen in confusion, the hounds
went to the dislodgement, with the men after them. The men surrounded
both the crag and the wooded knoll until they were sure that they had con-
tained the beast whose presence had been revealed by the voices of the blood-
hounds.' *hit:* anticipatory subject, lit. 'there was (within their ring)'. *blod-
houndes:* larger hounds (resembling the modern bloodhound), which were
used especially in boar-hunting, to attack the game at close quarters.
1438. 'And he came out menacingly straight across the line of men.'

On the sellokest swyn swenged out there,
Long sythen fro the sounder that soght for olde,   1440
For he was borelych and brode, bor alther-grattest,
Ful grymme when he gronyed; thenne greved mony,
For thre at the fyrst thrast he thryght to the erthe
And sparred forth good sped boute spyt more.
Thise other halowed 'Hyghe!' ful hyghe, and 'Hay! Hay!' cryed
Haden hornes to mouthe, heterly rechated.   1446
Mony was the myry mouthe of men and of houndes
That buskkes after this bor with bost and wyth noyse,
          To quelle.
     Ful oft he bydes the baye   1450
     And maymes the mute innmelle.
     He hurtes of the houndes, and thay
     Ful yomerly yaule and yelle.

Schalkes to schote at hym schowen to thenne,
Haled to hym of her arewes, hitten hym oft;   1455
Bot the poyntes payred at the pyth, that pyght in his scheldes,

---

1440. fro: MS for; soght: MS wight
1441. borelych and *supplied*

1440. 'which had long since left (*soght fro*) the herd on account of age'.
sounder is the technical term for a herd of wild pig; *for olde:* a ME idiom (*for* +
adj.) 'on account of age'.

1441. *brode:* the word is illegible: also, the half-line appears to lack a stress
(unless the first falls on *he*). For the emendation adopted above, cf. *The
Parlement of the Thre Ages* 32: *And ther-to borely and brode and of body grete* (of a
hart).

1443. *thre:* it is clear from 1438 and 1445 that this means 'three men'.

1452. *of the houndes:* 'some of the hounds'.

1456f. 'But the points which struck his shoulders were blunted (*payred*) by
the toughness (*pyth*) (of them) and none would penetrate the bristles (*barbes*)
of his brow.' Standing at bay, the boar presents to the archers the toughened
skin of his shoulders and the coarse hair of his brow; either is capable of deflect-
ing an arrow, however hard it may strike (1458f). See Savage, *MLN* 52 (1937),
36–8. *Barbes* has usually been understood as 'arrow-heads' (*MED* 3(a)) but the
pronoun *non* (antecedent *poyntes*) is an adequate subject for *wolde bite*, and *of
his browe* is more naturally construed with *barbes* than with *bite*, which is
usually followed by *in* or *on* (cf. 426, 1162).

And the barbes of his browe bite non wolde;
Thagh the schaven schaft schyndered in peces,
The hede hypped ayayn weresoever hit hitte.
Bot when the dyntes hym dered of her drye strokes,   1460
Then, braynwod for bate, on burnes he rases,
Hurtes hem ful heterly ther he forth hyes;
And mony arwed therat and on lyte drowen.
Bot the lorde on a lyght horce launces hym after,
As burne bolde upon bent his bugle he blowes,   1465
He rechated, and rode thurgh rones ful thyk,
Suande this wylde swyn til the sunne schafted.
This day wyth this ilk dede thay dryven on this wyse,
Whyle oure luflych lede lys in his bedde,
Gawayn, graythely at home in geres ful ryche   1470
          Of hewe.
      The lady noght foryate
      To com hym to salue;
      Ful erly ho was hym ate,
      His mode for to remue.   1475

Ho commes to the cortyn and at the knyght totes.
Sir Wawen her welcumed worthy on fyrst,
And ho hym yeldes ayayn ful yerne of hir wordes,
Settes hir sofly by his syde and swythely ho laghes
And wyth a luflych loke ho layde hym thyse wordes: 1480
'Sir, yif ye be Wawen, wonder me thynkkes,
Wye that is so wel wrast alway to god

1473. To com: MS Com to

1473. Given the similarity of *c* and *t* in the handwriting of the time, the MS reading *com to* is a fairly easy scribal error for *to com*; the emendation is not strictly necessary but greatly improves both syntax and metre.
1474f. *was hym ate:* no doubt deliberately ambiguous: 'Very early she visited him (or 'was pestering him') in order to bring about a change in his attitude.'
1478. *ful yerne of hir wordes:* possibly 'using very eager language'; *yerne*, however, may be adverbial and *of hir wordes* dependent on *yeldes ayayn:* 'she quickly replied to him'.
D*

And connes not of compaynye the costes undertake,
And if mon kennes yow hom to knowe, ye kest hom of your
    mynde:
Thou has foryeten yederly that yisterday I taght te   1485
Bi alder-truest token of talk that I cowthe.'
'What is that?' quoth the wyghe. 'Iwysse I wot never.
If hit be sothe that ye breve, the blame is myn awen.'
'Yet I kende yow of kyssyng,' quoth the clere thenne,
'Wherso countenaunce is couthe, quikly to clayme;   1490
That bicumes uche a knyght that cortaysy uses.'
'Do way,' quoth that derf mon, 'my dere, that speche,
For that durst I not do, lest I devayed were.
If I were werned, I wer wrang, iwysse, yif I profered.'
'Ma fay,' quoth the meré wyf, 'ye may not be werned;   1495
Ye ar stif innoghe to constrayne wyth strenkthe, yif yow lykes,
Yif any were so vilanous that yow devaye wolde.'
'Ye, be God,' quoth Gawayn, 'good is your speche;
Bot threte is unthryvande in thede ther I lende,
And uche gift that is geven not with goud wylle.   1500
I am at your comaundement, to kysse when yow lykes;
Ye may lach when yow lyst and leve when yow thynkkes,
       In space.'
    The lady loutes adoun

1485. taght te: MS taghtte

1483. *compaynye* already has some of the amorous connotation of the modern 'keep company', as it has also in Chaucer's lines on the Wife of Bath:
      Housbondes at chirche dore she hadde fyve,
      Withouten oother compaignye in youthe (*CT* I(A), 460*f*)
1485*f*. 'you have quickly forgotten what I taught you (*te:* thee)' yesterday in the very truest teaching I could put into words.'
1490. 'to claim it immediately wherever favour is clearly shown'.
1493. Gawain is not, as at first appears, reproving her for freedom of conduct.
1494. 'If I proferred (a kiss) and were refused, I would indeed be wrong.'
1495. *Ma fay:* 'By my faith'.
1499. 'but force is (considered) ignoble in the land where I live'. Gawain skilfully counters her argument on her own terms and once more politely declares his unwillingness to take the initiative.

And comlyly kysses his face.   1505
Much speche thay ther expoun
Of druryes greme and grace.

'I woled wyt at yow, wye,' that worthy ther sayde,
'And yow wrathed not therwyth, what were the skylle
That so yong and so yepe as ye at this tyme,   1510
So cortayse, so knyghtyly, as ye ar knowen oute—
And of alle chevalry to chose, the chef thyng alosed
Is the lel layk of luf, the lettrure of armes;
For to telle of this tevelyng of this true knyghtes,
Hit is the tytelet token and tyxt of her werkkes   1515
How ledes for her lele luf hor lyves han auntered,
Endured for her drury dulful stoundes,
And after wenged with her walour and voyded her care
And broght blysse into boure with bountées hor awen—
And ye ar knyght comlokest kyd of your elde,   1520
Your worde and your worchip walkes aywhere,
And I haf seten by yourself here sere twyes,
Yet herde I never of your hed helde no wordes
That ever longed to luf, lasse ne more.
And ye, that ar so cortays and coynt of your hetes,   1525

1507. 'about the punishments and favours of love.' The phrase is reminiscent of Chaucer's: *his (the God of Love's) myrakles and his crewel yre* (*The Parlement of Foules* 11).

1512f. 'and from among the whole (code) of chivalry, the thing principally praised (*alosed*) is the faithful practice (*layk*) of love'. The syntax of the speech effectively suggests the informality of conversation (*cf.* 2446–58); after this long parenthesis (1512–9) giving the lady's views on the importance of love in the code of chivalry, the construction begun at 1509 is loosely resumed. *the lettrure of armes:* 'the (very) doctrine of knighthood'; as 1515–9 show, the rules of love are conceived as a set of guiding principles for active knighthood.

1514ff. 'for to speak of the striving (*tevelyng*) of true knights (for *this*, 'these', see 1139n), it is the rubric written at the head of their works, and the very words themselves, how men . . .'; *werkkes* contains a pun on 'deeds' and '(literary) works'—i.e. romances of chivalry.

1518. 'and later avenged and dispelled their sorrow through their valour'.

1519. i.e. they made their ladies happy by their achievements.

1523. *lasse ne more:* 'smaller or larger', i.e. 'at all'.

Oghe to a yonke thynk yern to schewe
And teche sum tokenes of trueluf craftes.
Why! ar ye lewed, that alle the los weldes,
Other elles ye demen me to dille your dalyaunce to herken?
    For schame!   1530
   I com hider sengel and sitte
   To lerne at yow sum game;
   Dos teches me of your wytte,
   Whil my lorde is fro hame.'

'In goud faythe,' quoth Gawayn, 'God yow foryelde!   1535
Gret is the gode gle, and gomen to me huge,
That so worthy as ye wolde wynne hidere
And pyne yow with so pouer a mon, as play wyth your knyght
With anyskynnes countenaunce; hit keveres me ese.
Bot to take the torvayle to myself to truluf expoun   1540
And towche the temes of tyxt and tales of armes
To yow, that (I wot wel) weldes more slyght
Of that art, bi the half, or a hundreth of seche
As I am, other ever schal in erde ther I leve,
Hit were a folé felefolde, my fre, by my trawthe.   1545
I wolde yowre wylnyng worche at my myght,
As I am hyghly bihalden, and evermore wylle
Be servaunt to yourselven, so save me Dryghtyn!'
Thus hym frayned that fre and fondet hym ofte,
For to haf wonnen hym to woghe, whatso scho thoght elles;

1526. *a yonke thynk:* 'a young thing' (herself); *yern* is adverbial: 'eagerly'.
1534. *fro hame:* 'away from home'.
1540f. 'But to take upon myself the task (*torvayle*) of expounding true love (*to . . . expoun*, split infin.) and of treating of the subject matter (*temes of tyxt*) and stories of knighthood'.
1544. *other . . . leve:* 'or ever shall (be) as long as I live on earth' (*ther*—MS *þer*—is possibly a corrupt reading for *quel* 'while'—*cf.* 1035).
1550. 'in order to bring him to grief (wrong), whatever else she intended'. The poet appears to wish to exonerate the lady. Alternatively *woghe* (MS *woȝe*) can be interpreted as a verb 'woo' (so *TG-Davis n*) and the second half-line would then imply 'though she had no genuine desire for his advances'. However, the closest syntactical parallel (831) leads one to expect a noun rather than a verb here; also the whole tone of the comment (*cf. ondet* 'tempted' 1549)

Bot he defended hym so fayr that no faut semed,   1551
Ne non evel on nawther halve, nawther thay wysten
          Bot blysse.
          Thay laghed and layked longe;
          At the last scho con hym kysse,   1555
          Hir leve fayre con scho fonge,
          And went hir waye, iwysse.

Then ruthes hym the renk and ryses to the masse,
And sithen hor diner was dyght and derely served.
The lede with the ladyes layked alle day   1560
Bot the lorde over the londes launced ful ofte,
Sues his uncely swyn, that swynges bi the bonkkes
And bote the best of his braches the bakkes in sunder
Ther he bode in his bay, tel bawemen hit breken
And madee hym mawgref his hed for to mue utter,   1565
So felle flones ther flete when the folk gedered.
Bot yet the styffest to start bi stoundes he made,
Til at the last he was so mat he myght no more renne
Bot in the hast that he myght he to a hole wynnes
Of a rasse, bi a rokk ther rennes the boerne.   1570
He gete the bonk at his bak, bigynes to scrape—
The frothe femed at his mouth unfayre bi the wykes—
Whettes his whyte tusches. With hym then irked

---

favours the sense 'wrong, sin' (or perhaps 'harm', in view of the possible consequences).

1552f. 'nor were they aware of anything but pleasure.'

1564. *hit breken:* 'broke it (his stand)'.

1565. 'and made him move out into the open despite all he could do (*mawgref his hed*)'.

1571ff. When at bay, the boar sharpens his lower tusks against his upper ones and scrapes the ground with his feet. The description of an angry boar in *The Seven Sages* is very similar:

> He wette (*sharpened*) his tossches and his fet,
> The erthe with his snowte he bet,
> Thourh the mouht the fom was wight.

(edited Karl Brunner, London, EETS, 1933, 34).

1572. 'the froth foamed hideously at the corners of his mouth'.

1573ff. *With hym . . . :* 'Then all the very brave men who stood round him

Alle the burnes so bolde that hym by stoden
To nye hym on-ferum, bot neghe hym non durst   1575
          For wothe;
     He hade hurt so mony byforne
     That al thught thenne ful lothe
     Be more wyth his tusches torne,
     That breme was and braynwod bothe.   1580

Til the knyght com hymself, kachande his blonk,
Sy hym byde at the bay, his burnes bysyde.
He lyghtes luflych adoun, leves his corsour,
Braydes out a bryght bront and bigly forth strydes,
Foundes fast thurgh the forth ther the felle bydes.   1585
The wylde was war of the wye with weppen in honde,
Hef hyghly the here; so hetterly he fnast
That fele ferde for the freke, lest felle hym the worre.
The swyn settes hym out on the segge even,
That the burne and the bor were bothe upon hepes   1590
In the wyghtest of the water. The worre hade that other,
For the mon merkkes hym wel, as thay mette fyrst,
Set sadly the scharp in the slot even,
Hit hym up to the hult, that the hert schyndered
And he yarrande hym yelde and yedoun the water   1595
          Ful tyt.
     A hundreth houndes hym hent,
     That bremely con hym bite;
     Burnes him broght to bent
     And dogges to dethe endite.   1600

There was blawyng of prys in mony breme horne,

---

became weary of trying to hurt (to nye) him from a distance (on-ferum), but
none of them dared to go near him because of the danger.'
  1578. 'that it then seemed very hateful (lothe) to everyone'.
  1595. yedoun: for yed doun 'went down'—'was carried downstream'.
  1600. to dethe endite: 'do him to death'.

Heghe halowing on highe with hatheles that myght;
Brachetes bayed that best, as bidden the maysteres,
Of that chargeaunt chace that were chef huntes.
Thenne a wye that was wys upon wodcraftes   1605
To unlace this bor lufly bigynnes.
Fyrst he hewes of his hed and on highe settes,
And sythen rendes him al roghe bi the rygge after,
Braydes out the boweles, brennes hom on glede,
With bred blent therwith his braches rewardes.   1610
Sythen he britnes out the brawen in bryght brode cheldes,
And has out the hastlettes, as hightly bisemes,
And yet hem halches al hole the halves togeder
And sythen on a stif stange stoutly hem henges.
Now with this ilk swyn thay swengen to home.   1615
The bores hed was borne bifore the burnes selven
That him forferde in the forthe thurgh forse of his honde
            So stronge.
        Til he segh Sir Gawayne
        In halle, hym thoght ful longe;   1620
        He calde, and he com gayn,
        His fees ther for to fonge.

The lorde ful lowde with lote and laghter myry,
When he seghe Sir Gawayn, with solace he spekes.
The goude ladyes were geten, and gedered the meyny;   1625
He schewes hem the scheldes and schapes hem the tale

1623. laghter: MS laghed (Davis)

1602. *Heghe:* though the same word as *highe* in *on highe* ('loudly'), is probably to be distinguished in sense here ('proud'). Such repetition with change of meaning (*traductio*) was regarded as a stylistic embellishment in the Middle Ages; *cf.* 2276n.
1603f. 'Hounds bayed at that beast, as the masters-of-game, who were the chief huntsmen of that difficult chase, commanded.'
1608. *bi the rygge after:* 'along the backbone'.
1613. 'moreover, he fastens the two complete sides together'.
1616f. *bifore . . . forferde:* 'in front of the very knight who had killed it'.
1620. *hym thoght ful longe:* 'it seemed a long time to him'—i.e. 'he was impatient'.

Of the largesse and the lenthe, the lithernes alse
Of the were, of the wylde swyn in wod ther he fled.
That other knyght ful comly comended his dedes
And praysed hit as gret prys that he proved hade,   1630
For suche a brawne of a best, the bolde burne sayde,
Ne such sydes of a swyn segh he never are.
Thenne hondeled thay the hoge hed; the hende mon hit praysed
And let lodly therat, the lorde for to here.
'Now, Gawayn,' quoth the godmon, 'this gomen is your awen
Bi fyn forwarde and faste, faythely ye knowe.'   1636
'Hit is sothe,' quoth the segge, 'and as siker true,
Alle my get I schal yow gif agayn, bi my trawthe.'
He hent the hathel aboute the halse and hendely hym kysses
And eftersones of the same he served hym there.   1640
'Now ar we even,' quoth the hathel, 'in this eventide,
Of alle the covenauntes that we knyt sythen I com hider,
          Bi lawe.'
             The lorde sayde, 'Bi Saynt Gile,
             Ye ar the best that I knawe!   1645
             Ye ben ryche in a whyle,
             Such chaffer and ye drawe.'

Thenne thay teldet tables trestes alofte,
Kesten clothes upon; clere lyght thenne
Wakned bi wowes, waxen torches   1650
Segges sette, and served in sale al aboute.
Much glam and gle glent up therinne
Aboute the fyre upon flet; and on fele wyse
At the soper and after, mony athel songes,

1630. 'and praised his action as giving proof of great accomplishment'.
1634. 'and made a show of abhorrence at it, in order to praise the lord.'
1637. *siker true:* qualifies *I* in 1638: 'and as surely true (as you are)'.
1644. *Saynt Gile:* St. Giles was a saint of the seventh century who lived as a hermit in a forest near Nimes with a hind for companion. This association makes him perhaps an appropriate saint for the hunting knight.
1647. 'if you carry on (*drawe*) such trade.' The knight means that Gawain has doubled his takings in one day!
1648. *trestes alofte:* 'upon trestles'; *cf.* 884*n*.

As coundutes of Krystmasse and caroles newe,   1655
With alle the manerly merthe that mon may of telle.
And ever oure luflych knyght the lady bisyde;
Such semblaunt to that segge semly ho made,
Wyth stille stollen countenaunce, that stalworth to plese,
That al forwondered was the wye and wroth with hymselven,
Bot he nolde not for his nurture nurne hir ayaynes   1661
Bot dalt with hir al in daynté, how-se-ever the dede turned
       Towrast.
    When thay hade played in halle
    As longe as hor wylle hom last,   1665
    To chambre he con hym calle
    And to the chemné thay past.

Ande ther thay dronken and dalten and demed eft newe
To norne on the same note on Newe Yeres Even;
Bot the knyght craved leve to kayre on the morn,   1670
For hit was negh at the terme that he to schulde.
The lorde hym letted of that, to lenge hym resteyed,
And sayde, 'As I am true segge, I siker my trawthe
Thou schal cheve to the Grene Chapel thy charres to make,
Leude, on New Yeres lyght, longe bifore pryme.   1675
Forthy thow lye in thy loft and lach thyn ese
And I schal hunt in this holt and halde the towches,
Chaunge wyth the chevisaunce bi that I charre hider.
For I haf fraysted the twys and faythful I fynde the.
Now "Thrid tyme, throwe best" thenk on the morne;   1680

1655. *coundutes:* 'Christmas songs' (a *coundute*, L *conductus*, was originally a passage sung while the priest was proceeding to the altar).

1661. *nurne hir ayaynes:* an idiom of uncertain meaning; the context appears to demand the sense 'repulse her (openly)' rather than 'return her advances'.

1662f. 'but behaved with complete courtesy towards her even though this might be misconstrued (*towrast:* awry).'

1666. *he:* the host; *hym:* Gawain.

1669. 'to do the same (lit. 'sing the same tune'?) on New Year's Eve'.

1671. *that he to schulde:* 'to which he had to go'; the verb of motion is omitted and *to* accordingly bears the stress and alliteration.

1678. 'exchange winnings with you (*wyth the*) when I return hither.'

1680. 'Now remember tomorrow the saying "Third time, throw best", . . .' From the game of dice: 'Third time lucky'.

Make we mery whyl we may and mynne upon joye,
For the lur may mon lach whenso mon lykes.'
This was graythely graunted and Gawayn is lenged;
Blithe broght was hym drynk and thay to bedde yeden
      With light.   1685
      Sir Gawayn lis and slepes
      Ful stille and softe al night;
      The lorde, that his craftes kepes,
      Ful erly he was dight.

After messe, a morsel he and his men token.   1690
Miry was the mornyng; his mounture he askes.
Alle the hatheles that on horse schulde helden hym after
Were boun busked on hor blonkkes bifore the halle yates.
Ferly fayre was the folde, for the forst clenged;
In rede rudede upon rak rises the sunne   1695
And ful clere castes the clowdes of the welkyn.
Hunteres unhardeled bi a holt syde;
Rocheres roungen bi rys for rurde of her hornes.
Summe fel in the fute ther the fox bade,
Trayles ofte a traveres bi traunt of her wyles.   1700
A kenet kryes therof; the hunt on hym calles;
His felawes fallen hym to, that fnasted ful thike,
Runnen forth in a rabel in his ryght fare,
And he fyskes hem byfore; thay founden hym sone.
And when thay seghe hym with syght thay sued hym fast,   1705
Wreyande hym ful weterly with a wroth noyse,
And he trantes and tornayees thurgh mony tene greve,

1696. castes: MS costes
1700. traveres: MS trayteres (Gollancz)

1695f. 'The sun rises red, its redness reflected upon a bank of cloud, and in its full brightness drives the clouds from the sky.'

1699. 'Some (of the hounds) hit upon the scent where the fox was lurking, (and) trail again and again across it (*a traveres*) in their wily ingenuity.'

1701. *A kenet kryes therof:* 'A small hound gives tongue at it (the scent)'.

1706. 'Vilifying him in no uncertain terms (*weterly:* clearly, truly) with a furious noise'.

Havilounes and herkenes bi hegges ful ofte.
At the last bi a littel dich he lepes over a spenné,
Steles out ful stilly bi a strothe rande,   1710
Went haf wylt of the wode, with wyles, fro the houndes.
Thenne was he went, er he wyst, to a wale tryster,
Ther thre thro at a thrich thrat hym at ones,
　　　　　Al graye.
　　　　　He blenched ayayn bilyve   1715
　　　　　And stifly start onstray.
　　　　　With alle the wo on lyve
　　　　　To the wod he went away.

Thenne was hit list upon lif to lythen the houndes,
When alle the mute hade hym met, menged togeder: 1720
Suche a sorwe at that syght thay sette on his hede
As alle the clamberande clyffes hade clatered on hepes.
Here he was halawed when hatheles hym metten,
Loude he was yayned with yarande speche;
Ther he was threted and ofte 'thef' called,   1725
And ay the titleres at his tayl, that tary he ne myght.
Ofte he was runnen at when he out rayked,
And ofte reled in ayayn, so Reniarde was wylé.
And ye! he lad hem bi lagmon, the lorde and his meyny,

1719. list upon lif: MS lif upon list (Morris)

1710. *bi a strothe rande:* 'at the edge (*rande*) of a wooded marsh'.

1711. 'thought (*went*) to have escaped (*wylt*) out of the wood by tricks, away from the hounds.'

1713f. 'where three fierce (hounds)—all greyhounds—came at him in a rush (*thrich*).'

1716. 'and leaped off violently in a changed direction (*onstray*).'

1719f. 'Then it was pleasure indeed to hear (*lythen*) the hounds, (their voices) mingled (*menged*) together, when all the pack had met up with him'.

1728. *Reniarde* (also *Renaude*): 'Reynard'—popular medieval name for the fox.

1729. *lad hem bi lagmon:* 'led them in a string'; *lagmon* is a rare word, perhaps related to *lag* n. 'last person in a race, etc.'. See Menner, *PQ* 10 (1931), 163–8, and *EDD*.

On this maner bi the mountes whyle myd-over-under,   1730
Whyle the hende knyght at home holsumly slepes
Withinne the comly cortynes, on the colde morne.
Bot the lady, for luf, let not to slepe,
Ne the purpose to payre that pyght in hir hert,
But ros hir up radly, rayked hir theder   1735
In a mery mantyle, mete to the erthe,
That was furred ful fyne with felles wel pured;
No howes goud on hir hede, bot the hawer stones
Trased aboute hir tressour be twenty in clusteres;
Hir thryven face and hir throte throwen al naked,   1740
Hir brest bare bifore, and bihinde eke.
Ho comes withinne the chambre dore and closes hit hir after,
Wayves up a wyndow and on the wye calles
And radly thus rehayted hym with hir riche wordes,
      With chere: 1745
      'A! mon, how may thou slepe?
      This morning is so clere.'

1738. howes: MS hwes

1730. *whyle myd-over-under:* an extremely vague indication of time, lit. 'until half-way past (through?) *undern*'; but *undern* is used very loosely in ME for 'mid-morning' or 'midday'. Perhaps best translated 'until well on in the day'.

1731. *holsumly:* 'for the good of his health'—with delicate ironic contrast.

1733. 'But the lady, on account of her wooing, did not allow herself to sleep nor did she allow the purpose which stuck in her heart to become blunted'; *for luf* (as appears later) is to be taken generally, though it obviously suits the poet's purpose for the time being to allow the reader to assume inclination on the lady's part. *Cf.* 1927n.

1738. 'No seemly coifs on her head, but skilfully-cut (*hawer*) jewels set (*trased*) about her hair-fret in clusters of twenty.' If Gollancz's suggestion is correct, that the MS *hwes* is a form of OE *hufe* (ME *howve*) 'head-covering, coif', the implication here is that it would have been a more seemly head-dress for a married woman. *Cf.* the Wife of Bath's paraphrase of I *Timothy* II, 9:

> 'In habit maad with chastitee and shame
> Ye wommen shul apparaille yow,' quod he,
> 'And noght in tressed heer and gay perree (*precious stones*),
> As perles, ne with gold, ne clothes riche.'   (*CT* III(D), 342*ff*)

He was in drowping depe,
Bot thenne he con hir here.

In drey droupyng of dreme draveled that noble,   1750
As mon that was in mornyng of mony thro thoghtes,
How that Destiné schulde that day dele hym hys wyrde,
At the Grene Chapel when he the gome metes
And bihoves his buffet abide withoute debate more.
Bot when that comly com he kevered his wyttes,   1755
Swenges out of the swevenes and swares with hast.
The lady luflych com, laghande swete,
Felle over his fayre face and fetly hym kyssed.
He welcumes hir worthily with a wale chere;
He segh hir so glorious and gayly atyred,   1760
So fautles of hir fetures and of so fyne hewes,
Wight wallande joye warmed his hert.
With smothe smylyng and smolt thay smeten into merthe,
That al was blis and bonchef that breke hem bitwene,
            And wynne.   1765
        Thay lauced wordes gode,
        Much wele then was therinne.
        Gret perile bitwene hem stod,
        Nif Maré of hir knyght mynne.

For that prynces of pris depresed hym so thikke,   1770
Nurned hym so neghe the thred, that nede hym bihoved
Other lach ther hir luf other lodly refuse.
He cared for his cortaysye, lest crathayn he were,
And more for his meschef yif he schulde make synne
And be traytor to that tolke that that telde aght.   1775

1752. dele hym *supplied* (Tolkien and Gordon)
1755. com *supplied* (Emerson)

1752f. Since he is not to meet the Green Knight until the next day, we must
construe: 'on that day when he meets the man at the Green Chapel'.
1768f. 'There was great peril between them,—unless Mary be mindful of
her knight.' The tenses of *stod* and *mynne* are partly governed by the rhymes;
but sudden transitions between past tense and present tense are common.

'God schylde!' quoth the schalk. 'That schal not befalle!'
With luf-laghyng a lyt he layd hym bysyde
Alle the speches of specialté that sprange of her mouthe.
Quoth that burde to the burne, 'Blame ye disserve
Yif ye luf not that lyf that he lye nexte,   1780
Bifore alle the wyes in the worlde wounded in hert,
Bot if ye haf a lemman, a lever, that yow lykes better,
And folden fayth to that fre, festned so harde
That yow lausen ne lyst—and that I leve nouthe!
And that ye telle me that now truly I pray yow;   1785
For alle the lufes upon lyve, layne not the sothe
            For gile.'
        The knyght sayde, 'Be Sayn Jon'
        (And smethely con he smyle)
        'In fayth I welde right non,   1790
        Ne non wil welde the while.'

'That is a worde,' quoth that wyght, 'that worst is of alle;
Bot I am swared forsothe—that sore me thinkkes.
Kysse me now, comly, and I schal cach hethen;
I may bot mourne upon molde, as may that much lovyes.' 1795
Sykande ho sweye doun and semly hym kyssed,
And sithen ho severes hym fro and says as ho stondes,
'Now, dere, at this departyng do me this ese:
Gif me sumwhat of thy gifte, thi glove if hit were,

1776. In ME the negative connotation of a prohibition is regularly repeated
in the noun clause and (but for the indicative *schal*) Gawain's thought might
be interpreted 'God forbid that that should happen', and is usually so punc-
tuated. The present punctuation (which is justified by *schal*, instead of *schulde*)
makes the expression of his determination stronger.

1778. *speches of specialté:* 'declarations of affection'.

1782*ff.* 'unless you have a sweetheart, someone dearer (*lever*) to you, who
pleases you better, and (have) pledged your word to that noble one, confirmed
(*festned*) so definitely that you do not care to break it (*lausen*)—and that I do
believe now!'

1786. *For alle the lufes upon lyve:* equivalent to 'For the love of God and all
the saints'.

1788. *Sayn Jon:* St. John the Apostle, by tradition supremely dedicated to
celibacy.

1799. *if it were:* 'if only'.

That I may mynne on the, mon, my mournyng to lassen.'   1800
'Now iwysse,' quoth that wye, 'I wolde I hade here
The levest thing, for thy luf, that I in londe welde,
For ye haf deserved, forsothe, sellyly ofte
More rewarde bi resoun then I reche myght.
Bot to dele yow, for drurye, that dawed bot neked!—   1805
Hit is not your honour to haf at this tyme
A glove for a garysoun of Gawaynes giftes.
And I am here an erande in erdes uncouthe
And have no men wyth no males with menskful thinges
(That mislykes me, ladé) for luf, at this tyme;   1810
Iche tolke mon do as he is tan—tas to non ille
              Ne pine.'
                    'Nay, hende of hyghe honours,'
                    Quoth that lufsum under lyne,
                    'Thagh I nade oght of youres,   1815
                    Yet schulde ye have of myne.'

Ho raght hym a riche rynk of red golde werkes,
Wyth a starande ston stondande alofte,
That bere blusschande bemes as the bryght sunne;
Wyt ye wel, hit was worth wele ful hoge.   1820
Bot the renk hit renayed and redyly he sayde,
'I wil no giftes, for Gode, my gay, at this tyme;

1815. nade: MS hade (Gollancz)

1805ff. 'But to give you, as a love-token (*drurye*), something of little worth (lit. 'that which profited little')!—it is not equal to your dignity for you to have a glove as a trophy (*garysoun*) given by Gawain.' 1805 can be interpreted 'But to make you a present for the sake of love—that would not be very fitting'; the punctuation and translation adopted above are, however, better syntactically (the use of *dele* without direct object is awkward) and also more in keeping with Gawain's intention not to *lodly refuse* (1772).

1808. *an* is the preposition: 'on a mission'.

1811f. *tas . . . pine:* 'do not take it amiss or be distressed.'

1814. *under lyne:* '(one) dressed in linen', i.e. 'lady'.

1815. May be emended to *hade noght*, with same sense, but the emendation of Gollancz (above) keeps the vocalic alliteration and also assumes a somewhat more probable miscopying.

I haf none yow to norne ne noght wyl I take.'
Ho bede hit hym ful bysily and he hir bode wernes
And swere swyfte by his sothe that he hit sese nolde;   1825
And ho soré that he forsoke and sayde therafter,
'If ye renay my rynk, to ryche for hit semes,
Ye wolde not so hyghly halden be to me,
I schal gif yow my girdel, that gaynes yow lasse.'
Ho laght a lace lyghtly that leke umbe hir sydes,   1830
Knit upon hir kyrtel, under the clere mantyle;
Gered hit was with grene sylke and with gold schaped,
Noght bot arounde brayden, beten with fyngres.
And that ho bede to the burne and blythely bisoght,
Thagh hit unworthi were, that he hit take wolde;   1835
And he nay that he nolde neghe in no wyse
Nauther golde ne garysoun, er God hym grace sende
To acheve to the chaunce that he hade chosen there.
'And therfore I pray yow displese yow noght
And lettes be your bisinesse, for I baythe hit yow never   1840
          To graunte.
     I am derely to yow biholde
     Bicause of your sembelaunt,
     And ever in hot and colde,
     To be your true servaunt.'   1845

'Now forsake ye this silke,' sayde the burde thenne,
For hit is symple in hitself? And so hit wel semes:
Lo! so hit is littel and lasse hit is worthy.
Bot whoso knew the costes that knit ar therinne,

1827. *to ryche for hit semes:* 'because it seems too costly'.

1833. *brayden, beten:* 'embroidered (and) inlaid', corresponding respectively to *grene sylke* and *gold*, 1832.

1835. *unworthy:* 'of little value'. As in 1847f, the lady is being modest—or pretending to be: cf. 1832f, 2038f, 2430–2.

1836. *nay:* (pa.t. of *nie* 'say no'): 'he said he would not by any means touch (*neghe*)'.

1844. 'and ever (will be) in all circumstances (or 'through thick and thin')'; cf. 1547f.

1847f. 'And so it seems, perhaps: look! it is no bigger than this and its value is even less (than it seems)'.

He wolde hit prayse at more prys, paraventure;   1850
For what gome so is gorde with this grene lace,
While he hit hade hemely halched aboute
Ther is no hathel under heven tohewe hym that myght,
For he myght not be slayn for slyght upon erthe.'
Then kest the knyght, and hit come to his hert   1855
Hit were a juel for the jopardé that hym jugged were:
When he acheved to the chapel his chek for to fech,
Myght he haf slypped to be unslayn the sleght were noble.
Thenne he thulged with hir threpe and tholed hir to speke.
And ho bere on hym the belt and bede hit hym swythe   1860
(And he granted and hym gafe with a goud wylle)
And bisoght hym for hir sake discever hit never
Bot to lelly layne fro hir lorde; the leude hym acordes
That never wye schulde hit wyt, iwysse, bot thay twayne,
　　　　For noghte.   1865
　　　　He thonkked hir oft ful swythe,
　　　　Ful thro with hert and thoght;
　　　　Bi that on thrynne sythe
　　　　Ho has kyst the knyght so toght.

Thenne lachches ho hir leve and leves hym there,   1870
For more myrthe of that mon moght ho not gete.
When ho was gon, Sir Gawayn geres hym sone,
Rises and riches hym in araye noble,
Lays up the luf-lace the lady hym raght,
Hid hit ful holdely ther he hit eft fonde.   1875

1853. *tohewe:* 'cut down, cut to pieces'; the word is calculated to make Gawain think of his own plight, just as *slyght* 'skill, stratagem' (1854) seems designed to suggest that the girdle may be a match for the Green Knight's magical powers (*cf.* 1858).

1856. 'It would be a godsend (lit. 'jewel') for the hazard assigned to him'.

1858. 'if he could only escape without getting killed it would be a fine stratagem.'

1859. 'Then he gave in to her insistence and allowed her to speak.'

1868f. 'by that time she had kissed the hardy (*toght*) knight three times,'— i.e. she then gave him a third kiss (*cf.* 1758, 1796). The apparently singular form *on thrynne sythe* is explained as the relic of an old dative pl. in *-um*; *cf. on his fote* 2229.

Sythen chevely to the chapel choses he the waye,
Prevely aproched to a prest and prayed hym there
That he wolde lyste his lyf and lern hym better
How his sawle schulde be saved when he schuld seye hethen.
There he schrof hym schyrly and schewed his mysdedes,   1880
Of the more and the mynne, and merci beseches,
And of absolucioun he on the segge calles;
And he asoyled hym surely and sette hym so clene
As domesday schulde haf ben dight on the morn.
And sythen he mace hym as mery among the fre ladyes,   1885
With comlych caroles and alle kynnes joye,
As never he did bot that daye, to the derk nyght,
            With blys.
        Uche mon hade daynté thare
        Of hym, and sayde, 'Iwysse,   1890
        Thus myry he was never are,
        Syn he com hider, er this.'

Now hym lenge in that lee, ther luf hym bityde!
Yet is the lorde on the launde ledande his gomnes.
He has forfaren this fox that he folwed longe;   1895
As he sprent over a spenné to spye the schrewe,
Theras he herd the howndes that hasted hym swythe,
Renaud com richchande thurgh a roghe greve,
And alle the rabel in a res ryght at his heles.
The wye was war of the wylde and warly abides,   1900
And braydes out the bryght bronde and at the best castes.
And he schunt for the scharp and schulde haf arered;

1878. lyste: MS lyfte (Burrow)

1878. *lyste his lyf:* 'hear his confession'; see Burrow, 1965, 105, and *TG-Davis* n.

1881. 'belonging to (*of*) the greater and lesser (sins), and begs for forgiveness'; contemporary penitential manuals classify the branches of sin minutely.

1883. *he:* the priest.

1884. *as:* 'as if'.

1897. 'at a place where he (the knight) heard the hounds in full chase' (*hasted hym* reflex.).

1902. *schulde haf arered:* 'was about to retreat'.

A rach rapes hym to, ryght er he myght,
And ryght bifore the hors fete thay fel on hym alle
And woried me this wyly wyth a wroth noyse.   1905
The lorde lyghtes bilyve and laches hym sone,
Rased hym ful radly out of the rach mouthes,
Haldes heghe over his hede, halowes faste,
And ther bayen hym mony brath houndes.
Huntes hyed hem theder with hornes ful mony,   1910
Ay rechatande aryght til thay the renk seghen.
Bi that was comen his compeyny noble,
Alle that ever ber bugle blowed at ones
And alle thise other halowed, that hade no hornes;
Hit was the myriest mute that ever mon herde,   1915
The rich rurd that ther was raysed for Renaude saule
            With lote.
        Hor houndes thay ther rewarde,
        Her hedes thay fawne and frote,
        And sythen thay tan Reynarde   1920
        And tyrven of his cote.

And thenne thay helden to home, for hit was niegh nyght,
Strakande ful stoutly in hor store hornes.
The lorde is lyght at the laste at hys lef home,
Fyndes fire upon flet, the freke therbyside,   1925
Sir Gawayn the gode, that glad was with alle—
Among the ladies for luf he ladde much joye.
He were a bleaunt of blue, that bradde to the erthe,
His surkot semed hym wel, that softe was forred,

1905. *me:* untranslatable in this construction ('ethic dative'); it conveys a colloquial or ironic tone, suggesting the involvement of the narrator; *cf.* 1932, 2014, 2144.

1907. *rach mouthes:* 'mouths of the dogs'.

1919. 'they fondle and stroke their heads'.

1927. *for luf:* 'on account of friendship'; the phrase is little more than a tag, however, a conventional accompaniment of *lady* (as perhaps in 1733).

1928. 'he wore a silk garment of blue, which reached to the ground'. Burrow, 1965, 111*f*, notes that blue is traditionally the colour of faithfulness; it is ironical that Gawain should wear it for his one act of duplicity.

And his hode of that ilke henged on his schulder;   1930
Blande al of blaunner were bothe al aboute.
He metes me this godmon inmyddes the flore
And al with gomen he hym gret and goudly he sayde,
'I schal fylle upon fyrst oure forwardes nouthe,
That we spedly han spoken, ther spared was no drynk.'   1935
Then acoles he the knyght and kysses hym thryes
As saverly and sadly as he hem sette couthe.
'Bi Kryst,' quoth that other knyght, 'ye cach much sele
In chevisaunce of this chaffer, yif ye hade goud chepes.'
'Ye, of the chepe no charg,' quoth chefly that other,   1940
'As is pertly payed the porchas that I aghte.'
'Mary,' quoth that other mon, 'myn is bihynde,
For I haf hunted al this day and noght haf I geten
Bot this foule fox felle—the Fende haf the godes!—
And that is ful pore for to pay for suche prys thinges   1945
As ye haf thryght me here thro, suche thre cosses
          So gode.'
               'Inogh,' quoth Sir Gawayn,
               'I thonk yow, bi the Rode,'
               And how the fox was slayn   1950
               He tolde hym as thay stode.

With merthe and mynstralsye, wyth metes at hor wylle,
Thay maden as mery as any men moghten,
With laghyng of ladies, with lotes of bordes,
(Gawayn and the godemon so glad were thay bothe),   1955

1941. porchas: MS chepes (*miscopied from* 1939); *see TG*; Gollancz: pray

---

1932. *me:* see 1905*n.*

1934. On the previous two evenings the host has been first.

1935. 'which we readily affirmed when the drink flowed freely.'

1938–41. ' "By Christ," said the other knight, "you have had a lot of good luck in obtaining this merchandise, if you found the markets (or 'prices') good." "Oh never mind the market," said the other knight quickly, "since the gain which I obtained is publicly paid." ' Some of the wit of these lines stems from the ambiguity of *chepe:* 'trade, bargain, market, price'.

1954. *lotes of bordes:* 'jesting speeches'.

Bot if the douthe had doted other dronken ben other.
Bothe the mon and the meyny maden mony japes,
Til the sesoun was seyen that thay sever moste;
Burnes to hor bedde behoved at the laste.
Thenne lowly his leve at the lorde fyrst   1960
Fochches this fre mon and fayre he hym thonkkes
'Of such a selly sojorne as I haf hade here.
Your honour at this hyghe fest the Hyghe Kyng yow yelde!
I yef yow me for on of youres, if yowreself lykes,
For I mot nedes, as ye wot, meve tomorne,   1965
And ye me take sum tolke to teche, as ye hyght,
The gate to the Grene Chapel, as God wyl me suffer
To dele on New Yeres Day the dome of my wyrdes.'
'In god faythe,' quoth the godmon, 'wyth a goud wylle
Al that ever I yow hyght halde schal I redé.'   1970
Ther asyngnes he a servaunt to sett hym in the waye
And coundue hym by the downes, that he no drechch had,
For to ferk thurgh the fryth and fare at the gaynest
          Bi greve.
          The lorde Gawayn con thonk   1975
          Such worchip he wolde hym weve.
          Then at tho ladyes wlonk
          The knyght has tan his leve.

With care and wyth kyssyng he carppes hem tille

1956. The clause is dependent on *moghten* (1953): 'as merry as any men
could . . . unless the company had been demented, or else drunk'—i.e. without
overstepping the bounds of propriety.

1962f. Usually punctuated as one sentence, on the assumption that *yow yelde*
governs *Of* ('repay you for') and that *Your honour . . . fest* is in loose apposition
to *sojorne*. However, in similar constructions *yelde* takes a direct object (*cf.* 1292,
2410, 2441—all in the speech of Gawain). The punctuation adopted here
makes *Of* dependent on *thonkkes* (*cf.* 1031*ff*); transition in mid-sentence from
indirect to direct speech is quite common in ME and is also found in OE.

1964. 'I pledge (lit. 'give') myself to you (as your servant) in return for
one of your men, if it pleases you' (*cf.* 1666*f*).

1966. *And:* 'if'.

1975. The subject is *Gawayn*.

And fele thryvande thonkkes he thrat hom to have;   1980
And thay yelden hym ayayn yeply that ilk.
Thay bikende hym to Kryst with ful colde sykynges;
Sythen fro the meyny he menskly departes.
Uche mon that he mette he made hem a thonke
For his servyse and his solace and his sere pyne   1985
That thay wyth busynes had ben aboute hym to serve;
And uche segge as soré to sever with hym there
As thay hade wonde worthyly with that wlonk ever.
Then with ledes and lyght he was ladde to his chambre
And blythely broght to his bedde to be at his rest.   1990
Yif he ne slepe soundyly say ne dar I,
For he hade muche on the morn to mynne, yif he wolde,
            In thoght.
        Let hym lye there stille;
        He has nere that he soght.   1995
        And ye wyl a whyle be stylle,
        I schal telle yow how thay wroght.

1985f. *and his sere . . . serve:* 'and for the special trouble they had each taken
to serve him with solicitude' (*that* stands for 'with which'; *aboute* 'engaged in').
    1988. *As:* 'as if'.
    1991. 'Whether or not he slept soundly I dare not say'. The next line
implies that he probably did not; *cf.* also 2006*ff.*

IV

Now neghes the New Yere and the nyght passes,
The day dryves to the derk, as Dryghtyn biddes.
Bot wylde wederes of the worlde wakned theroute;   2000
Clowdes kesten kenly the colde to the erthe,
Wyth nye innoghe of the northe the naked to tene.
The snawe snitered ful snart, that snayped the wylde;
The werbelande wynde wapped fro the hyghe
And drof uche dale ful of dryftes ful grete.   2005
The leude lystened ful wel, that ley in his bedde—
Thagh he lowkes his liddes ful lyttel he slepes;
Bi uch kok that crue he knewe wel the steven.
Deliverly he dressed up er the day sprenged,
For there was lyght of a laumpe that lemed in his chambre.   2010
He called to his chamberlayn, that cofly him swared,
And bede hym bryng hym his bruny and his blonk sadel.
That other ferkes hym up and feches hym his wedes
And graythes me Sir Gawayn upon a grett wyse.
Fyrst he clad hym in his clothes, the colde for to were,   2015
And sythen his other harnays, that holdely was keped:
Bothe his paunce and his plates piked ful clene,
The rynges rokked of the roust of his riche bruny,

2000. *wederes of the worlde:* see 504n.
2001-4. 'clouds drove the cold keenly down to the earth and there was bitter wind enough from the north to torment the unprotected flesh. The snow showered down sharply, stinging (*that snayped*) the wild animals; the whistling wind struck down from the high ground'.
2008. 'every time a cock crowed he was aware of the hour (*steven*)'. It was believed in the Middle Ages that cocks could tell the time by the sun and would crow exactly on the hour (as Chauntecleer does in Chaucer's *Nun's Priest's Tale*). In view of 2009, however, Cawley is probably right in seeing this as a reference to the belief that they crow 'three times during the night—at midnight, 3 a.m., and an hour before dawn. '*Cf.* 1412-5.
2010. *of:* 'from'.
2012. *and his blonk sadel:* 'and saddle his horse'.
2014. *me:* see 1905n.
2018. 'the rings of his splendid mail-coat rocked free of rust'; armour was rocked in a barrel of sand to remove rust.

And al was fresch as upon fyrst, and he was fayn thenne
        To thonk.   2020
    He hade upon uche pece,
    Wypped ful wel and wlonk;
    The gayest into Grece
    The burne bede bryng his blonk.

Whyle the wlonkest wedes he warp on hymselven—   2025
His cote wyth the conysaunce of the clere werkes
Ennurned upon velvet, vertuus stones
Aboute beten and bounden, enbrauded semes,
And fayre furred withinne wyth fayre pelures—
Yet laft he not the lace, the ladies gifte;   2030
That forgat not Gawayn, for gode of hymselven.
Bi he hade belted the bronde upon his balwe haunches,
Thenn dressed he his drurye double hym aboute,
Swythe swethled umbe his swange, swetely, that knyght;
The gordel of the grene silke that gay wel bisemed,   2035
Upon that ryol red clothe, that ryche was to schewe.

2019–24. 'and he gave hearty thanks (for that). He had on him (now) every piece, polished (*wypped*) most splendidly; the most elegant (knight) from here to Greece ordered the man (*the burne*) to bring his horse.'

2026. '—his surcoat with the badge of bright workmanship (or 'pure deeds'—*cf*. 631) set (*ennurned*) upon velvet, with potent gems inlaid and clasped everywhere (*aboute*), the seams embroidered, and beautifully lined within with fine furs—'; *vertuus:* jewels were thought to have power against various evils and diseases.

2033ff. 'then he—happily (*swetely*), that knight!—arranged his love-token twice about himself, wrapped it (*swethled*; or pp.) every inch (*swythe:* lit. 'much') about his waist; the girdle of green silk well suited the magnificent knight (*that gay*)'. It is also possible to read *The gordel of grene silk* as direct object of *swethled* and the rest of 2035 as a relative clause with relative pronoun omitted. The word-order of 2034 may be intended to convey an ironical tone (as at 2031).

2036. *ryol red clothe:* i.e. his surcoat, which forms a red background to the gold pentangle; on his shield the pentangle is painted *Ryally wyth red golde upon rede gowles* (633). The poet's emphatic (and ironic) reference to the juxta-e position of pentangle and girdle is suggestive, for in failing to hand over the latter to the host he has fallen short of the high virtues symbolized by the former.

Bot wered not this ilk wye for wele this gordel,
For pryde of the pendauntes, thagh polyst thay were,
And thagh the glyterande golde glent upon endes,
Bot for to saven hymself when suffer hym byhoved,   2040
To byde bale withoute dabate, of bronde hym to were
               Other knyffe.
     Bi that the bolde mon boun
     Wynnes theroute bilyve,
     Alle the meyny of renoun   2045
     He thonkkes ofte ful ryve.

Thenne was Gryngolet graythe, that gret was and huge,
And hade ben sojourned saverly and in a siker wyse:
Hym lyst prik for poynt, that proude hors thenne.
The wye wynnes hym to and wytes on his lyre   2050
And sayde soberly hymself and by his soth sweres,
'Here is a meyny in this mote that on menske thenkkes.
The mon hem maynteines, joy mot he have;
The leve lady, on lyve luf hir bityde!
Yif thay for charyté cherysen a gest   2055
And halden honour in her honde, the Hathel hem yelde
That haldes the heven upon hyghe, and also yow alle!

2053. he: MS thay (Gollancz)

2041f. *of bronde ... knyffe:* 'to defend him from sword or knife': parallel to *for to saven hymself* 2040; (cf. 384: *Wyth what weppen so thou wylt*).

2043–6. 'When the brave man accoutred (*boun:* ready) comes outside soon, he thanks all the noble household often and abundantly (*ful rive*).' None of the household, except his servant, are present on this occasion, of course; he has, in fact, already said goodbye and thanked them individually the night before (1979–90). The quatrain is again an anticipatory summary of the following stanza (cf. 341f).

2049. 'that proud horse was in the mood to gallop then, because of his (fine) condition (*for poynt*).'

2053f. 'The man (who) supports them, may he have joy; the dear lady—may she be loved while she lives!' Gollancz's emendation of 2053 is justified by the parallel structure of 2054.

2056. *And ... honde:* 'and dispense favour (hospitality)'.

2057. *and ... alle!:* addressed (*in petto*) to the whole household (cf. 2043–6n).
E

And yif I myght lyf upon londe lede any whyle,
I schuld rech yow sum rewarde redyly, if I myght.'
Thenn steppes he into stirop and strydes alofte;   2060
His schalk schewed hym his schelde, on schulder he hit laght,
Gordes to Gryngolet with his gilt heles,
And he startes on the ston, stod he no lenger
        To praunce.
            His hathel on hors was thenne,   2065
            That bere his spere and launce.
            'This kastel to Kryst I kenne,'
            He gef hit ay god chaunce.

The brygge was brayde doun, and the brode yates
Unbarred and born open upon bothe halve.   2070
The burne blessed hym bilyve and the bredes passed,
Prayses the porter bifore the prynce kneled—
Gef hym God and goud day, that Gawayn He save—
And went on his way with his wye one,
That schulde teche hym to tourne to that tene place   2075
Ther the ruful race he schulde resayve.
Thay bowen bi bonkkes ther boghes ar bare;
Thay clomben bi clyffes ther clenges the colde.
The heven was uphalt, but ugly therunder.
Mist muged on the mor, malt on the mountes;   2080

2061. *His schalk* (also *His hathel* 2065): the guide allotted to him, who acted
as his squire. He hands over Gawain's helmet and lance at 2143.

2068. 'He wished it good fortune for ever.' Alternatively, the line can be
read as part of Gawain's wish: 'may He give it good fortune for ever.'

2072f. '(he) compliments the porter (who) knelt before the prince (*cf.* 818)—
(and the porter) wished him good day and commended him to God, (praying)
that He would save Gawain—'. 2073 is a compressed, indirect-speech rendering
of three greetings: (*I*) *gif yow Gode* 'I commend you to God', (*God*) *gif yow
goud day* (see *OED good day*), and *God save yow*. The syllepsis *gif yow God and
goud day* may have been used in direct speech too. A close parallel to 2073f is
found in *Le Bone Florence*:

> And betaght hur god and gode day
> And bad hur wende on hur way

Cf. also 1029, 2068, and—for an indirect rendering of *God blesse yow*—1296n.)

2079. 'The clouds were high (*uphalt*: drawn up) but threatening beneath.'

Uch hille hade a hatte, a myst-hakel huge.
Brokes byled and breke bi bonkkes aboute,
Schyre schaterande on schores, ther thay doun schowved.
Wela wylle was the way ther thay bi wod schulden,
Til hit was sone sesoun that the sunne ryses   2085
      That tyde.
        Thay were on a hille ful hyghe;
        The whyte snaw lay bisyde.
        The burne that rod hym by
        Bede his mayster abide.   2090

'For I haf wonnen yow hider, wye, at this tyme,
And now nar ye not fer fro that note place
That ye han spied and spuryed so specially after.
Bot I schal say yow forsothe, sythen I yow knowe
And ye ar a lede upon lyve that I wel lovy: 2095
Wolde ye worch bi my wytte, ye worthed the better.
The place that ye prece to ful perelous is halden:
Ther wones a wye in that waste, the worst upon erthe,
For he is stiffe and sturne and to strike lovies,
And more he is then any mon upon myddelerde,   2100
And his body bigger then the best fowre
That ar in Arthures hous, Hestor, other other.
He cheves that chaunce at the Chapel Grene,
Ther passes non bi that place so proude in his armes
That he ne dynges hym to dethe with dynt of his honde;   2105
For he is a mon methles and mercy non uses.
For be hit chorle other chaplayn that bi the chapel rydes,
Monk other masseprest, other any mon elles,

2081. *myst-hakel*: 'cap-cloud' (lit. 'cape of mist'—a poetic compound of a type very common in OE but less so in ME alliterative poetry).
2082*ff*. 'Brooks bubbled and splashed on the hillsides round about, dashing white on the banks, where they (the riders) made their way down. The path which they had to take through the wood was very devious (*wylle*).'
2086. 'at that time of year'.
2096. 'if you would act according to my judgement it would be the better for you.'
2102. *Hestor*: a variant of *Hector* (of Troy).

Hym thynk as queme hym to quelle as quyk go hymselven.
Forthy I say the: as sothe as ye in sadel sitte,   2110
Com ye there, ye be kylled, may the knyght rede,—
Trawe ye me that truely—thagh ye had twenty lyves
        To spende.
            He has wonyd here ful yore,
            On bent much baret bende;   2115
            Ayayn his dyntes sore
            Ye may not yow defende.

'Forthy, goude Sir Gawayn, let the gome one
And gos away sum other gate, upon Goddes halve!
Cayres bi sum other kyth, ther Kryst mot yow spede!   2120
And I schal hy me hom ayayn; and hete yow fyrre
That I schal swere "Bi God and alle His gode halwes",
"As help me God and the halydam", and othes innoghe,
That I schal lelly yow layne and lauce never tale
That ever ye fondet to fle for freke that I wyst.'   2125
'Grant merci,' quoth Gawayn, and gruchyng he sayde,
'Wel worth the, wye, that woldes my gode,
And that lelly me layne I leve wel thou woldes;

2109. 'it seems to him as pleasant a thing to kill him as to remain alive himself.' Perhaps: 'killing is second nature to him.'

2111. 'if you go there you will be killed, if the knight has his way' (for *rede* 'manage', *cf.* 373). Sisam, however (*Fourteenth Century Verse and Prose*, 219*f*), suggests the emendation: *may* [*y*] *the, knyght, rede* 'I may warn you (*the*), knight'; (*the/ye* variation is exemplified also in 2110). In some ways this is to be preferred, for the guide does not otherwise refer to the guardian of the chapel as a knight and, indeed, his notion of him would make that title seem inappropriate (*cf.* 2137*n*). It would be pressing inference too far to suppose that the word *knyght* here is a slip of the tongue occasioned by his knowledge that the Green Knight is really Sir Bertilak, but *cf.* E. M. Wright, *JEGP* 34 (1935), 157–79.

2114. *ful yore:* 'for a long time'; Burrow notes that this conflicts with Sir Bertilak's own statement at 2459*ff*.

2123. *As ... halydam:* 'As may God and the holy object (*halydam*) help me'—a form of oath which originated in the practice of swearing on a sacred relic.

2125. 'that you ever attempted to flee because of any man I (ever) knew.'
2127. 'Good luck befall you, man, who wish for my good'.

Bot helde thou hit never so holde, and I here passed,
Founded for ferde for to fle, in fourme that thou telles,   2130
I were a knyght kowarde, I myght not be excused.
Bot I wyl to the chapel, for chaunce that may falle,
And talk wyth that ilk tulk the tale that me lyste,
Worthe hit wele other wo, as the Wyrde lykes
      Hit hafe.   2135
    Thaghe he be a sturn knape
    To stightel, and stad with stave,
    Ful wel con Dryghtyn schape
    His servauntes for to save.'

'Mary!' quoth that other mon, 'now thou so much spelles   2140
That thou wylt thyn awen nye nyme to thyselven
And the lyst lese thy lyf, the lette I ne kepe.
Haf here thi helme on thy hede, thi spere in thi honde,
And ryde me doun this ilk rake, bi yon rokke syde,
Til thou be broght to the bothem of the brem valay.   2145
Thenne loke a littel on the launde, on thi lyfte honde,
And thou schal se in that slade the self chapel
And the borelych burne on bent that hit kepes.
Now fares wel, on Godes half, Gawayn the noble!
For alle the golde upon grounde I nolde go wyth the,   2150
Ne bere the felawschip thurgh this fryth on fote fyrre.'

2129. 'but no matter how faithfully you kept it, if I passed this place'.
2131. *I myght not*: 'I could not'.
2132. 'But I am determined to go to the chapel whatever happens'.
2134*f.* 'whether good or ill come of it, as Fate sees fit to dispose.' *Wyrde*: the OE word for 'fate', already partially identified with Providence or 'the will of God' in OE (*cf.* 2138).
2137. *and stad with stave*: 'and armed with a club'. Gawain echoes the guide's description of the guardian of the chapel as a wild man of the woods, though there is no apparent reason for him to conceal the fact that he knows the Green Knight; if it is not a slip on the poet's part, we may perhaps interpret it as wishful thinking: Gawain would no doubt prefer an encounter with an ordinary *wodwos* (*cf.* 721) to another meeting with the Green Knight.
2142. 'and it pleases you to lose your life, I do not care to dissuade you.'
2144. *me*: see 1905*n*.
2151. *on fote fyrre*: 'one foot further'.

Bi that the wye in the wod wendes his brydel,
Hit the hors with the heles as harde as he myght,
Lepes hym over the launde, and leves the knyght there
                 Alone.   2155
     'Bi Goddes self,' quoth Gawayn,
     'I wyl nauther grete ne grone;
     To Goddes wylle I am ful bayn
     And to Hym I haf me tone.'

Thenne gyrdes he to Gryngolet and gederes the rake,   2160
Schowves in bi a schore at a schawe syde,
Rides thurgh the roghe bonk ryght to the dale.
And thenne he wayted hym aboute, and wylde hit hym thoght,
And seghe no syngne of resette bisydes nowhere.
Bot hyghe bonkkes and brent upon bothe halve   2165
And rughe knokled knarres with knorned stones;
The skues of the scowtes skayned hym thoght.
Thenne he hoved and wythhylde his hors at that tyde
And ofte chaunged his cher the chapel to seche.
He segh non suche in no syde—and selly hym thoght—   2170
Save, a lyttel on a launde, a lawe as hit were,
A balw berw bi a bonke the brymme bysyde,
Bi a forw of a flode that ferked thare;
The borne blubred therinne as hit boyled hade.
The knyght kaches his caple and com to the lawe,   2175
Lightes doun luflyly and at a lynde taches
The rayne of his riche, with a roghe braunche.
Thenne he bowes to the berwe, aboute hit he walkes,

2177. of: MS &

2161f. 'pushes in, past a rock (*schore*—the *rokke* of 2144), at the edge of a wood, rides down through the wooded slope right to the bottom.'

2166f. 'and rough, lumpy crags with rugged outcrops; the clouds seemed to him to be grazed (*skayned*) by (*of*) the jutting rocks (*scowtes*).'

2171–4. 'except, at a short distance across a glade, a sort of knoll, a smooth-surfaced barrow (*berw*) on the side of (*bi*) a slope beside the water's edge, by the channel (*forw*) of a stream which passed there; the burn gurgled in it (i.e. the channel) as if it was boiling.' For the construction of the last clause, *cf.* 2202.

Debatande with hymself what hit be myght.
Hit hade a hole on the ende and on ayther syde,   2180
And overgrowen with gresse in glodes aywhere,
And al was holw inwith, nobot an olde cave
Or a crevisse of an olde cragge—he couthe hit noght deme
            With spelle.
            'We! Lorde,' quoth the gentyle knyght,   2185
            'Whether this be the Grene Chapelle?
            Here myght aboute mydnyght
            The Dele his matynnes telle!'

'Now iwysse,' quoth Wowayn, 'wysty is here;
This oritore is ugly, with erbes overgrowen.   2190
Wel bisemes the wye wruxled in grene
Dele here his devocioun on the Develes wyse;
Now I fele hit is the Fende, in my fyve wyttes,
That has stoken me this steven to strye me here.
This is a chapel of meschaunce, that chekke hit bytyde!   2195
Hit is the corsedest kyrk that ever I com inne!'
With heghe helme on his hede, his launce in his honde,
He romes up to the roffe of tho rogh wones.
Thene herde he of that hyghe hil, in a harde roche
Biyonde the broke, in a bonk, a wonder breme noyse.   2200
What! hit clatered in the clyff as hit cleve schulde,

2183f. *he . . . spelle:* 'he could not say which it was.'
2186ff. 'Is this the green chapel? The Devil might well recite his matins here about midnight!' In monastic houses, matins, the first of the canonical hours, were sung before daybreak; however, midnight is probably mentioned here as an appropriate hour for the Devil's.
2193. 'Now I feel, in my five senses, that it is the Devil'.
2195. 'This is a chapel of doom, ill fortune befall it!' *that . . . hit:* 'which'.
2199f. Presumably *that hyghe hil* refers to the hill he is standing on (or the 'chapel' itself) and *in a harde roche Biyonde the broke, in a bonk* to the source of the noise.
2201. *What!:* as also in OE (*Hwæt!*), the word is an exclamation of surprise or a call for attention; here it may also be intended to echo the sound itself (*cf.* 1163—the sound of the arrow?)
2201-4. 'as if it (the cliff) would split, as if someone were grinding a scythe upon a grindstone (for syntax *cf.* 2174). What! it whirred and ground like water at a mill; what! it swished and rang, ghastly to hear.'

As one upon a gryndelston hade grounden a sythe.
What! hit wharred and whette as water at a mulne;
What! hit rusched and ronge, rawthe to here.
Thenne 'Bi Godde,' quoth Gawayn, 'that gere, as I trowe,   2205
Is ryched at the reverence me renk to mete
      Bi rote.
    Let God worche! "We loo!"
    Hit helppes me not a mote.
    My lif thagh I forgoo,   2210
    Drede dos me no lote.'

Thenne the knyght con calle ful hyghe,
'Who stightles in this sted, me steven to holde?
For now is gode Gawayn goande ryght here.
If any wye oght wyl, wynne hider fast,   2215
Other now other never, his nedes to spede.'
'Abyde,' quoth on on the bonke aboven over his hede,
'And thou schal haf al in hast that I the hyght ones.'
Yet he rusched on that rurde rapely a throwe

2206f. These lines have not been satisfactorily explained. The following interpretation (*cf. TG*, 117) suits the stress-pattern best, for it elevates *renk*, as the alliteration seems to demand: '(that contrivance, as I believe) is being prepared (*ryched*) in honour of (*at the reverence*) marking out (*to mete*, lit. 'measure') the field of combat (*renk*) for me, with due ceremony (*Bi rote*).' Though there is no direct evidence, *me renk to mete* is presumed to have a metaphorical sense 'to challenge me to a duel'; the syntactical pattern would be that of *me steven to holde* 2213. Other interpretations are possible if we allow an extra stress on *me* and put it before the caesura (perhaps cross-alliterating with *mete*): e.g. 'in honour of me, in order to meet a knight (*renk*) with due ceremony'.
    2208ff. 'Let God's will be done! (To cry) "Alas!" will not help me a bit. Even though I lose my life, no noise (*lote*) shall make me fear (*drede* v.).' *Cf.* the Vernon poem *Deo Gracias I*, 45–8:

> Though I weore out of bonchef brought,
>   What help weore to me to seye 'Allas!'
> In the nome of God, whatever be wrought,
>   I schal seie, 'Deo gracias.'

Minor Poems of the Vernon MS, edited by C. Horstmann and F. J. Furnivall (London, EETS, 1892–1901), II, 665.
    2215. *oght wyl:* 'wants anything'; *wynne:* subj.; 'let him come'.
    2219f. 'Still he swished on hastily (*rapely*) with that noise for a while (*throwe*) and turned back (*awharf*) to his sharpening before he would come down'.

And wyth whettyng awharf, er he wolde lyght;   2220
And sythen he keveres bi a cragge and comes of a hole,
Whyrlande out of a wro wyth a felle weppen:
A denes ax, newe dyght, the dynt with to yelde,
With a borelych bytte bende by the halme,
Fyled in a fylor, fowre fote large—   2225
Hit was no lasse, bi that lace that lemed ful bryght!—
And the gome in the grene gered as fyrst,
Bothe the lyre and the legges, lokkes and berde,
Save that fayre on his fote he foundes on the erthe,
Sette the stele to the stone and stalked bysyde.   2230
When he wan to the watter, ther he wade nolde,
He hypped over on hys ax and orpedly strydes,
Bremly brothe on a bent that brode was aboute,
          On snawe.
          Sir Gawayn the knyght con mete;   2235
          He ne lutte hym nothyng lowe.
          That other sayde, 'Now, sir swete,
          Of steven mon may the trowe.'

'Gawayn,' quoth that grene gome, 'God the mot loke!'

2221. The Green Knight (who is standing on the hill at the opposite side of
the stream from Gawain) appears to descend by some sort of hidden passage.
2225*f.* 'sharpened on a grindstone, four feet wide (i.e. from point to point)—
it was no less, by that belt which shone very brightly!' In describing the
earlier axe, the poet mentions a *lace* ('cord') which is wrapped about its handle
(217–20); if a similar cord is alluded to here, however, it is difficult to see how it
could play any part in an observer's assessment of the size of the blade. The
best solution is that *bi . . . bryght* is an oath on the green girdle (*cf.* the description
at 2038*f*), spoken *in petto* by Gawain; at the moment when he sees the axe, with
its huge blade, it is understandable that his thoughts should fly to his magic
charm. See S. Malarky and J. B. Toelken, *JEGP* 63 (1964), 14–20, (reprinted
in Howard and Zacher, 1968).
2233. 'a fiercely violent creature against a broad field'; the point of view
is Gawain's.
2234. *On snawe*: complements *strydes*.
2235–8. 'Sir Gawayn greeted the knight, (but) hardly bowed to him at all.
The latter said, "So, my dear sir, you can be trusted to keep an appointment." '
2239. *God the mot loke!*: 'God guard you!' *Cf.* the greeting of the old man
in Chaucer's *Pardoner's Tale* (*CT* VI(C), 715): 'Now, lordes, God yow see!'
E*

Iwysse thou art welcom, wye, to my place,   2240
And thou has tymed thi travayl as truee mon schulde;
And thou knowes the covenauntes kest us bytwene:
At this tyme twelmonyth thou toke that the falled
And I schulde at this Newe Yere yeply the quyte.
And we ar in this valay verayly oure one;   2245
Here ar no renkes us to rydde, rele as us likes.
Haf thy helme of thy hede and haf here thy pay.
Busk no more debate then I the bede thenne
When thou wypped of my hede at a wap one.'
'Nay, bi God,' quoth Gawayn, 'that me gost lante,   2250
I schal gruch the no grue, for grem that falles;
Bot styghtel the upon on strok and I schal stonde stylle
And warp the no wernyng to worch as the lykes
       Nowhare.'
    He lened with the nek and lutte   2255
    And schewed that schyre al bare,
    And lette as he noght dutte;
    For drede he wolde not dare.

Then the gome in the grene graythed hym swythe,
Gederes up hys grymme tole, Gawayn to smyte;   2260
With alle the bur in his body he ber hit on lofte,
Munt as maghtyly as marre hym he wolde.

2243. 'Twelve months ago at this time of year you were to take what fell to your lot'; *thou toke* could be pa.t. subj. or pa.t. indic. but since the Green Knight is summarizing the terms of the agreement rather than what happened we should interpret it as subj.

2250. *that . . . lante:* 'Who gave me a soul'.

2251. 'I shall not bear you the slightest ill-will (*no grue:* not a bit) whatever injury befalls me.'

2254. Usually rendered 'in any way at all'; but can be understood literally: 'anywhere', 'here or anywhere else'. Gawain implies that the remoteness of the valley is immaterial, provided that the Green Knight intends to stick to the single blow of the agreement. *Bot* (2252): 'only'.

2257f. 'and acted as if he feared nothing; he did not intend to flinch for fear.'

2262. 'aimed (a blow) at him as forcibly as if he intended to destroy (*marre*) him.'

Hade hit dryven adoun as drey as he atled,
Ther hade ben ded of his dynt that doghty was ever.
Bot Gawayn on that giserne glyfte hym bysyde,   2265
As hit com glydande adoun on glode hym to schende,
And schranke a lytel with the schulderes for the scharp yrne.
That other schalk wyth a schunt the schene wythhaldes
And thenne repreved he the prynce with mony prowde wordes:
'Thou art not Gawayn,' quoth the gome, 'that is so goud halden,
That never arwed for no here by hylle ne be vale,   2271
And now thou fles for ferde er thou fele harmes!
Such cowardise of that knyght cowthe I never here.
Nawther fyked I ne flaghe, freke, when thou myntest,
Ne kest no kavelacion in kynges hous Arthor.   2275
My hede flaw to my fote and yet flagh I never;
And thou, er any harme hent, arwes in hert.
Wherfore the better burne me burde be called
            Therfore.'
               Quoth Gawayn, 'I schunt ones   2280
               And so wyl I no more;
               Bot thagh my hede falle on the stones
               I con not hit restore.

'Bot busk, burne, bi thi fayth, and bryng me to the poynt—
Dele to me my destiné and do hit out of honde.   2285
For I schal stonde the a strok and start no more
Til thyn ax have me hitte—haf here my trawthe.'

2264. 'he who was ever brave (i.e. Gawain) would have died there from
his blow.'

2265. glyfte hym bysyde: 'glanced sideways'.

2273. cowthe I never here: 'I never did hear'; cf. 230n.

2276. The MS spelling of both flaw and flagh is flaȝ, accentuating the play
on words.

2277. er any harme hent: absolute use of the past participle; cf. the modern
'no offence taken'.

2285. out of honde: The fact that this is the earliest recorded instance of this
phrase (OED and MED), as of Haf at the (2288), reinforces the impression that
the language of the speeches is often extremely up-to-date and colloquial;
bring me to the poynt 'come to the point with me'—but also a play on words
(cf. 2392).

'Haf at the thenne!' quoth that other, and heves hit alofte
And waytes as wrothely as he wode were.
He myntes at hym maghtyly bot not the mon rynes,   2290
Withhelde heterly his honde er hit hurt myght.
Gawayn graythely hit bydes and glent with no membre
Bot stode stylle as the ston other a stubbe auther
That ratheled is in roché grounde with rotes a hundreth.
Then muryly efte con he mele, the mon in the grene: 2295
'So, now thou has thi hert holle hitte me bihovs.
Halde the now the hyghe hode that Arthur the raght
And kepe thy kanel at this kest, yif hit kever may!'
Gawayn ful gryndelly with greme thenne sayde:
'Wy, thresch on, thou thro mon! Thou thretes to longe.   2300
I hope that thi hert arwe wyth thyn awen selven.'
'Forsothe,' quoth that other freke, 'so felly thou spekes,
I wyl no longer on lyte lette thin ernde
          Right nowe.'
          Thenne tas he hym strythe to stryke   2305
          And frounses bothe lyppe and browe.
          No mervayle thagh hym myslyke
          That hoped of no rescowe.

He lyftes lyghtly his lome and let hit doun fayre
With the barbe of the bitte bi the bare nek.   2310
Thagh he homered heterly, hurt hym no more
Bot snyrt hym on that on syde, that severed the hyde.

2293f. 'but stood as steady as the rock, or else a stump that is anchored
(ratheled) in rocky soil with a hundred roots.'
2297. 'May the noble order (hyghe hode—i.e. the order of knighthood)
which Arthur bestowed upon you keep you now and (may it) preserve your
neck (kanel) at this stroke, if it is able to accomplish it!' Although Gawain does
not realize it at this point, the outcome of the beheading game is made depen-
dent on his conduct during his last three days in the castle. The Green Knight
is saying, 'Let us see if your knighthood enabled you to resist the temptations
of the third day.'
2301. 'I believe that you have struck fear into your own heart (lit. 'that
your heart is afraid of yourself ').'
2307f. 'No wonder if it displease him who expected no rescue.'
2311f. no more Bot: 'no more than (to)'.

The scharp schrank to the flesche thurgh the schyre grece,
That the schene blod over his schulderes schot to the erthe.
And when the burne segh the blode blenk on the snawe,   2315
He sprit forth spenne-fote more then a spere lenthe,
Hent heterly his helme and on his hed cast,
Schot with his schulderes his fayre schelde under,
Braydes out a bryght sworde and bremely he spekes—
Never syn that he was barne borne of his moder   2320
Was he never in this worlde wye half so blythe—
'Blynne, burne, of thy bur! Bede me no mo!
I haf a stroke in this sted withoute stryf hent
And if thow reches me any mo I redyly schal quyte
And yelde yederly ayayn—and therto ye tryst—   2325
        And foo.
        Bot on stroke here me falles—
        The covenaunt schop ryght so,
        Festned in Arthures halles—
        And therfore, hende, now hoo!'   2330

The hathel heldet hym fro and on his ax rested,
Sette the schaft upon schore and to the scharp lened
And loked to the leude that on the launde yede,

2320. barne: MS burne (Andrew)
2329. Festned: Cawley's reading (MS *nearly illegible*); fermed, Menner;
        fettled, Gollancz

2316. *spenne-fote*: 'with feet together'; Gawain's instinctive reaction is an
unprepared standing-jump.
2318. *under* is an adv. 'underneath, down': 'with his shoulders he jerked
down his fair shield'. Gawain is carrying his shield slung on his shoulder in
readiness (*cf.* 2061, and contrast 621); the jerk is evidently a practised movement
to make it slide down the left arm while he draws his sword with the other
hand.
2320f. The redundancy and slight incoherence of the poet's description
suggest a jumble of feelings (*cf.* 2334f).
2326. 'and in hostility': i.e. 'in earnest'. Gawain is saying that he will no
longer consider himself bound by the rules of the game, but will fight.
2327. 'Only one stroke falls to my lot here'.
2331. *heldet hym fro*: 'moved away from him (i.e. Gawain)'.

How that doghty, dredles, dervely ther stondes,
Armed ful awles; in hert hit hym lykes.   2335
Thenn he meles muryly wyth a much steven
And, wyth a rynkande rurde, he to the renk sayde,
'Bolde burne, on this bent be not so gryndel.
No mon here unmanerly the mysboden habbes,
Ne kyd bot as covenaunde at kynges kort schaped.   2340
I hyght the a strok and thou hit has—halde the wel payed.
I relece the of the remnaunt of ryghtes alle other.
Iif I deliver had bene, a boffet paraunter
I couthe wrotheloker haf waret, to the haf wroght anger.
Fyrst I mansed the muryly with a mynt one   2345
And rove the wyth no rof-sore. With ryght I the profered
For the forwarde that we fest in the fyrst nyght;
And thou trystyly the trawthe and truly me haldes:
Al the gayne thow me gef, as god mon schulde.
That other munt for the morne, mon, I the profered: 2350
Thou kyssedes my clere wyf, the cosses me raghtes.
For bothe two here I the bede bot two bare myntes
          Boute scathe.
     True mon true restore;
     Thenne thar mon drede no wathe.   2355
     At the thrid thou fayled thore,
     And therfor that tappe ta the.

2339f. 'No one has treated (mysboden) you discourteously here, nor acted
otherwise than as the covenant at the king's court laid down.'

2342. 'I release you from all remaining obligations whatever.'

2343f. 'If I had been quick, I could perhaps have repaid a blow more harshly
(and) have done you harm (anger).'

2347. In the phrase the fyrst nyght the host appears to conflate the evening
before the first hunt, when the agreement was first made (fest), with the evening
of the hunt, when it was carried out; the morne of 2350 is evidently the day of
the second hunt.

2348. 'and you faithfully and honestly kept (lit. 'keep') your pledge to me'.

2354f. 'A true person must (mon) restore truly; then one (mon) need (thar)
fear no danger.'

2356. thore: 'there', 'in that respect'—i.e. in honesty.

2357. ta the: imperative sing. (reflex.), '(you must) take'.

For hit is my wede that thou weres, that ilke woven girdel.
Myn owen wyf hit the weved, I wot wel forsothe.
Now know I wel thy cosses and thy costes als,   2360
And the wowyng of my wyf. I wroght hit myselven;
I sende hir to asay the, and sothly me thynkkes
On the fautlest freke that ever on fote yede.
As perle bi the white pese is of prys more,
So is Gawayn, in god fayth, bi other gay knyghtes.   2365
Bot here yow lakked a lyttel, sir, and lewté yow wonted;
Bot that was for no wylyde werke, ne wowyng nauther,
Bot for ye lufed your lyf—the lasse I yow blame.'
That other stif mon in study stod a gret whyle,
So agreved for greme he gryed withinne;   2370
Alle the blode of his brest blende in his face,
That al he schrank for schome that the schalk talked.
The forme worde upon folde that the freke meled:
'Corsed worth cowarddyse and covetyse bothe!
In yow is vylany and vyse, that vertue disstryes.'   2375
Thenne he kaght to the knot and the kest lawses,
Brayde brothely the belt to the burne selven:
'Lo! ther the falssyng—foule mot hit falle!

2359. *Myn . . . weved:* 'My own wife gave it to you'.

2361. *the wowyng of my wife:* 'my wife's wooing (of you)'.

2361*f.* While the shape-shifting and the beheading game are later attributed to the agency of Morgan (2446*ff*), the Green Knight himself here emphatically assumes responsibility for the testing of Gawain in the castle.

2362. *me thynkkes:* either 'you seem to me' or 'it seems to me (that you are)'.

2363. 'the most (*cf.* 137*n*) faultless knight who ever lived (lit. 'walked').'

2364. 'As the pearl in comparison with (*bi*) the white (i.e. dried) pea is of greater value'; *pese* is the old singular form.

2365. *in god fayth:* perhaps more than an exclamation—'in respect of good faith'.

2366. *here:* 'in this respect'; *yow lakked a lyttel* is impersonal: 'a little was lacking to you', i.e. 'you fell short a little'. The construction of *lewté yow wonted* is similar.

2367. *wylyde werke:* probably 'intricate (skilled) workmanship' (i.e. of the girdle); *cf.* 2430–2 and (for the author's statement of Gawain's motives) 2037–40.

2372. *that . . . talked:* '(at) what the man said'.

For care of thy knokke, cowardyse me taght
To acorde me with covetyse, my kynde to forsake: 2380
That is larges and lewté, that longes to knyghtes.
Now am I fawty and falce, and ferde haf ben ever
Of trecherye and untrawthe—bothe bityde sorwe
　　　　And care!
　　　　I biknowe yow, knyght, here stylle,   2385
　　　　Al fawty is my fare.
　　　　Letes me overtake your wylle
　　　　And efte I schal be ware.'

Thenn loghe that other leude and luflyly sayde,
'I halde hit hardily hole, the harme that I hade.   2390
Thou art confessed so clene, beknowen of thy mysses,
And has the penaunce apert of the poynt of myn egge,
I halde the polysed of that plyght and pured as clene
As thou hades never forfeted sythen thou was fyrst borne.
And I gif the, sir, the gurdel that is golde-hemmed;   2395
For hit is grene as my goune, Sir Gawayn, ye maye
Thenk upon this ilke threpe ther thou forth thrynges
Among prynces of prys, and this a pure token
Of the chaunce of the Grene Chapel at chevalrous knyghtes.
And ye schal in this Newe Yer ayayn to my wones   2400
And we schyn revel the remnaunt of this ryche fest

2382ff. 'Now I am sinful (*fawty*) and dishonourable, I who have always been afraid of treachery and dishonesty—may sorrow and care betide both of them.'

2387. 'Let me understand your wish' (i.e. in respect of 'penance'). For both men the scene takes on the character of a chivalric 'confession'; *cf.* 2390*ff*, 2445*n*.

2396-9. 'Because it is green like my gown (tunic), Sir Gawain, you may think about this bout of ours where you go back (lit. 'mingle forth') among noble princes, and this will be (*this:* an ellipsis for 'this is') a perfect (or 'noble') token of the exploit of the Green Chapel in the dwellings of (*at*) chivalrous knights.' Note that it is Gawain (2433*ff*) who stresses the humbling effect of the girdle; the Green Knight evidently has in mind a social scene, like that of 2513-20.

2400. The infinitive 'come' is understood after *schal* 'must'; *ayayn:* 'back'.

2401. *the remnaunt:* probably adverbial, '(for) the remainder'.

Ful bene.'
Ther lathed hym fast the lorde
And sayde, 'With my wyf, I wene,
We schal yow wel acorde,
That was your enmy kene.'   2405

'Nay forsothe,' quoth the segge, and sesed hys helme
And has hit of hendely and the hathel thonkkes,
I haf sojorned sadly—sele yow bytyde,
And He yelde hit yow yare that yarkkes al menskes!   2410
And comaundes me to that cortays, your comlych fere,
Bothe that on and that other, myn honoured ladyes,
That thus hor knyght wyth hor kest han koyntly bigyled.
Bot hit is no ferly thagh a fole madde
And thurgh wyles of wymmen be wonen to sorwe;   2415
For so was Adam in erde with one bygyled,
And Salamon with fele sere, and Samson, eftsones—
Dalyda dalt hym hys wyrde—and Davyth, therafter,
Was blended with Barsabe, that much bale tholed.
Now these were wrathed wyth her wyles, hit were a wynne huge
To luf hom wel and leve hem not, a leude that couthe.   2421
For thes wer forne the freest, that folwed alle the sele
Exellently, of alle thyse other under hevenriche

2408. *has hit of*: 'takes it off'.

2417f. *eftsones, therafter*: 'next' or 'again' (in the succession of items in the list).

2419. *that much bale tholed*: 'who suffered much grief'; qualifies *Davyth* (*cf.* 145–6n). See II Samuel XII, 7–20.

2420–4. 'Since these were troubled by their wiles, it would be a great advantage (*wynne*: 'gain', or possibly 'joy') to love them well and not trust them (*leve*: 'believe'), if a man could (lit. 'for a man who could'). For these were of old (*forne*) the noblest, those who were pre-eminently (*exellently*) favoured by fortune (*sele*) (lit. 'those whom all prosperity followed pre-eminently'), of all those (lit. 'those others') upon earth (*under hevenriche*) who have wandered in mind.' The sense is: 'I have mentioned only the most noteworthy examples of the stupefying influence of women on men.' For the force of *thise other, cf.* 1139n, 1914. For the sense of *mused* 'wandered in mind, doted', *cf.* Gavin Douglas *Aeneid* IV, Prologue, 16: *Your curious thochtis quhat bot musardry* (in a list of love's contrarieties), and the OF, ME *musard* 'dreamer'.

That mused;
And alle thay were biwyled   2425
With wymmen that thay used.
Thagh I be now bigyled,
Me think me burde be excused.

'Bot your gordel,' quoth Gawayn, '—God yow foryelde!—
That wyl I welde wyth guod wylle, not for the wynne golde, 2430
Ne the saynt, ne the sylk, ne the syde pendaundes,
For wele ne for worchyp, ne for the wlonk werkkes;
Bot in syngne of my surfet I schal se hit ofte,
When I ride in renoun remorde to myselven
The faut and the fayntyse of the flesche crabbed,   2435
How tender hit is to entyse teches of fylthe.
And thus, when pryde schal me pryk for prowes of armes,
The loke to this luf-lace schal lethe my hert.
Bot on I wolde yow pray, displeses yow never:
Syn ye be lorde of the yonder londe that I haf lent inne   2440
Wyth yow wyth worschyp—the Wye hit yow yelde
That uphaldes the heven and on hygh sittes—
How norne ye yowre ryght nome, and thenne no more?'
'That schal I telle the truly,' quoth that other thenne:

2425–8. 'And all these were deceived (*biwyled*) by women with whom they had relations. If I now am taken in, it seems to me that I ought to be excused.' The contradiction between this and everything else Gawain says about his own culpability should alert us to the almost jocular tone of this stanza (note especially 2414, 2420*f*). In spite of the reader's first impressions, Gawain's chivalry and social tact are most in evidence here: in order to avoid directly implicating Bertilak's wife in his condemnation of himself he falls back on the ecclesiastical commonplace of the 'eternal Eve'. (*Cf.* Brewer, 1966.)

2431. 'nor for the girdle (itself) nor for the long (*syde* adj.) pendants'. Note the chiasmus, 2430–1: *golde . . . saynt . . . sylk . . . pendaundes.* The speech from 2429 to 2438 is rhetorical in tone; perhaps Gawain is a little inclined to dramatize his predicament.

2436. 'how liable it is to catch (*entyse*) blemishes (*teches*) of sin.' The analogy between sin and disease is a medieval commonplace; *cf.* J. Huizinga, *The Waning of the Middle Ages,* 221.

2438. 'the act of looking at this love-girdle shall humble (*lethe*) my heart.'
2439. *on:* 'one thing'.

'Bertilak de Hautdesert I hat in this londe.   2445
Thurgh myght of Morgne la Faye, that in my hous lenges,
And koyntyse of clergye, bi craftes wel lerned—
The maystrés of Merlyn mony ho has taken,
For ho has dalt drury ful dere sumtyme
With that conable klerk; that knowes alle your knyghtes   2450
         At hame.
    Morgne the goddes
    Therfore hit is hir name;
    Weldes non so hyghe hawtesse
    That ho ne con make ful tame—   2455

'Ho wayned me upon this wyse to your wynne halle
For to assay the surquidré, yif hit soth were
That rennes of the grete renoun of the Rounde Table;
Ho wayned me this wonder your wyttes to reve,
For to haf greved Gaynour and gart hir to dye   2460

2448. has *supplied* (Madden)

2445. *de Hautdesert:* Since the Green Knight is here revealing his everyday name, *Hautdesert* must be the name of his castle rather than another designation of the Green Chapel. On the other hand the introduction of the title ('of the high hermitage') at this point underlines the fact that the Green Knight performs some of the confessional functions of the hermits of the spiritualized French Arthurian *Quest del saint Graal;* see Smithers, 1963.

2446ff. The loose conversational structure of this speech is comparable to that of 1508ff. Sir Bertilak picks up the thread in 2456, after the digression on the fame and history of Morgan.

2447. 'and (her) skill in learning, (she who is) well-instructed in magic arts—she has acquired many of the miraculous powers (*maystrés*) of Merlin, for she has formerly had very intimate love-dealings with that excellent (*conable*) scholar, as all your knights at home know.'

2454f. 'There is no one so exalted in pride (*hawtesse*) whom she cannot humble completely—'

2456. *upon this wyse:* i.e. in his green guise.

2457-61. 'to make trial of your pride, (to see) if (the report) which is current, of the great renown of the Round Table, is true. She sent this marvel to deprive you of your senses, in order to distress Guenevere and cause her to die from terror at that man who spoke in supernatural manner (*gostlych*)'; *me* (2459) has possibly been miscopied from 2456, but can be taken as ethic dative, especially in this position in the line (see 1905n and *cf.* other examples there).

With glopnyng of that ilke gome that gostlych speked
With his hede in his honde bifore the hyghe table.
That is ho that is at home, the auncian lady;
Ho is even thyn aunt, Arthures half-suster,
The duches doghter of Tyntagelle, that dere Uter after   2465
Hade Arthur upon, that athel is nowthe.
Therfore I ethe the, hathel, to com to thyn aunt.
Make myry in my hous: my meny the lovies
And I wol the as wel, wye, bi my faythe,
As any gome under God, for thy grete trauthe.'   2470
And he nikked hym naye, he nolde bi no wayes.
Thay acolen and kyssen and kennen ayther other
To the Prynce of paradise, and parten ryght there
          On coolde.
              Gawayn on blonk ful bene   2475
              To the kynges burgh buskes bolde,
              And the knyght in the enker grene
              Whiderwarde-soever he wolde.

Wylde wayes in the worlde Wowen now rydes
On Gryngolet, that the grace hade geten of his lyve;   2480
Ofte he herbered in house and ofte al theroute,

2461. glopnyng: MS gopnyng;   gome: MS gomen
2472. and kennen *supplied* (Tolkien and Gordon); bikennen, Madden

---

2464. See 110n.

2465f. 'the daughter of the duchess of Tintagel (Igerne), upon whom the noble Uther later begot Arthur, who is now glorious.' The pointed contrast between Arthur's shameful origins (he was born out of wedlock) and present renown recalls one of the themes of the opening stanza of the poem (there in connection with Aeneas and Felix Brutus).

2469f. 'and I bear you as much good will, sir, as (I do) any man on earth, because of your great integrity.'

2471. See 706n, 1045n.

2477f. See 460n.

2479f. 'Gawain, whose life had been reprieved, now rides wild pathways in the world on Gringolet'.

2481. *in house*: 'where he had a roof over his head'.

And mony a venture in vale he venquyst ofte
That I ne tyght at this tyme in tale to remene.
The hurt was hole that he hade hent in his nek
And the blykkande belt he bere theraboute,   2485
Abelef, as a bauderyk, bounden bi his syde,
Loken under his lyfte arme, the lace, with a knot,
In tokenyng he was tane in tech of a faute.
And thus he commes to the court, knyght al in sounde.
Ther wakned wele in that wone when wyst the grete   2490
That gode Gawayn was commen; gayn hit hym thoght.
The kyng kysses the knyght and the quene alce,
And sythen mony syker knyght that soght hym to haylce,
Of his fare that hym frayned; and ferlyly he telles,
Biknowes alle the costes of care that he hade,   2495
The chaunce of the chapel, the chere of the knyght,
The luf of the ladi, the lace at the last.
The nirt in the nek he naked hem schewed
That he laght for his unleuté at the leudes hondes
      For blame.   2500
        He tened when he schulde telle;
        He groned for gref and grame.

2482. he: MS & (Gollancz)

2482f. 'and many times overcame hazards in valleys, which I do not intend at this time to relate (*remene*: recall).' *in vale* is little more than a tag; *cf. in erde*, etc. Gollancz's interpretation of 2482 need not be accepted in its entirety but his emendation (MS *&* to *he*) would seem to be necessary for two reasons: it normalizes the structure in respect of the relative clause (antecedent: *venture*), and it resolves the ambiguity of *venquyst ofte* which (as it stands in the MS) could mean 'was often vanquished'. It is not improbable that the scribe copied the ampersand from the line above, instead of *he*.

2488. 'in order to signify that he had been found guilty of a fault.'

2489. *al in sounde:* 'safe and sound' (perhaps with some reference to his wound; *cf.* 2484).

2490. *the grete:* either 'the prince' (i.e. King Arthur) or 'the nobles'. The latter reading is to be preferred (2491 *him* 'to them') in view of the references to individuals in 2492f.

2494. *and ... telles:* 'and he tells his amazing story'.

2499f. 'which he received at the knight's hands as a reproach (*blame*) for his faithlessness (*unleuté*).'

The blod in his face con melle,
When he hit schulde schewe, for schame.

'Lo! lorde,' quoth the leude, and the lace hondeled,   2505
'This is the bende of this blame I bere in my nek.
This is the lathe and the losse that I laght have
Of couardise and covetyse, that I haf caght thare;
This is the token of untrawthe that I am tan inne.
And I mot nedes hit were wyle I may last;   2510
For mon may hyden his harme bot unhap ne may hit,
For ther hit ones is tachched twynne wil hit never.'
The kyng comfortes the knyght, and alle the court als
Laghen loude therat and luflyly acorden
That lordes and ladis that longed to the Table,   2515
Uche burne of the brotherhede, a bauderyk schulde have,
A bende abelef hym aboute, of a bryght grene,
And that, for sake of that segge, in suete to were.
For that was acorded the renoun of the Rounde Table
And he honoured that hit hade, evermore after,   2520
As hit is breved in the best boke of romaunce.
Thus in Arthurus day this aunter bitidde—
The Brutus bokes therof beres wyttenesse.

2506. in *supplied*; on, Gollancz
2511. mon: MS non (Andrew)

2506–9. 'this (the belt) is the ribbon of this reproof (the scar) which I carry in my neck. This is the injury and the damage which I have obtained because of cowardice and covetousness, which infected me there. This is the token of infidelity in which I have been detected.' Gawain adopts the girdle as the ribbon of an 'order' of shame (contrast 2519*f*). The very fact that he identifies the belt and the scar as twin tokens of his fault makes the passage difficult to construe: *laght* means 'took' in relation to the belt, 'received' in relation to the punishment; the identification becomes complete in *hit* 2510. With *caght*, *cf. entyse* 2436*n*.
    2510. *wyle . . . last:* 'as long as I may live'.
    2511. 'for one may conceal one's offence but one cannot remove it'.
    2519. 'For that was agreed (to be) the glory of the Round Table'.
    2521. *Cf.* 690*n*.
    2523. *Brutus bokes:* 'chronicles of Britain', Brutus being the legendary founder; *cf.* 13, 2524.

Sythen Brutus, the bolde burne, bowed hider fyrst,

After the segge and the asaute was sesed at Troye,   2525

      Iwysse,

    Mony aunteres herebiforne

    Haf fallen suche er this.

    Now that bere the croun of thorne,

    He bryng us to His blysse!   AMEN   2530

2527f. 'many exploits of this kind have happened in times past (*herebiforne* = *er this*).'

HONY SOYT QUI MAL PENCE.

HONY SOYT . . .: the Garter motto appears to have been added to the poem in order to associate it with that order (instituted by Edward III about 1348). Its colour, however, is blue and (despite some similarity of theme in Polydore Vergil's well-known account of its founding) it is not likely that the poet intended any such direct connection.

Glossary

This is a glossary of words which may give difficulty to the reader, and is designed solely for the interpretation of the text. It does not aim to repeat explanations already given in the notes. Normal alphabetical order is observed.

In looking up a word, the reader should first look for the line-reference in question; if this is not recorded, the most common meaning (which is usually entered first without line-references, or with a few references followed by 'etc.') may be assumed to apply.

a *pron. (unstressed)* she, 1281

abelef *adv.* diagonally, 2486, 2517

abode *n.* stay, delay, 687

abof, above(n) *adv. & prep.* above, 184, 2217, *etc.;* upon it, on top, 153, 166, 856; in a higher place, 73; in the place of honour, 112

achaufed *pa.t.* warmed, 883

acheve *v.* obtain, accomplish; **a. to** reach (*cf.* **cheve**)

acole *v.* embrace

acorde *v.* agree; match, 602, 631; reconcile, 2380, 2405; *n.* agreement, 1384

adoun *adv.* down

after *prep., adv. & conj.* after, afterwards, for; along, 218, 1608; to match, 171

afyaunce *n.* trust, 642

agayn *adv.* in reply, in return

aghlich *adj.* fearsome, 136

aght(e) *pa.t.* owned; had, got, 1941

agreved *pp.* overcome (with), 2370

al *conj.* even though, 143; *adv. see* **al(le)**

alce *see* **als(e)**

alder *adj.* older, elder

algate *adv.* anyway, at any rate, 141

al(le) *adv.* everywhere, completely

aloft(e) *prep. & adv.* upon, up, at the top

als(e), alce *adv.* as, 1067; also, as well

alther-grattest *adj.* greatest of all, 1441

alvisch *adj.* other-worldly, 681

amende *v.* improve, 898

anamayld *pp.* enamelled, 169

and *conj.* and, if

anelede *pa.t.* pursued, 723

angardes *n.* of arrogance (arrogant), 681

anious *adj.* troublesome, 535

anyskynnes *adj.* of any kind (at all), 1539

apende *v.* appertain

apert *adj. & adv.* exposed, 154; open(ly), 2392

apparayl *n.* ornamentation, 601

arayed, -de *pp.* prepared

are *adv.* before, 239, 1632, 1891

armes *n.* feats of arms, chivalry, 95, 631(?), 1513, 1541, 2104(?), 2437; armour (and weapons), 204, 281, 567, 590, 2104(?); coat-of-arms, 631(?)

arsoun(e)s *n.* saddle-bows, 171, 602

arwe *adj.* afraid, 241

arwe *v.* be afraid

aryght *adv.* in proper fashion, 1911

as *adv. & conj.* as, like, as if; where, 1004

aske *v.* ask (for); demand, 530, 1327

askes *n.* ashes, 2

askyng *n.* request

asoyled *pa.t.* absolved, 1883

as(s)ay *v.* test

asswythe *adv.* immediately, 1400

astit, -y- *adv.* at once, in a moment, 31, 1210

at(e) *prep. & adv.* at; to, 929, 1671; of, 359 *etc.*; from, 328, 391, 646 1977, *etc.*; according to, 1006, 1546; for, 648

athel *adj.* noble, glorious

at(t)le *v.* intend, 27; pretend, 2263

auen *see* **aune**

auncian *adj.* aged, venerable; *as n.,* 948

aune, auen, awen, owen *adj. & pron.* own

aunter *see* **aventure**

auntered *pa.t.* ventured, risked, 1516

auter *n.* altar, 593

auther *see* **other**

Ave *n.* Ave Maria, 757

aventure, awenture, aunter *n.* strange happening, marvel, 27, *etc.*; exploit, 95, 489

aventurus *adj.* daring, 93

avyse, awyse *v.* devise, 45, 1389; contemplate, 771

awen *see* **aune**

awenture *see* **aventure**

awles *adj.* fearless, 2335

awyse *see* **avyse**

ay *adv.* always, 26, *etc.*; all the time, 562, *etc.*; in each case, 73, 128, 190

ayayn *adv.* back; *prep.* against, 2116; **-es** towards, 971

ayled *pp.* troubled, 438

ayther *adj & pron.* each, both, 939, 1356, 1357, 2180; **ayther o.** each other, 841, 1307, 2472

aywhere *adv.* everywhere

bade *see* **byde**

bald(e)ly *adv.* boldly, vigorously

bale *n.* calamity; grief, 2419

balw(e) *adj.* smooth and rounded

barayne *adj.* barren (not breeding), 1320

barbe *n.* point, 2310

barbican *n.* fortified gateway, 793

bare *adj.* without armour, 277, 290; mere, 2352; *adv.* openly, 465; only, 1066; **-ly** positively, 548

baret *n.* battle, strife; enmity (with God), 752

barne *n.* (a) child, 2320 (MS **burne**)

barred *pp.* decorated with bars, 159, 600

barres *n.* decorative bars, 162

bastel *n.* tower; **b. roves** roofs of towers, 799

batayl *n.* (a) duel, 277

bate *n.* baiting, persistent attacks, 1461

bauderyk *n.* baldric, belt, strap

bawemen *n.* archers, 1564

bay(e) *n.* baying of hounds; defensive stance; **byde (at) the b.,** *or* **in his b.** stand at bay

bayn *adj.* obedient

baythe(n) *v.* agree (to), grant

be *see* **be(ne), bi**

beau sir (my) handsome lord, 1222

becom(e), bed(d)e, begynne *see* **bicum, bid(d)e, bigyn(n)e**

beholde, byholde *v.* (**behelde** *pa.t.,* **bihalden, biholde** *pp.*) behold; *pp.* obliged

beknowe(n), *see* **biknowe**

belde *n.* courage, 650

bele *adj.* gracious, pleasant, 1034

bende *n.* band, ribbon, 2506, 2517

bende *pa.t.* (bent); arched, 305; *pp.* curved (**bi:** in line with), 2224; caused, 2115

bene *adv.* pleasantly, happily

be(ne) *v.* (**was, wer(en)** *pa.t.,* **ben(e)** *pp.*) be

bent *n.* field, battlefield; bank (of stream), 1599; **burne on b.** warrior, 1465, 2148; **bent-felde** hunting field, 1136

ber *n.* beer, 129

berdles *adj.* beardless, 280

bere *v.*, (**ber(e)** *pa.t.*, **born(e)** *pp.*) bear, lift, wear; swing, 2070; keep, 2151; spread, 1819; press, 1860; **b. lyf,** live

beres *n.* bears, 722

best *superl. adj. & adv.* best, 78, 1216, *etc.*; of highest rank, 73, 550, 1325 (nobles); bravest, 259; sturdiest, 2101; **of the b.** from among the best, 38, *etc.*; in the best manner, 889, 1000

best *n.* beast

beten *pa.t.* beat, 1437; *pp.* inlaid, embroidered, 78, 1833, 2028

bette *pp.* kindled, 1368

bever-hued *adj.* the colour of beaver, 845

bi, be, by *prep.* by, beside, according to; against, 2310; *for phrases see also the nouns*, **contray, skyl, sythes,** *etc.*; *conj.* until, 1006; by the time that, 1169; when, 2032; **b. that** *adv.* by that time, 597, 1868; then, 2152; *conj.* by the time that, 443, *etc.*; when, 1678, 1912, 2043

bicum, bicome, be-, by- *v.* become; arrive (at), 460

bid(de), bedde, bede *v.* (**bede** *pa.t.*, **boden** *pp.*) ask, 327, 1089, 2090; command, 344, 370, 1374, 1437, *etc.*; offer, 374, 382, 1824, *etc.*

big *adj.* strong; **-ly** *adv.* powerfully

big(g)e *v.* build

bigog! *interj.* by God!, 390

bigyn(n)e, begynne *v.* (**bygan** *pa.t.*) begin; found, 11

bihalde(n), biholde *see* **beholde**

bihynde *adv.* behind; inferior, 1942

bikenne, by- *v.* (**bikende** *pa.t.*) commend

biknowe, be- *v.* confess, acknowledge

bilive, bylyve *adv.* quickly

biseme *v. impers.* suit, become

bisides *see* **bisyde**

bisied *see* **busy**

bisiness *n.* importunity, 1840

bisyde *prep. & adv.* beside; at his side, 1083; alongside, 1582(?), 2088, 2230; *see also* **lay; bisides, bisydes** *adv.* round about, 76, 856, 2164

bite *v.* (**bot(e)** *pa.t.*) bite

bitidde *see* **bityde**

bit(te), bytte *n.* blade

bitwene *prep.* between; *adv.* at intervals, 611, 791, 795

bityde *v.* (**bitidde** *pa.t.*) happen

blame *n.* blame, reproach, guilt

blande *n.* **in b.** together, 1205

blande *pp.* trimmed, 1931

blasoun *n.* shield, 828

blaunmer, blaunner *n.* ermine, fur

ble(e)aunt *n.* silk (garment)

blenched *pa.t.* dodged

blende, blent *pa.t. & pp.* mingled

blended *pp.* deluded (**with:** by), 2419

blenk(e) *v.* shine

blesse *v.* bless; cross (oneself), 2071

blithe *see* **blythe**

blonk *n.* horse

blowe *v.*[1] blow, bloom, 512

blowe *v.*[2] (**blew, blowed** *pa.t.*) blow

bluk *n.* trunk, torso, 440

blunder *n.* turmoil, strife, 18

blusch *n.* gleam, 520

blusche *v.* look; **-ande** *presp.* flashing, 1819

blycande, blykkande *presp.* shining

blykke *v.* shine, 429

blynne *v.* cease (**of:** from), 2322

blysful *adj.* delightful, 520

blythe, -i- *adj.* glad, happy; bright, lovely, 155, 162; *adv.* happily, 1684; **-ly** *adv.* gaily, happily

bobbaunce *n.* pomp, pride, 9

bobbe *n.* bunch, clump, 206

bode *n.* bidding, 852; offer, 1824

boden *see* **bid(de)**

bo(e)rne *n.* burn, stream

boffet *see* **buffet**

bold(e) *adj.* valiant, 2476; *as n.* valiant men, warriors, 21

bole *n.* trunk, 766

bolne *v.* swell, 512

bonchef *n.* happiness, 1764

bone *n.* boon, request, 327

bonk(k)(e) *n.* hillside; bank, 785, 1571; shore, 700

bor *n.* boar

borde *n.*¹ table, 481

borde *n.*² band (of material), 159, 610

bordes *see* **bo(u)rde**

borelych *adj.* massive, huge

borgh(e), **borne** *see* **burgh(e)**, **bo(e)rne**

bornyst, burnyst *pp.* burnished

bost *n.* clamour, 1448

bot *prep., conj. & adv.* but, except, only; **b. (if)** unless, 716, 1782, *etc.*; **no more b.** only to the extent of, 2312; **never b.** only, 547; **noght b.** only, 1267, completely, 1833

bot(e) *see* **bite**

both(e) *adj., pron. & adv.* both, 111, *etc.*; each, 2070, 2165; as well, 129, *etc.*

bothem *n.* bottom, 2145

botouns *n.* buttons, 220

boun *adj.* ready; setting off, 548

bounden *see* **bynde**

bounté *n.* virtue, merit

bo(u)rde *n. & v.* joke, jest; **bourdyng** *n.* jesting, 1404

boure *n.* bower, bedroom

bout(e) *prep.* without

bowe *v.* go, come

brace *n.* arm-pieces, 582

brach(et)es *n.* hounds

brad *pp.* grilled, 891

brath, brawden *see* **brothe, brayde**

brawen, brawne boar's flesh, meat; **b. of a best** well-fleshed boar, 1631

brayde *v.* (**brayd(e)(n)** *pa.t.*, **brayden, brawden** *pp.*) draw, pull;

take, 621; fling, 2377; gush, 429; *pp.* embroidered, woven, 177, 220, 580, 1833; **b. doun** let down, 2069

braynwod *adj.* maddened

bredden *pa.t.* flourished, multiplied, 21

bredes *n.* boards, 2071

brek(e)(n) *pa.t.* broke; opened, 1333; burst forth, 1764

brem(e) *adj. & adv.* fierce, wild, loud; firmly, 781; **-ly(ch)** *adv.* loudly, fiercely; quickly, 779

brenne *v.* (**brenned** *pa.t.*, **brent, brende,** *pp.*) burn; broil, 1609; *pp. adj.* refined (by fire) *or* burnished, 195

brent *adj.* steep, 2165

bresed *adj.* bristly, 305

brether *n.* brothers(-in-arms), 39

breve *v.* declare, tell; reveal, 1436

brit(t)en *v.* ruin, 2; destroy, 680; cut open, 1339; **b. out** cut up, 1611

brod(e) *adj. & adv.* broad, wide; **ful b.** with eyes wide open, 446

broke *n.* brook

bronde, bront *n.* sword; charred stick, brand, 2

brothe, brath *adj.* fierce; **-ly** *adv.*

broun *adj.* brown; burnished, 426

bruny, bryné *n.* coat of mail

bryddes *n.* birds

brydel *n.* bridle

bryg(g)e *n.* drawbridge

bryghtest *adj.* fairest, 1283

bryné *see* **bruny**

buffet, bo- *n.* blow

bult *see* **bylde**

bur *n.* onslaught, blow; force, 2261

burde *n.* maiden, lady

burde *v. impers.* **me b.** I ought (to)

burgh(e), borgh(e) *n.* castle, city

burn(e), buurne *n.* man, warrior, knight; sir, 1071, *etc.*

burnyst *see* **bornyst**

busk *n.* bush, 182, 1437

busk(ke) *v.* hasten, prepare; dress, 1220

busy *v.* (**bisied** *pa.t.*) stir, 89; *reflex.* bestir oneself, 1066

busyly, bysily *adv.* earnestly

busynes *n.* solicitude, 1986

by *see* **bi**

byde, bide *v.* (**bode, bade** *pa.t.*) stay, wait (for), endure. *See also* **bay(e)**

bygan *see* **bigyn(n)e**

byhode *pa.t.* behoved, 717

byholde, bykenne *see* **beholde, bikenne**

bylde *v.* (**bult** *pa.t.*) build, 509; live, dwell, 25

bylyve *see* **bilive**

bynde *v.* bind; **bounden** *pp.* bound, 192, 2486; lined, 573; adorned, 600, 609, 2028

bysily, bytte *see* **busyly, bitte**

cace, case *n.* affair, 546, 1196; chance, 907; **uche a c.** everything that turned up, 1262

cach(che), kach *v.* (**caght, kaght,** *pa.t. & pp.*) take, seize, 133, 368, 434, 1118, 1305; **c. to,** 2376; receive, obtain, 643, 1011, 1938; catch, 1225; urge on, spur, 1581, 2175; hasten, go, 1794; **c. up** lift, 1185

calle, k- *v.* call (out); **c. of** beg for, ask for, 975, 1882; signal, 1421

can *see* **con**

capados *n.* hood, cape, 186, 572

caple *n.* horse, 2175

care *n.* sorrow, trouble; **c. of** concern for, 2379

care *v.* be concerned

carneles *n.* battlements, 801

carole *n.* courtly ring-dance with singing

carp, karp *n.* talk, conversation

carp(pe) karp *v.* speak, say, talk; **here c.** hear tell, 263

carye, case *see* **cayre, cace**

cast, kest *n.* speech, 1295; stroke, 2298; fastening, 2376; device, trick, 2413

cast, kest *v.* cast; direct, aim, 228, 1901; speak, utter, 64, 249, 2275; arrange, 2242, consider, 1855

cayre, carye, kayre *v.* ride

cemmed *pp.* combed, 188

chace *n.* the chase, 1416; hunt, 1604

charge *v.* charge, 451; put on, 863

charre *v.* turn aside (*reflex.*), 850

charres *n.* business affairs, 1674

chaunce *n.* chance, fortune; **for c. that** whatever, 2132; adventure, exploit, 1081, *etc.*

chauncely *adv.* fortuitously, 778

chaunge *v.* change, exchange. *See* **cher(e)**

chauntré *n.* singing of mass, 63

chef *adj.* chief; **chefly, chevely** *adv.* quickly, especially, first of all

chek(ke) *n.* bad luck; doom, 1857

chelde, chemné *see* **schelde, chymné**

chepen *v.* haggle, 1271

cher(e), schere *n.* face, expression; mien, manner, conduct; cheerfulness, friendliness, 562, 1259, *etc.*; company, 1034; mood, 711*n*, 883; **chaunge c.** look about, 711*n*, 2169

cheryche, -se *v.* welcome, entertain

ches *see* **chose**

cheve *v.* get, 1271, 1390; come, 63; **c. to** reach, 1674; **c. that chaunce** bring it about, 2103

chevely *see* **chef**

chevisaunce, -y-c- *n.* winnings; acquisition, 1939

chose *v.* (**ches, chosen** *pa.t.*, **chosen** *pp.*) choose; perceive, 798; make one's way, go, 451, *etc.* (*also* **c. the gate, waye**); accept, 1838

chylde *n.* (**chylder** *pl.*) child

chymbled *pp.* muffled up, 958

chymné, chemné *n.* fireplace; chimney, 798

chyne *n.* chine, backbone, 1354

clamberande *presp.*, **clambred** *pp.* clustering, crowding

clanly *adv.* completely, 393

clannes *n.* purity, 653

clater *v.* splash, echo; crash, 1722

clene *adj. & adv.* clean, 885; bright, 158, 161, 163, 576, 854, 2017; pure, 1013, 1883, 2393(?); completely, 146, 154, 1298, 2391, 2393(?); neatly, perfectly, 792

clenge *v.* cling; shrink, 505

clepe *v.* call, 1310

cler(e) *adj.* bright, lovely (*& as n.*); pure, 631, 885

clomben *pa.t.* climbed, 2078

close *v.* close, fasten, 572, 1742; enclose, contain, 578, 1298; encircle, 186; **closed fro** free from, 1013

clothe *n.* (table-)cloth; **clothes** (table-)cloths, coverings, 876, 1649; (bed-)clothes, 1184, 2015

clyff(e), k- *n.* crag, hillside

cnoke *v.* strike, 414

cofly promptly, 2011

colde *see* **coolde**

comaunde, cu- command; commend, 2411

comfort *n.* pleasure

comfort *v.* amuse, 1099; console, 2513

comloker,-est *see* **comly(ch)**

comly(ch) *adj.* (**comloker,-est** *compar. & superl.*) comely, fair, fine; *as n.* noble (fair) one, 674, 1755, 1794; **comlyly, comly(che)** *adv.* fittingly, 360, 648, *etc.*; courteously, 1307, *etc.*

com(me), cum *v.* (**com(e)(n)** *pa.t.*, **com(m)en, cum(m)en** *pp.*) come, arrive, go

con *v.* (**cowthe, couth(e)** *pa.t. & pp.*) be able, can, know how (to). *See* **con, can** *auxil. v.*

con, can *auxil. v.* (*orig. fr.* (*be-*)*gan*, confused *w. prec.*) did, 230*n*, 275, 340, 362, 1042, *etc.*; **cowthe** *pa.t. used in same way?*, 2273

constrayne *v.* force, 1496

contray *n.* region, 734; **bi c.** across country, 734

conveye *n.* escort to gate, see off, 596

co(o)lde *adj.* cold; melancholy, 1982; *as n.* (wintry) ground, 2474

coprounes *n.* finials, 797

cors, cource *n.*[1] course (of a meal), 116*n*, 135

cors *n.*[2] body, 1237*n*

corsour *n.* horse, charger, 1583

cort(a)yn *n.* bed-curtain

cortays(e) *adj.* courteous, refined; *as n.* gracious lady, 2411; **-ly** *adv.* graciously

cort-feres *n.* fellow courtiers, 594

corvon *pp.* carved, 797

cosse *n.* kiss

cost *n.* nature, 546; *pl.* qualities, 1272, 1849; manners, 944, 1483; actions, 2360; observances, 750; **c. of care** hardships, 2495

cosyn *n.* cousin (nephew), 372

cote *n.* coat, tunic; coat-armour (*cf.* 586*n*), 637, 2026

cothe *pa.t.* quoth, said

coundue *v.* conduct, 1972

countenance *n.* expression, 335; *pl.* looks, 1659; custom, 100; favour, approval, 1490, 1539

co(u)rtaysy(e) *n.* courtesy, chivalry

couth(e) *see* **con**

couthly *adv.* familiarly, 937

covenaunt, -aunde *n.* agreement, compact; *pl.* conditions

coverto(u)r *n.* caparison (ornamental cloth covering for horse's trappings), 602; counterpane, 855, 1181

covetyse *n.* avarice

cowters *n.* elbow-pieces, 583

cowthe, coynt *see* **con, quaynt**

crabbed *adj.* harsh, 502; perverse, 2435

craft *n.* (display of) skill; *pl.* arts; sports, 1688

crafty *adj.* skilfully made, 572

craftyly *adv.* skilfully, 797

crakkande *presp.* ringing, 1166

crakkyng *n.* blare, 116

crathayn *n.* churl, 1773

crave *v.* ask for; claim, 1384

Crede *n.* Apostle's Creed

cresped *pp.* curled, 188

crevisse *n.* fissure, 2183

cropure, cropore *n.* crupper

croun *n.* crown; top of head, 419, 616

cry(e), kry *n.* cry; blast, 1166

cum(men), cumly *see* **com(me), comly(ch)**

curious *adj.* fine, ornate, 855

dabate *see* **debate**

dalyaunce *n.* courtly conversation

dame *n.* lady, 470; ladies, 1316

dar *v.* (**durst** *pa.t.*) dare

dare *v.* shrink, cower, 315, 2258

daylye, daly *v.* converse, flirt

daynté, dayntye *n.* honour, courtesy; delight (in,) 1889; *pl.* luxuries, delicacies, 121, *etc.*; *adj.* charming, 1253

debate, da- *n.* resistance

debonerté *n.* courtesy, 1273

dece, des *n.* dais

defende *v.* defend; forbid, 1156

dele *v.* (**dalt(en)** *pa.t. & pp.*) deal (out), mete out; perform, 2192; partake of, 1968; converse, 1668; bestow (on), 1266, 1805; **d. un-**

tyghtel behave freely, let oneself go, 1114

delful *adj.* grievous, 560

deliverly *adv.* quickly, nimbly, 2009

delyver *v.* assign, 851; despatch, 1414

deme *v.* think; think fit, 1082; agree, 1089, 1668

denes ax *n.* Danish axe, battle-axe, 2223 (*see* 288*n*)

depaynt(ed) *pp.* painted, portrayed

deprece, deprese *v.*¹ subjugate, 6; press, 1770

deprece *v.*² release, 1219

dere *adj.* (**derrest** *superl.*) dear, 470, 754; costly, precious, 121, 193, 483(?), 571; noble, splendid, 75, 2465; festal, 92, 1047; pleasant, charming, 47, 564, 1012, 1026; intimate, 2449; *as n.* noble man, 678, 928; *superl.* most noble one(s) (Guenevere?), 445; **derrest** *adv.* (?) most nobly, 483

der(e) *n.* deer

dered *pa.t.* hurt, 1460

derely *adv.* courteously, in courtly style; deeply, 1842

derf, derve *adj.* bold, strong, zealous; dreadful, 1047; painful, 558, 564; **-ly** *adv.* boldly, quickly

derne *adj.* confidential, 1012; **-ly** *adv.* secretly, 1188

derve, -ly *see* **derf**

derworthly *adv.* sumptuously, 114

des *see* **dece**

destiné *n.* destiny, fate

devaye *v.* refuse

deve *v.* strike down, 1286

devised *pp.* related, 92

deye, dye *v.* die

dight, dyght *v.* prepare, 1559, 1689, 2223; place, 114; appoint, 295, 678, 1884; *reflex.* direct oneself, 994

dille *adj.* stupid, 1529

dint *see* **dynt**

discever, -cover *v.* reveal

discrye *v.* discern, 81

displese *v. reflex.* be offended, 1839, 2439

disport *n.* pleasure, 1292

dispoyled *pp.* divested, 860

dit *pp.* fastened, 1233

do *v.* do, make; put, 478, 1492; have, cause to (be), 1327; *reflex.* go, 1308; *pp.* finished, 928, 1365

doel *n.* grief, 558

doghty *see* **dughty**

dole *n.* part, 719

dom(e) *n.* judgement, 1216; doom, 1968; right, 295

donkande *presp.* moistening, 519

dor(e) *n.* door

doser *n.* tapestry, backcloth, 478

doted *pp.* demented; frenzied, 1151

doublefelde *adv.* in double helpings, 890

dounes, downes *n.* hills

doute *n.* fear, 246, 442

douth(e) *n.* company

dowelle *v.* dwell, remain

draght *n.* drawbridge, 817

draveled *pa.t.* muttered, 1750

drawe, drowe *v.* (**drow(en)** *pa.t.*, **drawen** *pp.*) draw, pull; shut, 1188, 1233; **d. on lyte (on drye)** hold back, 1031, 1463

drechch *n.* delay, 1972

dres(se) *v.* arrange, 1000, 2033; postition, 75; direct, 445; proceed, 474 (*reflex.*), 1415; get up, 566, 2009; **upon grounde hym dresses** takes his stand, 417

drey *see* **drye**

driven, drof *see* **dryve**

drow(en) *see* **drawe**

drowping *n.* slumber, heaviness

drury(e) *n.* love, love-making; love-token, 1805, 2033

drye, drey *adj. & adv.* (**-ly** *adv.*) straight, unmoved, 335; long-suffering, 724; incessant, 1460,

(**-ly**), 1026; deep, 1750; heavily, 2263; **drawe on d.** detain, 1031

drye *v.* endure

Dryghtyn *n.* God, the Lord

dryve *v.* (**drof** *pa.t.*, **driven, -y-** *pa.t. & pp.*) drive; hurtle, 1151, 2263; pour (in), 121; strike, 389; pass (time), 1176, 1468; make, 558, 1020; **d. to** press against, 786, 1999; make for, 222

dubbed *pp.* adorned, 75, 193; arrayed, 571

dughty, -o- *adj.* brave; *as n.*, 2334

dulful *adj.* grievous, 1517

dunt *see* **dynt**

dut *n.* merriment, 1020

dut(te) *pa.t.* feared

dyght *see* **dight**

dyn *n.* noise

dynges *pres.* 3 *sg.* strikes, 2105

dyngne *adj.* worthy, 1316

dynt, dint, dunt(e) *n.* blow

eft(e) *adv.* again; next time, 898, 2388; then again, 641

eft(er)sones *adv.* again

egge *n.* edge, 212; weapon, 2392

eke *adv.* also, 90, 1741

elde(e) age, time

elles *adv. & conj.* besides, else; otherwise, 1082; provided that, 295

em(e) *n.* uncle

enbelyse *v.* adorn, grace

enbrauded, -aw-, -en *pp.* embroidered, 78, *etc.*

enfoubled *pp.* swathed, 959

enker *adv. or adj.* pure, intense

enn(o)urned *pp.* adorned; set

enquest *n.* question, 1056

entayled *pp.* embroidered, 612

er(a)nd(e) *n.* errand, mission, business

erbes *n.* plants

erde *n.* land, 1544, 1808; **in e.** on earth, 2416; (*as intensive*) real-life, 27; truly, 140; the best on earth, 881

er(e) *prep.*, *conj.* & *adv.* before; **e. this** until now

ernd(e) *see* **er(a)nd(e)**

erraunt *adj.* travelling, questing, 810

ese *n.* ease, pleasure

etayn *n.* giant

ete *v.* (**et(t)e** *pa.t.*) eat

ethe *adj.* easy, 676

ethe *v.* entreat

evel *n.* unpleasantness, 1552

even *adj.* & *adv.* straight, right; quits, 1641; actually, 2464

even *n.* eve (*i.e.* day before), 734, 1669

ever *adv.* ever, continually

evesed *pp.* clipped, 184

expoun *v.* expound; describe, 209; utter, 1506

fade *adj.* bold(?), 149

fage *n.* deceit; **no f.** in truth, 531

fale *adj.* brownish, dun, 728

falle *v.* fall; bend down suddenly, 1758; rush, 1425, 1702; happen, 23, *etc.*; happen to be, 483; betide, 2378; befit, 358, 890, 1303, 1358

falssyng *n.* deception, 2378

fange, fonge *v.* (**fonge(d)** *pp.*) take, get, receive; welcome, 816, *etc.*

fantoum *n.* apparition, 240

farand *adj.* splendid, 101

fare *n.* journey, fortune; track, 1703; behaviour, 1116, 2386; food, 694; celebration, 537

fare *v.* (**ferde(n)** *pa.t.*, **faren** *pp.*) go, travel; behave, bear oneself

faste *adj.* firm, binding, 1636

fast(e) *adv.* securely, 782; earnestly, insistently, 1042, 2403; swiftly, 1425, 1908, *etc.*

faut(e) *n.* fault, offence; sinfulness, 2435

fautles *adj.* (**-lest** *superl.*) faultless, perfect

fax *n.* hair, 181

fayl(y) *v.* fail, fall short; lack, 278

fayn *adj.* glad

fayntyse *n.* fallibility, deceitfulness, 2435

fayr(e) *adj.* fair, lovely; courteous, 1116; **the fayrer** the upper hand, 99; *adv.* humbly, courteously, gracefully, neatly

fayrye *n.* the supernatural, 240

fayth(e) *n.* (word of) honour

faythely *adv.* truly, 1636

faythful *adj.* trustworthy

fech *v.* (**fette** *pp.*) fetch, receive

fe(e)rsly *adv.* fiercely, proudly

felawschyp *n.* brotherly love, 652; company, 2151

felde *v.* fold, embrace, 841

fel(l)e *adj.* & *pron.* many; **feler** *compar.*; **felefolde** many times over, 1545

felle *adj.* fierce, daring; terrible, 2222; *as n.* fierce animal, 1585; **felly** *adv.* 2302

felle *n.*[1] fell, hill, 723

felle *n.*[2] fur, skin

Fende *n.* Devil

ferde *pa.t.* & *pp.* feared, afraid; **for f.** 2130, 2272

ferde(n) *see* **fare**

fere *adj.* proud, dignified, 103

fere *n.*[1] panoply, 267

fere *n.*[2] companion; wife, 2411; equal, 676

ferk(ke) *v.* go (quickly), ride, pass; **f. hym up** bestirs himself, 2013

ferly *adj.* exceptional, 716 (*or n.*); *adv.* (*also* **ferlyly**) marvellously, exceedingly, 388, *etc.*; *n.* marvel, 23, 2414

fer(re) *adv.* far; **fyrre, fire** *compar.* further, moreover

fersly *see* **fe(e)rsly**

fest *n.* festival; feast, 894

festned *pp.* confirmed

fetled *pp.* bound, fastened, 656

fetly *adv.* gracefully, neatly, 1758

fetures *n.* features, parts (of body), 145, 1761

feye *adj.* doomed, dead, 1067

fildore *n.* gold thread, 189

fire *see* **fer(re)**

flagh(e) *pa.t.* fled, 2274, 2276n

flat *n.* lowlands, 507

flaw(e) *pa.t.* flew, 459, 2276n

flete *pa.t.*, **floten** *pp.* flew, 1566; having drifted, 714

flet(te) *n.* floor; **upon (on this) f.** in (this) hall

flod(e) *n.* stream; **French f.** English Channel, 13

flokked in *pa.t.* assembled, 1323

flone *n.* arrow

flosche *n.* pool, 1430

floten *see* **flete**

fnast(ed) *pa.t.* snorted, panted

foch(che) *v.* take

folde *n.* earth; ground, 422; land, 23; **upon f.** on earth, living, 196, *etc.*; **forme . . . upon f.** very first, 2373

folde *v.* (**folden** *pp.*) fold; pack up, 1363; wrap, 959; **f. in** plait, 189; match, 499; assign, 359; pledge, 1783

fole *n.*1 horse

fole *n.*2 fool, 2414

folé, foly *n.* folly

folwe *v.* follow, pursue; **folwande** *presp.* matching, 859; in proportion(?), 145n

fonde *v.* try; tempt, 1549

fonde, fonge *see* **fynde, fange**

foo *adj.* wicked, 1430; *adv.*, 2326

foo *n.* foe, 716

for *conj.* for, because; but(?), 147n

for *prep.* for, because of; before, 965, 1822; in spite of, 1854, 2132, 2251

forbe *prep.* beyond, 652

forfaren *pp.* headed off, 1895

forfeted *pa.t.* transgressed, 2394

forlondes *n.* headlands, *or* low-lying lands near the sea, 699

forme *adj.* first, 2373; *as n.* beginning, 499

forme *see* **fo(u)rme**

forred, furred *adj.* lined (with fur)

forsake *v.* refuse, 1826, 1846; deny, 475, 2380

forsothe *adv.* indeed, in truth

forst *n.* frost, 1694

forth(e) *n.* ford

forthi, forthy *conj.* therefore

forward(e) *n.* agreement; *pl.* terms

forwondered *adj.* astonished, 1660

foryate *pa.t.*, **foryeten** *pp.* forgot(ten)

foryelde *v.* recompense

fot(e) *n.* (**fote(s), fete** *pl.*) foot

fotte *v.* receive, 451

foule, fowle *adj.* ugly, 717; poor, 1329, 1944; *as n.* evil, 2378

founde *v.* hasten, go, come

fourches *n.* legs, haunches, 1357

fo(u)rme *n.* shape, figure, outward appearance, 145n; manner, 1295, 2130

fowle *see* **foule**

foyne *v.* strike at, 428

foysoun *n.* abundance, 122

fraunchis(e) *n.* liberality, generosity

frayn *v.* ask; put to test, 489, 1549

frayst *v.* (**frayst(ed)** *pp.*) ask (for), seek; try, test, 503, 1679

fre *adj.* noble; *as n.* gracious lady, 1545, 1549, 1783; **-ly** *adv.* graciously

frek(e) *n.* warrior, man, knight

fremedly *adv.* as a stranger, 714

frenges *n.* fringes, 598

frenkysch fare refined manners, 1116

fres *pa.t.* froze, 728

fresch *adj.* bright, 2019; **the fresche** fresh food, 122; **freschly** *adv.* eagerly, 1294

fro *conj.* after, 8, 62

frounse *v.* crease, pucker, 2306

frount *n.* forehead, 959

fryth *n.* wood

F

ful *adj. & adv.* full, 44, 2005; fully very, quite, 41, 146, *etc.*

fust *n.* fist, hand, 391

fuyt, fute *n.* trail

fyched *pp. or pa.t.* fixed, established, 659

fyed *pa.t.* joined exactly (to their towers), 796

fyked *pa.t.* flinched, 2274

fylle *v.* carry out

fylthe *n.* sinfulness

fynde *v.* (**fonde, founden** *pa.t.*, **f(o)unde(n)** *pp.*) find; **fonde** *pa. subj.* would find, 1875

fyn(e) *adj. & adv.* fine, perfect(ly), complete(ly); *also* **fynly**, 1391

fynisment *n.* end, 499

fyr(e), fire *n.* fire, sparks

fyrre *see* **fer(re)**

fyrst *adj. & adv.* first; at first, 2227; **on f.** first, 9, 1477, 1934; in the beginning, 301, 491, 528, 2019; *as n.* first day, 1072 (*cf.* 491)

fyskes *v.* scampers, 1704

gafe *see* **gif**

game, gamnes *see* **gomen**

garysoun *n.* treasure; trophy, 1807

garytes *n.* watch-towers, 791

gast *adj.* afraid, 325

gate *n.* road, way (*cf.* **yate**); **bi g.** on the way, 696; **haf the g.** pass, 1154. *See also* **chose**

gaudi *n.* beadwork (?), dye(?), 167

gay(e) *adj.* lovely, handsome, elegant; *as n.* fair lady, 970, 1213, 1822; elegant knight, 2035; **gayly** *adv.* elegantly, 598, 1760

gayn *adj. & adv.* obedient *or* well-suited, 178; good, 1241, 2491; directly, 1621; **at the gaynest** most directly, 1973

gayn(e) *v.* serve, 584; enrich, 1829

geder(e) *v.* gather, assemble; lift up,

heave up, 421, 2260; pick up (path), 2160; **g. to** spur at, 777

gef *see* **gif**

gentyle, jentyle *adj.* noble; kind, 774; *as n.* noble man, 542

gere *n.* armour; apparatus, 2205; *pl.* bedclothes, 1470

gere *v.* dress, clothe; array, 791; make, 1832

geserne *see* **giserne**

get *n.* winning(s), 1638

gete *v.* (**gete(n)** *pa.t.*, **geten** *pp.*) get, capture; fetch, 1625

gif *v.* (**gef, gafe** *pa.t.*, **geven** *pp.*) give; bestow upon, wish; *reflex.* give in, 1861

gift(e), gyft *n.* gift; **of my g.** as a gift from me, 288, 1799, 1807

gilt *see* **gyld**

giserne, geserne *n.* battle-axe

glad *adj.* affable, 1926; **-ly** *adv.* gladly, cheerfully; **-loker** *compar.* with greater pleasure, 1064

gla(u)m *n.* din, noise

glaver *n.* babble, 1426

gle *n.* sound of revelry, music, *etc.*, 46, 1652; joy, 1536

glede(s) *n.* red-hot embers

glem *n.* shining, brightness

glemered *pa.t.* shone, glimmered, 172

glent *n.* glance, 1290

glent *pa.t.* glanced, 476; flinched, 2292; sprang, 1652; sparkled, glinted, 82, 172, 569, 604, 2039

glod *see* **glyde**

glode *n.* bright patch, 2181; **on g.** in a flash, 2266

glowande *presp.* shining, 236

glyde *v.* (**glod** *pa.t*) glide, come, go

glyght *pa.t.* looked

go *v.* go, walk

god(e) *n.* good, profit; goodness; *pl.* goods

god(e) *see* **go(u)d(e)**

god(e)mon *n.* householder, landlord

godly *see* go(u)d(e)

godlych *adj.* goodly, fine, 584

gome *n.* man, knight

gomen, game(n) *n.* (gommes, gamnes *pl.*) game, pleasure; merriment, 1376, 1933; sport (hunting), 1319, 1894; catch, 1635; process, 661; gomenly *adv.* happily, 1079

gorde *pp. see* gurde

gorde, -y- *v.* strike, spur

gorger *n.* neckerchief, wimple, 957

go(u)d(e) *adj.* good, worthy; go(u)dly *adv.* graciously, generously

goules, gowles *n.* gules, heraldic red

grame *n.* vexation, 2502

grattest *see* gret(e)

gra(u)nte *v.* grant; agree (to) gra(u)nt mercy, -i many (*lit.* great) thanks

graye *v.* become grey, 527

grayth(e) *adj.* ready; -ly *adv.* properly; readily, 1683; comfortably, 876, 1470

graythe *v.* prepare, 876, 2259; adorn, dress, 151, 666, 2014; install, seat, 74, 109.

grece, gres *n.* fat, flesh; skin, 2313

grem(e) *n.* wrath, vexation

grene *adj. & n.* green; *as n.* that g. the green man, 464; grener *compar.*

grenne *v.* grin, smile, 464

gres(se) *n.* grass. *See also* grece

gret *pa.t.* greeted

gret(e), grett *adj.* (grattest *superl.*) big, great; magnificent, 2014; boastful, 312, 325; grattest of gres fattest, 1326; grattest in grene greenest, 207

grete *v.* weep, 2157

greve *v.* trouble, distress, 1070, 2460; *intrans.* be troubled

greve *n.*¹ wood, thicket

greves *n.*² greaves (armour), 575

grome *n.* man, retainer

gronyed *pa.t.* snorted, 1442

ground *n.* ground; field, 508; land, region, 705; (up)on g. on earth, on the ground

gruchyng *presp.* ill-humouredly, 2126

gryed *pa.t.* shuddered, 2370

gryndel *adj.* fierce, angry; -ly *adv.*

gryndellayk *n.* ferocity, 312

Gryngolet *n.* (Gawain's horse)

gurde, gorde *pp.* girt

gyft *see* gift(e)

gyld, gilt *pp.* gilded

gyng *n.* company, 225

gyrde *see* gorde

habbes *see* have

hadet *pp.* beheaded (with: by), 681

haf(e) *see* have

halawed *see* halowe

halce, hals *n.* neck

halche *v.* embrace, salute, 939; enclose, 185; loop around, 218; fasten, 1852, 1613; interlace, 657

halde, holde *v.* (helde *pa.t.*, halden, holden *pp.*) hold, 436, *etc.*; contain, 124; possess, 627; keep, 698, 1043, 1158, 1677, 2129, 2297, *etc.*; govern, 53, 904, 1256, 2057; consider, 28, 259, 285, *etc.*; *pp.* bound, 1040; beholden, 1828; h. alofte keep up, 1125

hale, halle *v.* (hal(l)ed, *pa.t.*, halet *pp.*) draw, 1338; shoot (arrow), 1455; hasten, rush, 136, 458, 1049; sweep, 788

half, halve *n., adj. & adv.* half; side, 649, *etc.*; upon Godes h. for God's sake, in God's name

hal(le) *n.* hall, castle

halme *n.* handle

halowe, -awe *v.* shout (at)

halowing *n.* shouting, 1602

hals, halve *see* halce, half

halwes *n.* saints, 2122

han *see* **have**

hanselle *see* **hondeselle**

hap *n.* good fortune, happiness, 48

hapnest *adj.* most fortunate, 56

happe *v.* fasten, 655; wrap, 864; imprison, 1224

harden *v.* encourage

hardily *adv.* assuredly, 2390

hardy *adj.* bold

harled *pp.* entwined, 744

harme *n.* injury, offence

harnays *n.* armour, accoutrements

harnayst *pp.* armed, accoutred, 592

hasel *n.* hazel, 744

hasp(p)e *v.* buckle; clasp, 1388

hast(e) *n.* speed; **in (with) h.** quickly

hastlettez pig's offal, 1612

hasty *adj.* urgent, 1051; **-ily** *adv.* quickly

hathel *n.* man, knight; Lord, 2056

hat(te) *v.* (**-s** *pres.* 2 *sg.*) be called

hauberghe, hawbergh *n.* tunic of mail

have, haf(e) *v.* (**habbe(s), has, haven, haf, han,** *pres.*) have; take, 773, 1612, 1944, 2247, 2408; draw, 1051; accept, 1980; put, 1446; reach, 700; beget, 2466; **haf at the** take guard, 2288

havilounes *v.* doubles back, 1708

hawbergh *see* **hauberghe**

haylse, haylce *v.* greet

hed(e) *n.* head

hedles *adj.* headless, 438

hef *see* **heve**

heghe, heght *see* **high(e), hyght**

helde *v.* turn, come, go; sink, 1321; bow, 972, 1104

helde *see* **halde**

helder *compar. adv.* **never the h.** no more (for that), 376, 430

heles *n.* heels (spurs)

helme *n.* helmet

hem, hom *pron.* (to, for) them, 99, 301, *etc.*; themselves (*reflex.*), 1130, 1254, *etc.*; **hemself** (it pleased) them, 976; *reflex.*, 1085. *See also* **him**

heme *adj.* neat, 157; **hemely** *adv.* closely, 1852

hende *adj.* noble, gracious, courteous; *as n.* gracious knight, lady, 827, *etc.* **-ly** *adv.*

hendelayk *n.* courtesy, 1228

hendly *see* **hende**

heng(e) *v.* hang

henne *adv.* hence, 1078

hent *v.* take, receive, seize

hepes *n.* **(up)on h.** in a heap

her, hor *adj.* their, 54, 130, *etc.*

her, hir *adj. & pron.* (to, for) her, 76, 647, 955, 1002, *etc.*; herself (*reflex.*), 1193, 1735, *etc.*

herber *n.* lodging; *v.* lodge

here *n.*[1] warrior-band, 59; army, 2271

here *n.*[2] hair, 180, *etc.*

here *v.* (**herande** *presp.*, **herd(e)** *pa.t.*) hear

heredmen *n.* retainers, 302

herinne *adv.* in this place, 300

herk(k)en *v.* listen (to), hear

herle *n.* strand, 190

herre *see* **high(e)**

hersum *adj.* glorious, festal, 932

Hervest *n.* Autumn, 521

hes *n.* promise, 1090

hest *n.* command, bidding

hete *n. & v.* (**hyght** *pa.t.*, **hette** *pa.t. & pp.*) promise

hethen *adv.* hence, away

het(t)erly *adv.* fiercely, suddenly

hevé, hevy *adj.* heavy; serious, 496

heve *v.* (**hef** *pa.t.*) lift, raise; rise, 120

heven *v.* raise, 349

hewe, hue *n.* hue, colour

hewe *v.* cut; **hewen** *pp.* made, cut

high(e), heghe, hygh(e) *adj. & adv.*
(**herre** *compar.*) high, tall, 137, 281,
etc.; noble, 5, 57, 222, *etc.*; proudly,
349, 1417; solemn, important, 932,
1051; mature, 844; loud, 1165; **on
(ful) h.** loudly, aloud, 67, 307, 468,
1602; **upon h.** to the highest
degree, 48; **the h.** *sc.* ground, 1152,
etc.; **h. and lowe** great and small,
302, 1040; **-ly** *adv.* solemnly; up
on end, 1587

highlich *adj.* splendid, 183

hightly *adv.* fitly; **h. bisemes** is
right and proper, 1612

hil(le) *n.* hill, (castle-)mound; **on h.**
in (any) castle(?), 59 (*but cf.* 2271)

him, hym *pron.* him; them, 49,
1423, 1684(?), 1897, 2491 (*also* **hem,
hom**)

hit, hyt *pron.* it; **h. ar(n)** there are,
280, 1251

hit(te) *v.* hit, strike; jump, fall, 427

ho *pron.* she

hod(e) *n.*[1] hood, 155, *etc.*

hode *n.*[2] order of knighthood, 2297

hoge, huge *n.* huge

hoghes *n.* hocks, 1357

holde *n.* stronghold, 771; grasp, 1252

holde *see* **halde**

holde(ly) *adv.* carefully, faithfully

hol(l)e *adj.* whole; healed, 2484;
amended, 2390; **thi hert h.** all
your courage, 2296; **holly** *adv.*
completely

holt *n.* wood

holtwodes *n.* woods, 742

holyn *n.* holly, 206

hom *see* **hem**

homered *pa.t.* (hammered), struck,
2311

hond(e) *n.* hand; **out of h.** at once

hondeselle, hanselle *n.* (*collect.*) New
Year's presents, gratuities, 66;
omen, present (*iron.*), 491

hone *n.* delay, 1285

hoo! *interj.* stop!, 2330

hope *v.* think, believe; **h. of** expect,
2308

hor *see* **her**

hore *adj.* grey (with frost), 743

hors(s)(e), horce *n.* horse; horse's,
180, *etc.*

(h)ostel *n.* house; **bone h.** good
lodging, 776

hoved *pa.t.* paused, tarried

hoves *n.* hoofs, 459

hunt(e) *n.* huntsman

hye *n.* haste; **in h.** suddenly, 245

hy(e), hie *v.* hie, hurry

hygh(e) *see* **high(e)**

hyghe! *interj.* look out!, 1445

hyght, heght *n.* height; **upon h.**
towering, 332; aloft, 421

hyght *see* **hete**

hymself, hymselven, his- *pron.*
(*refl. & emph.*) him, himself; **with
h.** with him, 113 (*i.e.* Baldwin), 226

hypped *pa.t.* vaulted, 2232; **h. ayayn**
bounced back, 1459

hyt *see* **hit**

iche *see* **uch(e)**

iisseikkles *n.* icicles, 732

ilk(e) *adj. & pron.* same, very; **that i.**
the same; **of that i.** to match

ille *adv.* badly, amiss

ilyche *adv.* equally; **i.ful** kept up in
full, 44

inmyddes *prep. & adv.* amongst, 167;
in the middle (of), 1004, 1932

innermore *adv.* farther in, 794

innmelle *adv.* in the midst (of them),
1451

in(n)ogh(e), in(n)ow(e) *adj. & adv.*
enough, 404, *etc.*; many, in plenty,
77, 219, 514, *etc.*; very, 289, 803
(*iron.*?), 888

inore *adj.* inner, 649

inwyth *prep. & adv.* within

iwys(se), iwyis *adv.* indeed

jape *n.* jest, joke
jentyle *see* **gentyle**
joly *adj.* lively, 86; **jolilé** *adv.* gallantly, 42
joyfnes *n.* youth, 86
juste *v.* joust, 42; **justyng** *n.* jousting, 97.

karp *see* **carp**
kavelacion, c- *n.* argument, objection
kay *adj.* left, 422
kayre *see* **cayre**
kene *adj.* bold, brave; zealous, 482; bitter, 2406; **kenly** *adv.* eagerly, 1048; keenly, bitterly 2001
kenne *v.* (**kende** *pa.t.*) teach, 1484, 1489; commend, 2067, 2472
kepe *v.* keep, hold, possess; preserve, 2015, 2298; await, 1312; care, 546, 2142; take care, 372; attend to, 1688
kest(en) *see* **cast** *n. & v.*
kever *v.* manage (to); recover, 1755; find, get, 1221, 1254; give, 1539; come, 2221
klyf(fe) *see* **clyff(e)**
knape *n.* fellow, 2136
knarre *n.* rock, crag
knot *n.* knot; wooded mound
know(e) *v.* know, acknowledge; observe, 1272
knyghtly *adv.* in courtly manner, 974; **-ly** *adj.* courtly, 1511
knyt, knit(ten) *pa.t. & pp.* tied, 1331, 1831; agreed on, 1642; woven, 1849
koynt *see* **quaynt**
kyd(de) *pp. & adj.* (made) known, 263(?), 1520; behaved (towards), 775, 2340; renowned, 51, 263(?)
kyn *n.* kinds (of)
kynde *adj.* proper, courtly, 473; **kyndely** properly, fittingly, 135
kynde *n.* nature, true character; race, offspring, 5; **the worldes k.** mankind, 261

kyrf *n.* blow, 372
kyrtel *n.* gown, 1831
kyth *n.* land, country

lace *n.* cord, 217; belt, 1830, *etc.*
lach(che) *v.* (**laght, leghten** *pa.t.*) catch, seize, take, 127, 234, *etc.*; receive, 2499, 2507, *etc.*; **laght** *pp.* drawn back, 156; **l. leve** take leave, 595, *etc.*
lachet *n.* loop
lad(de), laft, laght *see* **lede, leve, lach(che)**
lakked *v.* disparaged, 1250
lappe *n.* flap, fold
lappe *v.* embrace, 973; *pp.* wrapped, 217, enclosed, 575
large *adj.* broad
larges(se) *n.* width, 1627; liberality, 2381
lasse *compar. adj. & adv.* (**lest** *superl.*) smaller, less, 87, *etc.*
lassen *v.* lessen, diminish, 1800
last *pa.t.* lasted, 1665
lathed *pa.t.* invited, 2403
lauce(n), -us-, -ws- *v.* loosen, break, undo; utter, 1212, 1766, 2124
launce *v.* shoot, gallop
launde *n.* glade, field, grassy plain
lawe *n.*[1] mound, hillock
lawe *n.*[2] style, 790; **bi l.** formally, 1643
lay *v.* lay, 97, *etc.*; bestow upon, 1480; **l. hym bysyde** turn aside, parry, 1777; **l. up** put away, 1874
layk *n.* game, fun; holiday, 1023
layke *v.* play, amuse oneself
laykyng *n.* playing, 472
layne *v.* conceal; **l. yow (me)** keep your (my) secret
layt(e) *v.* seek
lede, leude, lude *n.* man, knight, prince, 98, *etc.*; sir, 449, *etc.*; (*collective*) people, 833, 1113, 1124; **leudles** *adj.* companionless

lede v. (**lad(de)** *pa.t.*) lead; pursue, 1894; live, experience, 1927, 2058

lee n. shelter, castle

lef, leve adj. (**lever** *compar.* **levest** *superl.*) beloved, dear, 1133, *etc.*; delightful, pleasant, 49, 909, 1111; **that lever wer** *impers.* = who would rather, 1251

leg(g)e adj. liege, sovereign

leghten, leke *see* **lach(che), louke**

lel(e) adj. loyal, faithful, true; **lelly** adv., 449, *etc.*

leme v. shine

lende v. (**lent** *pa.t.*) approach, 971; go, 1319; dwell, remain, 1100, *etc.*

leng(e) v. stay; **hym l.** let him stay, 1893; *pp.* persuaded to stay, 1683

lenger *see* **long(e)**

len(k)the n. length; **on l.** afar, for a long time

lent *see* **lende**

Lentoun n. Lent, 502

lepe v. (**lopen** *pp.*) leap, run; gallop, 2154 (*reflex.*)

lere n.[1] ligature, 1334

lere, lyre n.[2] cheek, face, 318, 943, 2228; flesh, 418; coat, 2050

lese v. (**lost** *pp.*) lose

lest *see* **lasse**

let(t)(e) v.[1] let allow; utter, speak, 1086, 1206; behave, pretend, 1190, *etc.*; cause, 1084; **l. se** show, 299, 414

lette v.[2] hinder, dissuade, 1672, 2142, 2303

leude, leudles *see* **lede**

leve n. leave; leave-taking, 1288

leve v.[1] allow, 98

leve v.[2] (**laft** *pa.t.*) leave; leave off, 1502; relinquish, 369; omit, 2030

leve v.[3] believe, 1784, 2128, 2421

leve v.[4] live, 1035, 1544

leve(st) *see* **lef**

lewed adj. uninstructed, 1528

lewté n. loyalty, good faith

ley *see* **lye**

lif, lyf, lyve n. life; person, 1780; **(up)on l.** alive, on earth; indeed, 2095; **l. haden** lived, 52

light(e) *see* **lyght(e)**

like, lyke v. like, 694; please, 87, *etc.*; *impers.* it pleases (him, *etc.*), 289, *etc.*; **liked** was pleased, 893; **l. ille** displease, 346

lis *see* **lye**

lithernes n. viciousness, 1627

lode n. train; **on (in his) l.** with her (him), in train

lodly adv. with a show of repugnance

lofden *see* **luf**

loft(e) n. upper room; **(up)on l.** aloft, up

loghe, lowe adj. & adv. low; **on l.** down, 1373; **-ly** humbly

loghe *pa.t.* laughed, 2389

loke v. look, watch, appear; take care, 448; guard, 2239

loken *see* **louke**

lome n. tool, weapon, 2309

londe n. land, 411, *etc.*; meadows, 1561; **in l.** on earth, in the land, 35, 486, *etc.*

long(e) adj. & adv. long, 139, *etc.*; adv. a long time, 36, 88, *etc.*; **lenger** *compar.*, 1043, *etc.*

longe v. belong, pertain (to)

longynge n. anxiety, 540

lopen *see* **lepe**

lord(e) n. lord; husband, 1231, *etc.*

los n. renown

lote n. speech, word, sound; echoes, 119; clamour, 1917; voice, 244, 1623

lothe, lathe n. injury, 2507; **withouten l.** without offence, ungrudged

louke, lowke v. (**leke, louked** *pa.t.*, **loken** *pp.*) shut, 2007; *intrans.* fasten, 217, 628, *etc.*; *pp.* enclosed, enshrined *or* linked, 35; framed, 765

loupe *n.*[1] loop, 591
loupe *n.*[2] loop-hole, 792
loute *v.* (**lut(te)** *pa.t. & pp.*) bow, bend; come, go, 833, 933; defer (to) 248
louve, lowe *v.* praise; be praised, 1399
lovelokkest, lovely(ch), lovy(e), *etc. see* **lufly(ch), luf**
lowande *presp.* shining, brilliant
lowe *see* **loghe, louve**
lowke, lude *see* **louke, lede**
luf *n.* love, affection, friendship; wooing, 1733, 1810, 2497
luf, lovy(e) *v.* (**lofden** *pa.t.pl.*) love; feel inclined, like, 126
luf-laghyng *n.* flirtatious wit, 1777
lufly(ch), lovely(ch) *adj.* (**loveloker** *compar.*, **lovelokkest, luflyest** *superl.*) gracious, courteous, beautiful, comely, 38, *etc.*; *also iron.*, 433 (precious), *etc.*; l. loke look of love, 1480; *adv.* (*also* **luflyly**) courteously, in friendly manner, 369, 595, 981, *etc.*; kindly, 254; gladly, 1606
lur *n.* loss; penalty, 1284, 1682
lurk(k)e *v.* laze, doze, 1180; *pp.* with eyes closed, 1195
lye *v.* (**lyges, lys, lis** *pres. 3 sg.*, **lay, ley** *pa.t.*) lie; be in residence, 37; stay in bed, 88
lyft(e) *adj.* left
lyfte *n.* heaven, 1256
lyft(e) *pa.t. & pp.* lifted, raised
lyges *see* **lye**
lyght *adj.* active, energetic, 87, 1119, 1464; swift(ly), 199; **set at l.** think lightly of, 1250; **lyghtly** *adv.* swiftly, 292, 328, 423, *etc.*; easily, 1299
lyght *n.* first light, dawn, 1675
lyght(e), light(e) *v.* dismount, come down; *pa.t.*, 822; *pp.*, 1924
lyghtly *adj.* brilliant, dazzling, 608

lyk *v.* taste, 968
lyke *adj.* similar, 187; *as n.* the same, 498
lykkerwys *adj.* delicious, 968
lym(m)e *n.* limb
lymp(e) *v.* happen, befall
lynde *n.*[1] tree
lyndes *n.*[2] loins, 139
lyre *see* **lere**
lys *see* **lye**
lyst(e) *v.* it pleases, it pleased
lystyly *adv.* cunningly, cleverly
lyte *adj.* little; *pl.* few, 701
lyte *n.*, **on l.** in delay, hesitation
lut(te) *see* **loute**

mace *see* **make**
mach *v.* match, 282
madde *v.* behave stupidly, 2414
maghtyly *adv.* forcibly
make *v.* (**mace, mas** *pres. 3 sg.*, **maked, mad(e)(n)** *pa.t.*) make; create, 869; do, 1073, 1674; perform, 43; **m. god chere** behave cheerfully, 562
males *n.* bags
malt *pa.t.* condensed, trickled, 2080
maner *n.* custom, 90; kind, 484; way, 1730; *pl.* manners, 924
manerly *adj.* polite, dignified, 1656
mansed *pa.t.* threatened, 2345
Mary *n.* (the Virgin) Mary; marry!, 2140
mas *see* **make**
masse, -e- *n.* (service of) Mass
masseprest *n.* ordained priest, 2108
mat(e) *adj.* frightened, subdued, 336; exhausted, 1568
may *n.* woman, 1795 (*2nd*)
may(e) (**mowe, may** *pres. pl.*, **myght, moght(en)** *pa.t.*) can, may; **what he m.** (*sc.* do) what he was doing, 1087
mayn *adj.* great, 94, *etc.*; strong, 497
mayster *n.* lord, master

mele *v.* speak, say

melle *v.* mingle, flow, 2503

melly *n.* quarrel, 342; battle, 644

mended *pa.t.* improved, 883

mene *v.* mean, 233

mensk *adj.* gracious, 964

mensk(e) *n.* courtesy, honour; **-ed** *pp.* adorned, 153; **-ful** *adj.* fine, noble (& *as n.*); **-ly** *adj.* fittingly, with honour

meny *see* **me(y)ny**

menyng *n.* understanding, 924

mere *adj.* noble, 924

mere *n.* rendezvous, 1061

meré *see* **mery**

merk *n.* appointed place, rendezvous, 1073

merkkes *v.* aims at, 1592

merthe, mirthe, my(e)rthe *n.* joy, pleasure, amusement; merriment, 71, 106, 985, *etc.*; pleasant subjects, 541, 1763

mervayl(e) *n.* wonder, marvel; **had m.** wondered, 233

mery, meré, miry, myry *adj.* merry, good-humoured, bonny, *etc.*; fine, 1691; elegant, 142, 153, 878, 1736; **meryly, mur-** *adv.* merrily, cheerfully; playfully, 2345; splendidly, elegantly, 740

meschef *n.* guilty plight, 1774

mes(se) *n.* 'breakfast' (a light meal), 999; dish, food, 1004; Mass, 1690

messewhyle *n.* time of Mass, 1097

mete *adj.* reaching, 1736; **-ly** *adv.* properly

mete *n.* food, 45, *etc.*; meal, 71, 543, *etc.*

methless *adj.* intemperate, 2106

meve, mue *v.* influence, 90; initiate, 985; proceed, go, 1312, 1565, 1965; **m. to** portend, 1197; rouse, 1157

me(y)ny *n.* retinue, household

miche, mirthe, miry *see* **much(e), merthe, mery**

F*

mislyke *v.* displease

misy *n.* marsh, 749

mo *adj. & adv.* more (*usu.* in number)

moght(en) *see* **may**

molaynes *n.* bit-studs, 169

molde *n.* earth

mon *n.* man; **uche m.** everyone; **no m.** nobody; *pl.* **men(ne)** people, 28, 147, *etc.*; *as indef. pron.* one, anyone, 565, 1077, *etc.*

mon *v.* must, 1811, 2354

mone *n.*[1] moon

mone *n.*[2] appeal, 737

moni, mony *adj. & pron.* many (a); **m. on** many a one, 442

mor *n.* moor, 2080

more *adj. & adv.* greater, larger, more; **most** *superl. adj.* biggest, greatest, 137, 141, *etc.*; *adv.* 51, 638, *etc.*

morn(e), moroun *n.* morning; morrow, next day, 995, 1404, 1670, 1884, 2350

mornyng *see* **mournyng**

most(e) *see* **more, mot**

mot *v.* (**most(e)** *pa.t.*) may, 342, 387, *etc.*; must, have to, 1287, 1958, 1965, 2510

mote(s) *n.* notes of the horn

mote *n.* moat; castle, 635, 910, 2052

mount(e) *n.* hill; **bi m.** among the hills, 718

mounture *n.* mount, horse, 1691

mo(u)rnyng *n.* sorrow; **in m. of** oppressed by, 1751

mowe *see* **may(e)**

much(e), miche, mych *adj., adv. & n.* abundant, 182; big, strong, 2336; a lot (of), much, 558, *etc.*; **thus m.** as much as this, as follows, 447; **muchwhat** many things, 1280

muckel *n.* size, 142

mue *see* **meve**

muged *pa.t.* drizzled, lay damp, 2080

munt *see* **mynt, mynte**

muryly *see* **mery**

mute *n.* pack of hounds; sound (of a hunt), 1915

muthe, mouth(e) *n.* mouth, voice

mych *see* **much(e)**

myddelerde *n.* the earth, 2100

myght *n.* power; **at my m.** to the best of my ability, 1546

mynde *n.* mind, memory; **gos in m.** is questionable, 1293

myn(n)e *v.* remember, think about; remind, declare

mynt, -u- *n.* feint

mynte *v.* (**mynte, munt** *pa.t.*) aim (a blow), swing

myre *n.* mire, swamp, 749

myrthe, myry *see* **merthe, mery**

mysdede *n.* sin

mysses *n.* faults, 2391

naf *v.* have not, 1066; **nade** *pa.t.* 724, 763

naght *n.* night, 1407

naked *adj.* naked, bare; *as n.* (bare) flesh, 423, 2002

nakerys *n.* kettledrums, 1016; **nakryn** *g.pl. or adj.* of kettledrums, 118

nar *v.* are not, 2092

nas *v.* was not, 726

nauther, naw-, nou- *adj., adv. & conj.* neither, either, nor

naylet *pp.* nailed, studded, 599

nayted *pp.* celebrated, repeated (*a pun*), 65

ne *adv. & conj.* not, nor

nede(s) *adv.* of necessity

nedes *n.* needs, business, 2216

negh(e) *adv. & prep. see* **n(i)egh(e)**

negh(e) *v.* approach; reach, 1054

neked *n.* (a) little

neme *see* **nyme**

ner(r)(e) *adv.* near(er), nearly

neven *v.* name, call, mention

never *adv.* never; not at all, 376, 399, 430, *etc.*; **n. bot** only, 547

new(e) *adj.* new, fresh; *adv.* newly, anew

n(i)egh(e) *adv. & prep.* near(ly), close. *See also* **ner(r)(e)**

nirt *n.* cut, nick, 2498

noght *adv. & n.* nothing, not (at all). *See also* **bot**

nolde *pa.t.* would not

nome *n.* name

nome(n) *see* **nyme**

no(n) *adj.* no; **non(e)** *pron.* none, no one

nones: for the n. indeed, 844

norne, -u- *v.* propose, offer; urge, 1771; call, 2443

not *v.* know not, 1053

note *n.*[1] note, tune, 514, 1669

note *n.*[2] task, business

note *pp. adj.* notorious, 2092

nothyng *adv.* not at all, 2236

nouthe, nowthe *adv.* now

nouther *see* **nauther**

nowthe *see* **nouthe**

noyce, noyse *n.* sound, 118, *etc.*; music, 134

nurne *see* **norne**

nurture *n.* good breeding

nye *n.* trouble, difficulty, 58, 2141

nyme, neme *v.* (**nome** *pa.t.*, **nomen** *pp.*) take, 809, 993; undertake, 91; **n. to** take upon, 2141; **n. for ... bi nome** designate, 1347

nys *adj.* foolish, 323, 358

nys *v.* is not, 1266

of *adv.* off, 773, 983, 1332, 2249, *etc.*

of *prep.* of; from, 183, *etc.*; out of, 1087; because of, 86, 922; in respect of, 143, 355, 1478, 2238, *etc.*; with 172, 1455, 2167, *etc.*; by, 64; for, 96, 755, 975, *etc.*

oghe *v.* ought, 1526

oght *n.* anything

okes *n.* oaks

on *adj.* one, 30 (= a), 206, 314, 372, 771, 2151, 2252, 2312, *etc.*; **on(e)** *pron.* one, 137, 223, *etc.*; **that o.** the one, 952, *etc.*

on *prep.* on, 4, *etc.*; at, 479, 491, *etc.*; to, 1701; about, 683, 1800, 2052, *etc.*; by, 47; in, 1722, 1730, *etc.*; **on huntyng,** *etc.* a-hunting, 1102, 1143; **on lyve** alive, on earth, 385, 1717, *etc.*; indeed, 2095

one *adj.* alone; single, 2249, 2345; **hym (oure) o.** (by) himself, ourselves

ones *adv.* once; **at o.** together; **at thys o.** here and now, 1090

onewe *adv.* anew, 65

onsware, answare *v.* answer

or *conj.* than, 1543

oritore *n.* chapel, 2190

orpedly *adv.* boldly, 2232

oryght *adv.* in proper fashion, 40

ostel *see* **(h)ostel**

other *adj. & pron.* other, 24, 90, *etc.*; second, 1020, 2350; another, the other, 98, 501, 628; *pl.* others, 64, 551, 628, 673, *etc.*; **that o.** the other, 110, 386, *etc.*; **an o.** otherwise, 1268; **non o.** nothing else, 1396; **ayther o.** *see* **ayther**

other, auther *adv. & conj.* or, 96, *etc.*; **o . . . o(or)** either . . . or, 88, 702, *etc.*; or else, 1956, 2293

otherwhyle *adv.* at other times, 722

oute *adv.* far and wide, 1511

outtrage *adj.* extraordinary, 29

overal *adv.* all over, 150; in all parts, 630

overclambe *pa.t.* climbed over, 713

overloked *pa.t.* looked over their heads, 223

overwalt *pp.* overthrown, 314

overyede *pa.t.* went by, 500

pane *n.* garment (piece of material), 154; *pl.* panels, 855

paraventure, -aunter *adv.* perhaps

passe *v.* (**passed, past(e)** *pa.t.*) pass, go, travel; cross, 2071; surpass, 654, 1014; **-age** *n.* journey

Pater *n.* Paternoster, Lord's Prayer, 757

patrounes *n.* masters, 6

paumes *n.* flat ends of antlers, 1155

paunce *n.* abdominal armour, 2017

paye *v.* please, satisfy, pay

payne *n.* hardship, 733

paynted *pp.* painted, 800; portrayed, 611

payre *v.* be blunted, deteriorate

payttrure *n.* breast-harness, 168, 601

pelure *n.* fur, 154, 2029

pented *pa.t.* pertained to, 204

pertly *adv.* openly, publicly

pes *n.* peace, 266

piche *v.* (**pyght** *pa.t.,* **piched, -y-** *pp.*) place, fasten; strike, 1456

piked *pp.* polished, 2017

pine, pyne *n.* pain, 747; annoyance, 1812; trouble, 1985; difficulty, 123

place *n.* house, dwelling; room, 123

plate *n.* piece of armour

plesaunt *adj.* courteous, obliging, 808

plyght *n.* danger, 266; guilt, 2393

plytes *n.* plights, 733

poudred *pp.* scattered, 800

poynt *n.* point; question, 902; virtue, 654; good condition, 2049

prayere *n.* meadow, 768

prece, -s- *v.* hurry

prestly *adv.* promptly

preue *adj.* valiant, 262

prevé *adj.* discreet; **-ly** *adv.* in private

prik, -y- *v.* gallop, 2049; incite, 2347

princes *n.* princess, lady, 1770

pris *see* **prys**

proude, prowde *adj.* proud; splendid, 168, 601

pryk *see* **prik**

pryme *n.* the first canonical hour (6 a.m.), sunrise, 1675

prys, pris *n.*¹ value, 79, 1277, 1850; excellence, 912, 1249, 1630; renown, 1379; **of p.** valuable, 615, 2364; excellent, noble, 1770, 2398; *adj.* 1945

prys *n.*² 'capture' (call on horn)

prysoun *n.* prisoner, 1219

pure *adj.* pure, perfect; noble, 262, etc.; *adv.* perfectly, 808; **purely** *adv.* completely, fully, perfectly

pured *pp.* refined, 633, 912; purified, 2393; trimmed (to one colour), 154, 1737

pyched, pyght *see* **piche**

pyne *v. reflex.* take pains; *n. see* **pine**

pysan *n.* gorget, throat-armour, 204

quaynt, coynt, koynt *adj.* skilful, elaborate, 999; ornate, 877; fastidious (about), 1525; **-ly(ch)** *adv.* gracefully, daintily; cleverly, 2413

queldepoyntes *n.* quilted seats, 877

quelle *v.* kill; end, 752

queme *adj.* fine, pleasant

querré *n.* 'quarry', heap of game, 1324

quik(ly) *see* **quyk**

quit-clayme *v.* renounce, 293

quoth, cothe *pa.t.* said

quyk, quik *adj. & adv.* alive, 2109; lively, restive, 177; quickly, 975; **-ly** *adv.*, 1324, 1490

quyssewes *n.* thigh-pieces, 578

quyssynes *n.* cushions, 877

quyte *v.* requite, repay

race *n.* blow, 2076; **on r.** headlong, 1420

rach(ch) *n.* hound

rad *adj.* afraid, 251

rad(ly) *adv.* quickly

raged *adj.* ragged, trailing, 745

raght *see* **rech(e)**

rake *n.* steep path

rape *v.* rush, hurry; *reflex.*, 1309

rased *pa.t.* snatched, 1907

rases *pres. 3 sg.* charges, 1461

rasse *n.* ledge, bank, 1570

rawes *n.* hedgerows, 513

rayke *v.* go, depart; *reflex.*, 1735; **out r.** break cover, 1727

rayled *pp.* arrayed, set; spread, 745; *pa.t.*, 952

raysoun, resoun *n.* speech, discourse, 227, 392; *pl.*, 443; **bi r.** correctly, 1344; by rights, 1804

rechate *v.* sound the recheat (to call the hounds together)

rech(e) *v.* (**raght** *pa.t.*) reach, 432; extend, 183; offer, give, 66, 1804, 1817, *etc.*; confer upon, 2297

rechles *adj.* carefree, 40

recorded *pa.t.* repeated, 1123

recreaunt *adj.* cowardly

redé *adj.* ready, 1970

red(e) *v.* advise, guide

red(y)ly *adv.* quickly, soon; without hesitation, 373, 392

refourme *v.* restate, 378

rehayte *v.* urge on, exhort

reherse, -ce *v.* repeat, mention

rekenly *adv.* nobly, worthily, 39; graciously, promptly, 251, 821

rele *v.* roll, 304; swerve, 1728; sway (in combat), 2246; *reflex.* swagger(?), 229

remorde *v.* bewail, lament, 2434

renay *v.* refuse

renk *n.* man, knight

rennande *presp. see* **renne**

renne *v.* (**ran, runnen** *pa.t.*, **runnen** *pp.*) run; be current, 310, 2458

require *v.* ask, 1056

rere *v.* raise, 353

res *n.* rush

resette *n.* habitation, 2164

resoun *see* **raysoun**

resteyed, -a- *pa.t. & pp.* persuaded, 1672; turned back, 1153

reverence *v.* salute, 251

rich(ch)(e), -y-, -u- *v.* prepare; deck out (*infl. by* **rich** *adj.*); proceed, move forward, 8, 367, 1898; direct, 1223; decide(?), 360n; turn, 303

rich(e), -y- *adj.* noble, costly, splendid; wealthy, 1646; *as n.* noble steed, 2177; *pl.* nobles, 66, *etc.*; **-ly** *adv.* nobly, 931; pompously, arrogantly, 308; plentifully, 163

rimed hym *pa.t.* cleared his throat(?), drew himself up(?), 308

roche *n.* rock, 2199

rocher *n.* rocky bank

Rode *n.* Rood, Cross, 1949

roffe *n.* roof

rof-sore *n.* cut, gash, 2346

rogh(e), rugh(e) *adj.* rough; *adv.* roughly, 1608

rome *v.* wind one's way, 2198

rones *n.* bushes, 1466

ronge *pa.t.* (**r(o)ungen** *pa.t. pl.*), rang

ronk *adj.* luxuriant, 513

ronkled *pp.* wrinkled, 953

ropes *n.* cords, 857

rote *v.* rot, decay, 528

roun *v.* whisper, 362

rouncé *n.* horse, 303

roungen *see* **ronge**

rous *n.* praise, fame, 310

rout *n.* jerk, 457

rove *see* **ryve**

roves *see* **bastel**

ruch(ch)e *see* **rich(ch)(e)**

rudeles *n.* (window?) curtains, 857

ruful *adj.* terrible, 2076

rugh(e), rungen *see* **rogh(e), ronge**

runisch *adj.* rough, wild; **-ly** *adv.*

rurd(e) *n.* noise; voice, 2337

ruthes *pres. 3 sg.* bestirs, 1558

ryal, ryol *adj.* royal; **-ly** *adv.*

ryalme *n.* realm, kingdom

rych(e) *see* **rich(e), rich(ch)(e)**

ryd(d)(e) *v.* take away (from), 364; part, 2246; **r. of** clean off, 1344

ryght hym *pa.t.* proceeded, 308

ryne *v.* touch, 2290

rynk *n.* ring, 1817, 1827

rynkande *presp.* ringing, 2337

ryol *see* **ryal**

rys *n.* twig; **bi r.** in the wood, 1698

ryve *v.* (**rove** *pa.t.*) cut

sadly *adv.* firmly, deliberately; long enough, 2409

saf, save *prep. & conj.* except

sale *n.* hall

salue *v.* greet, 1473

salure *n.* salt-cellar, 886

same *adj. & pron.* same; **of the s.** in the same way, to match

same(n) *adv.* together, 50, 363, 673, 744, 940, 1318, 1345

samen *v.* (**samned** *pa.t.*) bring (be brought) together

sanap *n.* napkin, overlay, 886

save *see* **saf**

savered *pp.* flavoured, 892

saverly *adv.* feelingly, 1937; in comfort, 2048

sawe *n.* speech, words; prayer, 1202

sayned *pa.t.* crossed (himself)

sayn(t) *n.*[1] girdle; *n.*[2] saint

scathe *n.* injury, 2353; a pity, 674

schad(d)e *see* **schede**

schafte *n.* shaft; spear, 205

schafted *pa.t.* shone low, set, 1467

schal *v.* (**schyn** *pres.pl.*) shall, will, must; **schulde(n)** *pa.t.* would, ought to, had to

schalk *n.* man

schamed *pa.t.* was embarrassed, 1189

schankes, -o- *n.* legs

schape *v.* (**schop, schaped** *pa.t.*, **schapen, schaped** *pp.*) fashion, make, 213, 662, 1210; recount, 1626; ordain, 2138, 2328, 2340; *pp.* (= **chaped**) mounted (with), 1832

scharp *adj.* sharp; *as n.* blade, 424, 1593, 1902, 2313, 2332

schawe *v. see* **schewe**

schede *v.* (**schad(d)e** *pa.t.*) sever, 425; fall, be shed, 506, 727, 956

(s)chelde *n.* shield; shoulder (of boar), 1456; slab (of meat), 1611, 1626

schende *v.* destroy, 2266

schene *adj.* bright; *as n.* bright weapon

schere *n. see* **cher(e)**

schere *v.* (**schorne** *pf.*) cut

schewe, schawe *v.* show, reveal, 27, 1880, *etc.*; *intr.* show, appear, 420, *etc.*; produce, offer, 315, 619, 2061; **to s.** in appearance, 2036

schinande *presp. adj.* shining, 269

scho *pron.* she

schome, scham(e) *n.* shame

schonkes, schop *see* **schankes, schape**

schore *n.* bank (of stream); rock, 2161

schow(v)e *see* **schuve**

schrank(e) *pa.t.* winced; sank, 425, 2313

schrewe *n.* villain, 1896

schrof *pa.t.* confessed, 1880

schulde(n) *see* **schal**

schunt *n.* sudden deflection, 2268

schunt *pa.t.* started aside, 1902; flinched, 2280

schuve, schow(v)e *v.* push, press, thrust; **s. to** push forward, 1454

schy(i)r(e)(e) *adj.* fair, white, 317, 425, 772 (*cf.* 743), 956, *etc.*; bright, 506, 619; *as n.* white flesh, 1331, 2256; **schyrly** *adv.* completely (*cf.* **clanly**), 1880

schyn *see* **schal**

schynder *v.* sunder, break (apart)

scurtes *see* **skyrtes**

seche *pron.* such, 1543

sech(e) *v.* (**soght** *pa.t.*) seek; come, go, 685, 1052, 1438, 2493

seg(g)e *n.*¹ siege, 1, 2525

segg(e) *n.*² man, knight, 96, 115, *etc.*; person, 1987; sir, 394; *pl.* men, people, 673, 822, *etc.*

segh(e) *see* **se(ne)**

seker *see* **siker**

sele *n.* good fortune

self, selven *adj.* same, very, 751, 2147; *as n.* self, himself, 51, 1616, 2301, *etc.*

selly *adj.* (**sellokest** *superl.*) marvellous, 1962; strange, 2170; *as n.* marvel, 28, 239, 475; **selly(ly)** *adv.* exceedingly, 963, 1194, 1803

selure *n.* canopy, 76

selven *see* **self**

semb(e)launt *n.* appearance, 148; sign, 468; demeanour, 1273; demonstration (of regard), 1658; kindness, 1843

semblé *n.* throng, 1429

seme *adj.* gracious, 1085; *cf.* **semly(ch)**

seme *n.* ornamental strip of material inserted in, or laid over, a seam

seme *v.* seem, appear, 201, 235, *etc.*; be fitting *or* proper 73, 679 (*sc.* to be); suit, 848, 1929; seem fitting, 1005

semly(ch) *adj. & adv.* (**semloker** *compar.*) seemly, fitting, 348, 1198; handsome, 685; *compar.* lovelier (*sc.* gem), 83; **that s.** the handsome knight, 672; *adv.* becomingly, 622 (**semlyly**), 865, 882, 888; with pleasure, 916; sweetly, 1658, 1796

sendal *n.* silk, 76

sene *adj.* outward, 148; plain, 341. See also **se(ne)** *v.*

se(ne) v. (segh(e), sy(e) pa.t., sen(e) pp.) see. *See also* sene adj.

sengel adj. alone, 1531

sere adj. various, different, 124, 889, 2417; several, 822; adv. severally, 632; sere twyes on two different occasions, 1522

serlepes adv. in turn, 501

sertayn adv. for sure, 174

serve(n) v.¹ serve

serve v.² deserve, 1380

servyse, -ce n. service; (in church), 751, 940

sese v.¹ cease, 1, 134, 2525

sese v.² seize; touch, take, 1825

sesoun n. season; time, 1958, 2085

sete adj. excellent, 889

sete n. seat; wenten to s. took their places, 72, 493

sete(n) *see* sitte

sette v. (sett(e) pa.t.) put, place; strike (blow), 372; establish, found, 14; invent, 625; *reflex.* seat oneself, 437, *etc.*; devote (oneself), 1246; make, 1883; lay the table, 1651; pp. ingrained, 148; s. at light make light of, 1250; s. solace find pleasure, 1318; s. on his hede call down on him, 1721; s. hym on *reflex.* charge at, 1589

settel n. seat, 882

sever v. separate, part, depart

sewe n. stew, broth

seye v. (seyen pp.) go, come

sidbordes n. side-tables, lower tables, 115

side, syde n. side; direction, 659, 2170

siker, seker, syker adj. true, 403; trustworthy, 96, 111, 115, 2048, 2493; sure, 265

siker v. promise, pledge

sille n. floor; on s. in the hall, 55

sister-sunes n. nephews, sister's sons, 111

sithe, sythen adv. & conj. after, afterwards, then, since

sitte, -y- v. (sate, sete(n) pa.t., seten pp.) sit

skere adj. innocent, pure, 1261

skete adv. quickly, 19

skyfted pp. alternated, 19

skyl(le) n. reason

skyrtes, scurtes n. skirts, lower parts of a saddle or garment, 171, 601, 865

slade n. valley

slaked pa.t. died away, 244

sleght, slyght n. skill; stratagem; skilled demonstration, 916

slepe pa.subj. slept, 1991

sleye adj. intricate, subtle

slot n. hollow at base of throat

slowe pa.t. slew, killed, 1321

slyght *see* sleght

smal(e) adj. slender, slim, 144, 1207; fine, 76

smartly adv. promptly, 407

smethely adv. gently, 1789

smolt adj. gentle, 1763

smothe adj. pleasant, friendly, 1763; smothely adv. deftly, 407

smyte v. (smeten pa.t.pl.) smite; fall, 1763

snyrt pa.t. snicked, touched, 2312

so adv. then, 218

soberly adv. reverently, solemnly

soft(e) adj. soft, gentle; adv. (*also* sof(t)ly) softly, comfortably

soght *see* sech(e)

sojo(u)rne v. stay; pp. lodged, 2048

solace n. pleasure; entertainment, 1985

sone adv. immediately, quickly, soon

sop n. morsel, 1135

sore adj. painful, cruel

soré adj. sorry

soth(e) adj. true; as a fact, 348; n. truth, 355, 1786, *etc.*; word, 1825, 2051; for s. truly, 403; adv. in truth, 84; truly, 2110

sothen *pp.* boiled, 892

sothly *adv.* truly, 976, 1095, 2362

soure *adj.* unpleasant, 963

sourquydry, surquidré *n.* pride

sowme *n.* number, quantity, 1321

space *n.* time; **in s.** shortly, in due course

spare *adj.* restrained, tactful, 901

sparlyr *n.* calf (of leg), 158

sparred *pa.t.* sprang, 1444

spede *v.* prosper, bless; further, hasten, 979

spelle *n.* speech, words

spelle *v.* say, 2140

spend *pp.* fastened, 587; **spenet** *pa.t.* clung, 158

spende *v.* spend; utter, 410

spenné *n.* fence, hedge

sperre *v.* strike, spur, 670

spores, spures *n.* spurs

sprenged *pa.t.* (dawn) broke

sprent *pa.t.* leapt, 1896

sprit *pa.t.* jumped, 2316

spur(y)ed *pp.* asked

spyces *n.* spices, 892; spiced cakes, 979

spye, -i- *v.* inquire; look for, 1896

spyt *n.* (doing) injury, 1444

stabled *pp.* established, 1060

stad *pp.* set down, 33; provided, armed, 2137; **was s.** found himself, 644

stalke *v.* step warily, 237; stride, 2230

stal(l)e *n.*, **in s.** erect, 104, 107

stange *n.* pole, 1614

starande *presp.* glittering, 1818

start(e) *v.* start, jump, leap

statut *n.* agreement, 1060

stayned *pp.* stained, coloured, 170

sted(de) *n.* place; **in s.** there, 439

sted(e) steed

stek *pa.t.* clung (to) 152; **stoken** *pp.* fastened, 782; established, fixed, 33; crammed (with), 494; imposed on, 2194

stel-bawe *n.* stirrup, 435

stel(e) *n.*[1] steel; armour, 570

stele *n.*[2] handle, 214, 2230

stele *v.* (**stel** *pa.t.*) steal; **stollen** *pp.* surreptitious, 1659

stel-gere *n.* armour, 260

stem(m)ed *pa.t.* stopped, paused

sterop, stirop *n.* stirrup

steven *n.*[1] voice

steven *n.*[2] appointment; time, 2008

stif(fe), styf *adj.* bold, brave, 34, 260, 823, *etc.*; firm, 431, 846; unflinching, 294; strong, 214, 322, 2099, *etc.*; vigorous, 104; powerful, 176, 1364; *adv.*, 671; **stifly** *adv.*, 287, 606, *etc.*

stightel, styghtel *v.* rule, be in command, 104, 2213; master, 2137; **s. the upon** limit yourself to, 2252

stille *adj. & adv.* motionless; silent; in peace and quiet, 1367, *etc.*; in private, 1085, 2385; secret, 1659; **-ly** *adv.* quietly

stoffed *pp.* lined, padded, 606

stoken *see* **stek**

stonde *v.* (**stod(e)(n)** *pa.t.*) stand, 107, *etc.*; be present, 1768; put up with (from), take (from), 294, 2286; **s. alofte** stand out, 1818

ston(e) *n.* stone, jewel; rock, 2230, 2282, 2293; pavement, 2063

ston-fyr *n.* flint-sparks, 671

ston-stil stone-still, 242

stonye *see* **stoune**

stor(e) *adj.* powerful, 1923; stern, harsh, 1291

stoundes *n.* times; **bi s.** at times

stoune, stowne, stonye *v.* astound

stoutly *adv.* strongly, loudly; securely, 1614

strakande *presp.* sounding (on horn)

straunge (stronge, 1028) *adj.* strange, visiting

strayne *v.* control, 176

strayt *adj.* close-fitting, 152

streght *adj.* (stretched); smooth, 152

stroke *pa.t.* struck, flew, 671

stronge *adj.* strong, powerful; (1028 *see* **straunge**)

strye *v.* destroy, 2194

stryf *n.* resistance, 2323

stryth(th)e *n.* stance

studie *v.* gaze (to see), ponder

study *n.* thought, 2369

sturn(e) *adj.* grim, formidable, 334, 494, 2136; massive, 143, 846, 2099; *as n.* redoubtable knight, 214; **-ly** *adv.* fiercely, 331

styf *see* **stif(fe)**

stythly *adv.* strongly, 431

sue *v.* follow, pursue

su(e)te *n.* kind, suit; **of a s.**, **of folwande s.**, **in s.** to match, 191, 859, 2518; **of his hors s.** matching that of his horse, 180

sum(me) *adj. & pron.* some

sumned *pp.* summoned, 1052

sumwhat *n.* something, 1799

sumwhyle *adv.* once upon a time, 625; sometimes, 720, 721

sure *adj.* reliable, 585; **-ly** *adv.*, 1883

surfet *n.* transgression, 2433

surkot *n.* surcoat, gown, 1929

surquidré *see* **sourquydrye**

swange *n.* middle, hips

sware *adj.* squarely built, 138

sware *v.* answer

swenge *v.* rush, hasten

swere *v.* (**swere** *pa.t.*) swear

swevenes *n.* dreams, 1756

sweye(d) *pa.t.* swung, 1429; dropped, 1796

swoghe *adj.* deathly, 243

swyeres *n.* squires, young knights, 824

swyn *n.* swine, boar

swynges *v.* rushes, 1562

swyre *n.* neck

swythe, -ly *adv.* quickly; strongly, earnestly, very much, 1479, 1860, 1866

syde *see* **side**

sy(e) *see* **se(ne)**

syfle *v.* (*reflex.*) blow, 517

syght *n.* sight, 1721; **in s.** manifest, 28; **se wyth (in) s.** set eyes on, 197, 226, 1705

syke *v.* sigh

syker *see* **siker**

sykyng *n.* sigh, sighing, 1982; *as presp.*, 753

sylverin, -en *adj.* of silver, 886; **the s.** the silver (dishes), 124

symple *adj.* plain

syn(ne) *prep., conj. & adv.* since

syre *n.* lord

sythen *see* **sithen**

sythe(s) *n.* times; groups (of five), 656; **bi s.** on occasions, 17

tables *n.* cornices, 789

tach(ch)e, tacche *v.* fasten, attach

ta(ke) *v.* (**tok(e)(n)** *pa.t.*, **tone**, **ta(ke)n(e)** *pp.*) take; acquire, receive, 1396, 2243, 2448; catch, 1210, 2509; give, 1966; commit, 2159; **tan** *pp.* situated, 1811; **t. to** take upon, 350, 1540; **t. on honde** undertake, 490

tale *n.* tale, account, speech

talenttyf *adj.* eager, 350

tapit *n.* wall-hanging, 77, 858; carpet, 568

tap(p)e *n.* tap, blow

tars *n.* rich fabric (from Tharsia), 77, 571, 858

tary *v.* tarry, delay

tas *imper.* take

tayt *adj.* merry, 988; well grown, 1377

teccheles *adj.* faultless, 916

teche *v.* (**taght** *pa.t.*) teach; direct, show, 401, 1069, *etc.*

tel *see* **til(le)**

telde *n.* house, dwelling

telde *v.* set up

tene *adj.* troublesome; perilous, 2075

tene *n.* trouble

tene *v.* torment, harrass; *intrans.* suffer torment, 2501

tent *n.* care; **in t.** in a mind, 624

terme *n.* tryst, appointment; expression, 917

thad *adj.* that, 686

thagh(e) *conj.* though, even if, 350, 438, *etc.*; if, 496, 2282, 2307, 2427

thanne *see* **then(n)(e)**

thare *adv.* there

that *conj.* that, so that

that *rel. pron.* who(m), which; what, that which, 291, 391, *etc.*

theder, thi-, thiderwarde *adv.* thither

then(n)(e), thanne *adv. & conj.* than, 24, 236, *etc.*; then, 116, 301, *etc.*

thenk(ke) *v.* (**thoght(en)** *pa.t.*) think, consider, remember; intend, 331, 1023. *See also* **thynk(ke)**

theraboute *adv.* (working) at it, 613; thereabouts, 705; round it, 2485

therafter *adv.* behind, after(wards); again, 2418

theralofte *adv.* on it, 569

therbyside *adv.* beside it, 1925

ther(e) *adv. & conj.* there; where, when, 195, 334, 349, *etc.*

ther(e)as *conj.* where

therfor(n)e *adv.* therefore, for that reason; for it, 1107

therinne *adv.* in that place; *rel.* in which, 17

theroute *adv.* out of it (them); out of doors

therto *adv.* at it, to it (them), 219, *etc.*; accordingly, 757

thertylle *adv.* to it, to that place

therwyth *adv.* with (by) it, thereupon

thewes *n.* manners

thik(ke), -y- *adj. & adv.* thick, 579; burly, thick-set, 138, 175; close(ly), dense(ly), 612, 769, 795, 801; insistently, 1770; hard, 1702

tho *adj.* those, the (*pl.*), 39, 68, *etc.*

thof, thogh *conj.* though

thoght(en) *v.* *see* **thenk(ke), thynk(ke)**

thonk(e) *n.* thank(s)

thore *adv.* there

thow, thou *pron.* thou; **the** *acc. & dat.* thee; **thi(n), thy(n)** *gen.* thy, thine

thrast *n.* thrust, onslaught, 1443

thrawen, throwen *pp.* twisted, drawn up, 194; laid, 1740; *adj.* muscular, 579

thred *n.* thread; limit, 1771

threte *v.* (**thrat** *pa.t.*, **threted** *pp.*) threaten, attack; urge, 1980

thrid, -y- *adj.* third

thro *adj. & adv.* earnest(ly); fierce, 1713, 2300; hectic, 1021; **-ly** *adv.*

throwen *see* **thrawen**

thrye(s), -se *adv.* thrice

thryght *pa.t. & pp.* pushed down, flattened, 1443; imprinted on, 1946

thrynge *v.* (**thronge** *pa.t.*) press, crowd

thryvande *adj.* hearty, 1980; **-ly** *adv.* 1080, 1380

thryve *v.*, **so mot I t.** as on my salvation, 387; **thryven** *pp.* lovely, 1740

thurgh(e) *prep.* through(out), 243, 691, *etc.*; because of, by means of, 91, 998, 1258, *etc.*; beyond, 645, 1080; *adv.* 1356

thurled *pa.t.* pierced, 1356

thwong *n.* thong, lace

thynk(ke) *v. impers.* (**thoght, thught** *pa.t.*) seem (to me, *etc.*); *sometimes confused with* **thenk**, *esp. in pa.t.*; seem good (to you), 1502

til(le), tyl *prep. & conj.* until; to, 673, 1979

tit(e), tyt *adv.* quickly

titleres *n.* hounds

tole *n.* tool, weapon

tolke *see* tulk

tolouse, tulé, tuly *n.* rich red fabric (from Toulouse), 77, 568, 858

tomorn(e) *adv.* tomorrow (morning)

tone *see* ta(ke)

toppyng *n.* forelock, 191

tor(e) *adj.* difficult

tornayees, torne *see* to(u)rnaye, t(o)urne

tortor *n.* turtle-dove, 612

tote *v.* peep, 1476

toun(e) *n.* court, 31, 614

to(u)rnaye *v.* double back, 1707; tourney, 41

t(o)urne, torne *v.* turn; return, 1099; t. to make towards, 2075; *pp.* changing, turbulent, 22

towch *n.* tone, strain, 120; hint, 1301; covenant, 1677

towen *pp.* come, 1093

trammes *n.* devices, plots, 3

trante *v.* twist, dodge, 1707

travayl *n.* journey, 2241

travayled *pp.* had a wearisome journey, 1093

trawe, trowe(e) *v.* believe, be sure, trust

trawthe, traweth, trauthe *n.* (word of) honour; integrity, 626, 2470; truth, 1050, 1057; pledge, 2348

trayst *adj.* sure, 1211

tried, tryed *pp.* choice, fine, distinguished

trifel, tryfle *n.* trifle, pleasantry, 108, 1301; detail, 165, 960 (*or* trefoil?)

trochet *pp.* pinnacled, 795

trowe(e) *see* trawe

trulof, tru(e)luf *n.* true love, 1527, 1540; true-love flowers, 612

tryed, tryfle *see* tried, trifel

tryst *v.* believe, depend (**therto**: upon that), 2325

trystor, -er *n.* hunting station

tulé, tuly *see* tolouse

tulk, tolke *n.* man, knight

turned *see* t(o)urne

tweyne, twayne *adj.* two

twynne *adj.*, **in t.** in two

twynne *v.* be separated, 2512

twynnen *pp.* plaited, 191

tyde *n.* time; **hyghe t.** festival

tyght *pp.* spread, 568, 858

tyme *n.* time, period, occasion, 22, *etc.*; **by tymes** on occasions, 41

tyrve *v.* strip (**of**: off), 1921

tytel *n.* right

uch(e), iche *adj.* each, every; *also* uche a, 742, *etc.*; **u. wy, hathel, lede**, *etc.* everyone, 126, 131, *etc.*

uchon(e) *pron.* each one, every one, 98, 657, 829, *etc.*

ugly *adj.* gruesome, 441; threatening, 2079; oppressive, 2190

umbe *prep.* about, round

umbefolde *v.* envelop, 181

unbene *adj.* cheerless, 710

umbeteye *pa.t.* enclosed, 770

umbetorne *adv.* round, 184

umbeweved *v.* enveloped, 581

unblythe *adj.* unhappy, 746

uncely *adj.* ill-fated, hapless, 1562

uncouthe *adj.* strange, 93, 1808

undertake *v.* discern, understand, 1483

unethe *adv.* hardly, 134

unhap *n.* misfortune, 438

unhap *v.* unfasten, 2511

unhardeled *pa.t.* unleashed, 1697

unlace *v.* cut up, 1606

unmete *adj.* monstrous, 208

unslye *adj.* incautious, 1209

unsparely *adv.* in plenty, 979

untyghtel *see* dele

upon *prep.* on, upon, 92, 159, 164, *etc.*; at, 9, 37, 301, *etc.*; by, 47; *adv.* on, 1649, 2021. *For phrases see also* **styghtel, wyse, high(e),** *etc.*

upryse *v.* (**upros, uprysen** *pa.t.*) rise up

use *v.* practise; have relations with, 2426

verayly *adv.* truly

verdure *n.* green(ness), 161

vesture *n.* clothing, 161

vilanous *adj.* ill-bred, 1497

voyde *v.* leave, 345; clear, rid, 634, 1342, 1518

vyage *n.* journey, 535

vylany(e) *n.* discourtesy, degeneracy

wade *v.* (**wod** *pa.t.*) wade, 2231; go (down in), 787

wage *n.* pledge, foretaste, 533; *pl.* wages, 396

waked *see* **woke**

wakened(e), wakned *pa.t.* woke up, 1194, 1200; revived, 2000, 2490; roused, 119; shone, 1650

wakkest *superl. adj.* weakest, 354

wale *v.* choose, 1276; take, 1238; look for, 398

wal(l)e *adj.* excellent, delightful

walke *v.* walk, 2178; travel, 1521

wallande *presp.* welling, surging

walt *see* **welde**

waltered *pa.t.* poured, rolled, 684

wan *see* **wynne** *v.*

wande *n.* staff, 215; bough(s), 1161

wane *adj.* lacking, 493

wap *n.* blow, 2249

war(e) *adj.* aware, wary; **ware!** (hunter's cry), 1158; **be w. of** see; **-ly** *adv.*; **-loker** *compar. adv.* more cautiously, 677

ware *v.* spend, use; pay back, 2344

warloker, warly *see* **war(e)**

warp *v.* (**warp** *pa.t.*) cast, put, 2025; utter, 224, 1423, 2253

warthe *n.* ford, 715

waryst *pp.* recovered, 1094

wast *n.* waist, 144

waste *n.* wasteland, 2098

wat(t)er *n.* (**wattres** *pl.*) water; (tears), 684; stream, 715

wathe *see* **wothe**

wax *v.* (**wex** *pa.t.*) grow, spread

way *adv.* away, aside, 1492

wayke *adj.* feeble, 282

wayne *v.* bring, send; direct, 984

wayte *v.* look; glare, 2289

wayth *n.* catch, game, 1381

wayve *v.* throw, wave

we (loo)! *interj.* alas!

wede *n.* garment, clothing; *pl.* clothes; **hegh w., bryght w.** armour

weghed *pa.t.* brought, carried, 1403

wel *adv.* well, certainly; much, 1276, *etc.*; very, 179, 684; admittedly, 1847; *as n.* good fortune, 2127 (*cf.* **wele**); good, 1267(?)

wela *adv.* very

welde *v.* (**walt** *pa.t.*) wield, 270; enjoy, use, 835, 837, 1528; pass (time), 485; possess, 231, 1064, 1542, *etc.*

wele *n.* wealth, costliness; happiness, good fortune

wel-haled *adj.* well pulled-up, 157

welkyn *n.* sky

wende *v.* (**wende, went(en)** *pa.t. & pp.*) go; **was w.** had come, 1712; turn, 2152

wene *v.* (**wende, went** *pa.t.* 669, 1711) think; know, 270, 1226

wener *adj.* lovelier, 945

Wenore *n.* Guenevere, 945

weppen *n.* weapon

werbles *n.* trills, 119

were *n.* defence. *See also* **werre**

were *v.*[1] (**were(d)** *pa.t.*) wear

were *v.*[2] defend; keep out, 2015

werk(ke) *n.* work, 494; workmanship, 2367; *pl.* deeds, 1515, 2026(?); ornamentation, 216, 1817, 2432; embroidery, 164, 2026(?)

werne *v.* refuse

wernyng *n.* refusal, resistance, 2253

werre *n.* fighting. *See also* **were**

werre *v.* fight, 720

wesche *pa.t.*, **waschen** *pp.* washed

weve *v.* proffer, give

wex *see* **wax**

what! *interj.* why! how!, *etc.*; *pron. & conj.* what; why, 563

whatso *pron. & adj.* (*also* **w(h)at . . . so**) whatever

whederwarde *adv.* in what direction, 1053

whel *see* **whil(e)**

whenso *adv.* whenever, 1682

wher(e) *adv.* where; wherever, 100; **whereso** wherever

whethen *adv.* whence (ever)

whiderwarde-soever *adv.* to whatever place, 2478

while, -y- *n.* time, while; moment, 30, 134, 1646, 1996; **the w.** for the time, 1791; **that . . . w.** during, 940, 985

whil(e), w(h)yl(e), whel *prep. & conj.* while, as long as; until, 536, 1072, 1180, *etc.*

wil, wyl(le), wol *v.* (**wolde, woled** *pa.t.*) will, wish (for), desire, intend

wit, wyt *v.* (**wot** *pres*, **wyst(e)(n)** *pa.t.*) know, learn, be sure

with, wyth *prep.* with; against; towards, 1926, 2220; among, 49; through, 1519, 2461, *etc.*; by (*agent*), 314, 384, 681, 949, 1119, 1153, 1229, *etc.*; in respect of, 418; (tired, afraid) of, 1573, 2301; **w. hymselven** with him, 113, inwardly, 1660; **w. this, that** thereupon, 316, 1305

wlonk *adj. & adv.* splendid(ly), fine; *as n.* noble man

wod *see* **wade**

wode *adj.* mad, 2289

wod(e) *n.* wood, forest

woke *pa.t.*, **waked** *pp.* stayed up late revelling

wolde, wol(ed) *see* **wil**

wombe *n.* stomach, 144

wonde *v.* shrink

wonde, woned *see* **won(y)(e)**

wonder *n.* wonder, amazement; **have w.** be amazed; marvel, 29, 480, 2459; disaster(?), 16; *as adv.* amazingly, 2200

wone *v. see* **won(y)(e)**

won(e) *n.* dwelling; *plural as collective* 'abode', 685, *etc.*; pleasure, 1238; multitude, company, 1269

wont *n.* lack, 131

wont *v. impers.* it (there) lacks

won(y)(e) *v.* (**wonde, woned** *pa.t.*, **wonde, wonyd, wont** *pp.*) live, dwell; remain, linger, 50, 257, 814

worch(e) *v.* (**wroght(en)** *pa.t.* **wroght** *pp.*) work, do, act, make, bring about

word(e) word, speech; fame, 1521

worlde *n.* world; nature, 504, 530, 2000

wormes *n.* dragons, 720

worre *adj.* worst (of it)

wor(s)chip, -schyp *n. & v.* honour

wort *n.* plant, 518

worth(e) *v.* become; be (future); befall (to)

worthilych *adj.* honoured, 343

worthy, -é *adj.* worthy, noble (*& as n.*); fitting, 819; valuable, 1848; *adv.* courteously, 1477; **-ly** *adv.* fittingly, becomingly, 72, 144; courteously, 1759; honourably, 1386, 1988

wot *see* **wit**

wothe, wathe *n.* danger

wounden *see* **wynde**

wowe *n.* wall

wrake *n.* vengeance, 16

wrast *pp.* turned, disposed, 1482

wrathed *pa.t.* were (not) made angry, 1509; troubled, 726, 2420 (*pp.*)

wro *n.* nook, 2222

wroght(en) *see* **worch(e)**

wroth *pa.t.* stretched, 1200

wroth(e) *adj.* angry, 70, 319, 525, 1660; fierce 1706, 1905; **-ly** *adv.* fiercely, 2289; **-loker** *compar. adv.* 2344

wruxled *pp.* wrapped, clad, 2191

wy! *interj.* oh!, bah!, 2300

wy(e) *n.* man, knight, person; Lord, 2441; sir, 252, 1039; *etc.*; **uch w.** everyone, 131; **no w.** no one, 384

wyf *n.* woman, lady, wife

wyght, -i- *adj.* strong, 261, 1762; piercing, 119; **wyghtest** swiftest current, 1591; **wyghtly** *adv.* quickly, 688

wyght *n.* creature, person, 1792

wylde *n.* wild animal(s)

wyle *see* **whil(e)**

wylle *n.* mind, temper, 57, 352; will, wish, desire, 255, 836, 1039, 1665, *etc.*; **at w.** abundant, 1371; **at (your) w.** as (you) wish, 1039, *etc.*; **bi yowre w.** if you please, 1065; **with (a) good w.** willingly, gladly, 1387, *etc.*

wylnyng *n.* wish, 1546

wylsum *adj.* out-of-the-way, 689

wynne *adj.* delightful, lovely; **-lych** perfect, 980

wynne *n.* joy, 15, 1765

wynne *v.* (**wan, wonnen** *pa.t.*, **won(n)en** *pp.*) win (*intrans.*), 70; win, get, 984, 1106, *etc.*; go, come, 461, 1365, 1537, *etc.*; bring, 831, 1550, *etc.*; *reflex.* reach, 402, 1569, 2231

wypped *pa.t.* whipped, slashed, 2249

wyrde *n.* fate, Destiny

wyse *n.* manner, way; **in no w.** by no means, 1836; **in feghtyng w.** in battle array; **upon spare w.** discreetly, 901; **upon a grett w.** magnificently, 2014

wysse *v.* guide

wyst(e)(n), wyt *v.* see **wit**

wysty *adj.* desolate, 2189

wyte *v.* look, 2050

wyt(t)(e) *n.* mind, intelligence, skill, wisdom; sense, 677; *pl.* senses

yare *adv.* soon, 2410

yark(k)e *v.* prepare, institute; **y. up** open, 820

yar(r)ande *presp. adj.* snarling

yate *n.* gate

yaule *v.* howl, 1453

yayned *pp.* greeted, 1724

ye *n.* (**yen** *pl.*) eye, 82, *etc.*

yede(n), yod *pa.t.* went, walked

yederly *adv.* promptly, quickly

yelde *v.* (**yelde(n), yolden** *pa.t.*, **yolden** *pp.*) deliver, give, 67, 2223; make available, 820; return, repay, 453, 1038, *etc.*; bring back, 498; reply, 1478; *reflex.* yield, surrender, 1215, 1595

yelpyng *n.* valiant boasting, 492

yep(e) *adj.* young, new, 60; youthful, active, vigorous, 105, 284, 1510; fresh, blooming, 951; **-ly** *adv.* promptly

yeres yiftes *n.* New Year's gifts, 67

yern(e) *adj.* & *adv.* quick(ly), eager(ly), 498, 1478, 1526

yerne *v.*[1] desire, 492

yerne, yirne *v.*[2] run, pass, 498, 529

yet *adv.* still, moreover; nevertheless, 465, *etc.*; even, 1009

yette *v.* grant, 776

yeye *v.* cry (like a pedlar), 67; appeal, 1215

yif, if, iif *conj*. if, whether; **bot i.**
  unless
yirne *see* **yerne**
yod *see* **yede(n)**
Yol *n*. Yule
yolden *see* **yelde**

yolwe *adj*. yellow, sallow, 951
yomerly *adv*. miserably, 1453
yrn(e) *n*. iron, 215; weapon, 2267;
  pl. armour, 729

Zeferus *n*. the West Wind, 517